JUL 08

CH

If You're Trying to

Get Better Grades
& Higher Test Scores in
Reading and Language

You've Gotta Have This Book!

Grades 4-6

By Imogene Forte
& Marjorie Frank

Incentive Publications, Inc.
Nashville, Tennessee

Illustrated by Kathleen Bullock
Cover by Geoffrey Brittingham
Edited by Patience Camplair

ISBN 0-86530-644-3

1   2   3   4   5   6   7   8   9   10   08   07   06   05

PRINTED IN THE UNITED STATES OF AMERICA
www.incentivepublications.com

Contents

GET SHARP . . . IN GRAMMAR, USAGE, MECHANICS, AND SPELLING   67

GET SHARP . . . IN READING AND WORD MEANING 183

Get Ready

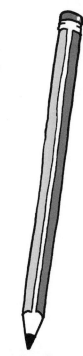

Get ready to get smarter. Get ready to be a better student and get the grades you are capable of getting. Get ready to feel better about yourself as a student. Lots of students would like to do better in school. (Lots of their parents and teachers would like them to as well!) Lots of students CAN do better, but it doesn't happen overnight. And it doesn't happen without some thinking and trying. So, are you ready to put some energy into getting more out of your learning efforts? Good! The first part of getting ready is wanting to do better—motivating yourself to get moving on this project of showing how smart you really are. The **Get Ready** part of this book will help you do just that: get inspired and motivated. It also gives you some wonderful and downright practical ways to organize yourself, your space, your time, and your homework. More importantly, it gives tips you can use right away to make big improvements in your study habits.

Get Set

Once you have taken a good, hard look at your goals, organization, and study habits, you can move on to other skills and habits that will set you up for more successful learning. The **Get Set** part of this book gives you ready-to-use tools for sharpening thinking skills and helping you get the most out of your brain. Then, it adds a quick and effective crash course on finding information in the library, on the Internet, and from many other sources. Top this off with a great review of tools and skills you need for good studying. It is all right here at your fingertips—how to read carefully, listen well, summarize, outline, take notes, create reports, study for tests, and take tests. Take this section seriously, and you are bound to start making improvements immediately.

Get Sharp

Now you are ready to mix those good study habits and skills with the content that you want to learn. The **Get Sharp** sections of this book contain all kinds of facts and explanations, processes and definitions, lists and how-to information. These sections cover the basic areas of language arts that you study in school—grammar, usage, mechanics, and spelling; writing and speaking; reading, vocabulary, and word use. They are loaded with the information that you need to do your language homework. You will find this part of the book to be a great reference tool PLUS a *How-To Manual* for many language topics and assignments. Keep it handy whenever you do an assignment in the language arts.

How to Use This Book

Students

Students—this can be the ultimate homework helper for your language assignments and preparation. Use the *Get Ready* and the *Get Set* sections to strengthen your general preparation for study and sharpen your study skills. Then, have the book nearby at all times when you have language work to complete at home, and use the *Get Sharp* sections to . . .

 . . . reinforce a topic you have already learned

 . . . get fresh and different examples of something you have studied

 . . . check up on a fact, definition, or detail of language

 . . . get a quick answer to a language question

 . . . get clear on something you thought you knew but now aren't sure about

 . . . guide you in reading and writing processes (such as how to write an essay)

 . . . check yourself to see if you have a fact or process right

 . . . review a topic in preparation for a test.

Teachers

This book can serve multiple purposes in the classroom. Use it as . . .

 . . . a reference manual for students to consult during learning activities or assignments

 . . . a reference manual for yourself to consult on particular rules terms, forms, and skills

 . . . an instructional handbook for particular language topics

 . . . a remedial tool for individuals or groups who need a review of a particular language topic

 . . . a source of advice for parents and students regarding homework habits

 . . . an assessment guide to help you gauge student mastery of language processes or skills

 . . . a source of good resources for bridging home and school

  (For starters, send a copy of the letter on page 17 home to each parent. Use any other pages, particularly those in the "Get Ready" and "Get Set" sections as send-home pieces.)

Parents

The *Get Ready* and *Get Set* sections of this book will help you to help your child improve study habits and sharpen study skills. It can serve as a motivator and a guide, taking the burden off of you! Then, use the *Get Sharp* sections as a knowledge and process back-up guide for yourself.

It is a handbook you can consult to . . .

 . . . refresh your memory about a language process, term, rule, or fact

 . . . clear up confusion about grammar rules, writing forms, reading skills, and many other language questions

 . . . provide useful homework help to your child

 . . . reinforce the good learning your child is doing in school

 . . . gain confidence that your child is doing the homework right

GET READY →

Get Motivated

Dear Student,

Nobody can make you a better student. Nobody can even make you WANT to be a better student. But you CAN be. It's a rare kid who doesn't have some ability to learn more, do better with assignments and tests, feel more confident as a student, or get better grades. YOU CAN DO THIS! You are the one (the only one) who can get yourself motivated.

"WHY would you want be a better student?" If you don't have an answer to this, your chances of improving are not so hot. If you do have answers, but they're like Charlie's (page 15), your chances of improving still might be pretty slim. Charlie figured this out, and decided that these are NOT what really motivate him. Now, we don't mean to tell you that it's a bad idea to get a good report card, or get on the honor roll, or please your parents.

But—if you are trying to motivate yourself to be a better student, the reasons need to be about YOU. The goals need to be YOUR goals for your life right now. In fact, if you are having a hard time getting motivated, maybe it is just BECAUSE you are used to hearing a lot of "shoulds" about what other people want you to be. Or maybe it is because the goals are so far off in some distant future that it is impossible to stay focused on them.

So it's back to the question, "Why try to be a better student?" Consider these as possible reasons why:

- to make use of your good mind—NOT cheating yourself out of something you could learn to do or understand

- to get involved—to change learning into something YOU DO instead of something that someone else is trying to do TO you

- to take charge and get where YOU WANT TO GO (It's YOUR life, after all.)

- to learn all you can FOR YOURSELF—because the more you know, the more you think, and the more you understand, the more possibilities you have for what you can do or be in your life RIGHT NOW and in the future

Follow the suggestions for getting motivated as you think about this question. (See page 15.) Then, write down a few reasons of your own to inspire you toward putting your brain to work, showing how smart you are, and getting even smarter. (See page 16.)

Sincerely,

Imogene and Marjorie

Most of these reasons don't motivate me much at all!

Why SHOULD I Be a Better Student?

To please my parents?
To please my teachers?
To impress my friends?
So people will like me better?
To keep from embarrassing my parents?
To do better than my brother or sister?
So that teachers will treat me better?
To do as well as my parents did in school?
To get the money and favors my parents offer for good grades?
To get well-prepared for high school?
To get a high-paying job?
To get a good report card?
To get into college?

How to Get Motivated

1. Think about why you want to do better as a student.

2. Think about what you could gain now from doing better.

3. Get clear enough on your motivations to write them down.

4. Set some short-term goals *(something you can improve in a few weeks)*.

5. Think about what gets in the way of you doing your best as a student.

6. Figure out a way to change or eliminate something that interferes.

   (Use the form on page 16 to record your thoughts and goals.)

My **Get Motivated** goals.

Get Ready Tip #1
Set realistic goals. Choose something you actually believe you can do. And, you'll have a better chance of success if you set a short time frame for your goal.

Why do I want to be a better student?

(Write reasons that are really true for you.)

1. _____
2. _____
3. _____
4. _____

What changes could I make that would help me in the near future?

(Write two short-term goals—things that you could improve in the next month.)

1. _____
   _____
2. _____
   _____

What gets in the way of good grades or good studying for me?

(Name the distractions or other things that keep you from doing your best as a student.)

1. _____
2. _____
3. _____
4. _____

What distraction am I willing to eliminate?

(Choose one of the distractions above that you'd be willing to change for the next month.)

1. _____

Dear Parent:

What parent doesn't want his or her child to be a good student? Probably not many! But how can you help yours get motivated to do the work it takes? You can't do it for her (or him). But here are some ideas to help students as they find it within themselves to get set to be good students:

- Read the letter to students (page 14). Help your son or daughter think about where she or he wants to go, what reasons make sense to her or him for getting better grades, and what benefits he or she would gain from better performance as a student.

- Help your child make use of the advice on study habits. (See pages 18–28.) Reinforce the ideas, particularly those of keeping up with assignments, going to class, and turning in work on time.

- Provide your child with a quiet, comfortable, well-lit place that is available consistently for study. Also provide a place to keep materials, post reminders, and display schedules.

- Set family routines and schedules that allow for good blocks of study time, adequate rest, relaxing breaks, and healthy eating. Include some time to get things ready for the next school day and some ways for students to be reminded about upcoming assignments or due dates.

- Demonstrate that you value learning in your household. Read. Show excitement about learning something new yourself. Share this with your kids.

- Keep distractions to a minimum. You may not be able to control the motivations and goals of your child, but you can control the telephone, computer, Internet, and TV. These things actually have on-off switches. Use them. Set rules and schedules.

- Help your child gather resources for studying, projects, papers, and reports. Try to be available to take her or him to the library, and offer help tracking down a variety of sources. Try to provide standard resources in the home (dictionary, thesaurus, computer, encyclopedia, etc.).

- DO help your student with homework. This means helping straighten out confusion about a topic (when you can), getting an assignment clear, discussing a concept or skill, and perhaps working through a few examples along with the student to make sure he or she is doing it right. This kind of involvement gives a chance to extend or clarify the teaching done in the classroom. Remember that the end goal is for the student to learn. Don't be so insistent on the student "doing it himself" that you miss a good teaching or learning opportunity.

- Be alert for problems, and act early. Keep in contact with teachers, and don't be afraid to call on them if you see any signs of slipping, confusion, or disinterest on the part of your child. It is easier to reclaim lost ground if you catch it early.

- Try to keep the focus on the student's taking charge for meeting his or her own goals, rather than on making you happy. This can help get you out of a nagging role and place some of the power in the hands of the student. Both of these will make for a more trusting, less hostile relationship with your child on the subject of schoolwork. Such a relationship will go a long way toward supporting your child's self-motivation to be a better student.

Sincerely,

Imogene and Marjorie

Get Organized

Mike has learned a lot about rainforests,
but he is not able to show what he's learned,
because he is so disorganized. Don't repeat Mike's mistakes.

Get Your Space Organized

Find a good place to study. Choose a place that . . .

> . . . is always available to you

> . . . is comfortable

> . . . is quiet and as private as possible

> . . . has good lighting

> . . . is relatively uncluttered

> . . . is relatively free of distractions

> . . . has a flat surface large enough to spread out materials

> . . . has a place to keep supplies handy (See page 19 for suggested supplies.)

> . . . has some wall space or bulletin board space for posting schedules and reminders

Get Ready Tip #2
Set up your study space before school starts each year. Make it cozy and friendly, a safe place for getting work done. Put a little time into making it your own, so it's a place you like—not a place to avoid.

Get Your Stuff Organized

Gather things that you will need for studying or for projects, papers, and other assignments. Keep them organized in one place, so you won't have to waste time looking for things.

Here are some suggestions:

Supplies to Have Handy

a good light
a clock or timer
a bulletin board or wall
pencils, pens, erasable pens
erasers
colored pencils or crayons
markers
highlighters
notebook paper
scratch paper
drawing paper
computer paper
index cards
sticky notes
posterboard
folders
ruler
compass
tape
scissors
calculator
glue, rubber cement
paperclips, push pins
stapler, staples
standard references:
dictionary
thesaurus
current almanac
world maps
language handbook
writer's guide
encyclopedia (set or CD)
homework hotline numbers
homework help websites

Get Ready Tip #3

Have a place to put the things you bring home from school. This might be a shelf, a box, or even a laundry basket. Put your school things in there every time you come in the door so that important stuff doesn't get lost in the house, or moved, or used by other family members.

Get Set with a place to keep supplies:

(a bookshelf, a file box, a paper tray, a drawer, a plastic dishpan, a plastic bucket, a carton, or a plastic crate)
Always keep everything in the same place. Return things to it after you use them.

Also have:

an assignment book
a notebook for every subject
a book bag or pack to carry things
a schedule for your week
(or longer)

Better Grades & Higher Test Scores / READING & LANGUAGE gr. 4–6
Copyright ©2005 by Incentive Publications, Inc., Nashville, TN.

Get Your Time Organized

It might be easy to organize your study space and supplies, but it is probably not quite as easy to organize your time. This takes some work. First, you have to understand how you use your time now. Then, you'll need to figure out a way to make better use of your time. Here is a plan you can follow right away to help you get your time organized:

Think about how you use your time now.

1. For one week, stop at the end of each day, think back over the day, and record what you did in each hour-long period of time for the whole day.

2. Then, look at the record you've kept to see how you used your time.

   Ask yourself these questions:

   - *Did I have any clear schedule?*

   - *Did I have any goals for when I would get certain things done?*

   - *Did I ever think ahead about how I would use my time?*

   - *How did I decide what to do first?*

   - *Did I have a plan or did I just get things done in haphazard order?*

   - *Did I get everything done or did I run out of time?*

   - *How much time did I waste?*

Let me see— how did I use my time today?

I forgot to set my alarm and I had no time for breakfast.

I wrote notes to friends instead of doing a book report in English class.

I got some good exercise after school, playing soccer with my friends.

From 8:00–9:00 pm, I played games on my PlayStation.

I started my homework at about 9:30 pm.

Get Ready Tip #4
When you plan your week's schedule, don't make it too tight or too rigid. Leave room for unexpected events.

3. Next, start fresh for the upcoming week. Make a plan for how to use your time. Include after-school activities, meals, study time, family activities, time for sports and fun, time for social activities and special events, and enough time for sleep.

4. Keep a calendar for each week or month.

5. Make sure you have an assignment notebook. Write on your calendar to remind yourself of major tests and assignments due.

6. Make a Daily To-Do List *(For each day, write the things that must be done by the end of that day.)*

Week of October 7 - 13

S 7	M 8	T 9	W 10	Th 11	F 12	S 13
Jamie's birthday party 5 pm	Soccer game after school	Math test	Science project due	Book report due	Math Chapter 4 review due	Get supplies for art project
	Plan for book report due	Dentist appointment 4 pm		Grammar quiz	Map due	Soccer game 10 am
		Note cards for science project due		Get Europe books at library	Football game 7 pm	

Monday TO DO List

study for math test
finish novel
plan book report
finish English exercises,
Chapter III
return library books
type science projects

Tueday TO DO List

finish Europe map
add diagrams to
science project
review for Thurs.
grammar quiz
work on book report
math homework

Wednesday TO DO List

finish book report
do web research
on France
review for grammar quiz
plan art project
math homework

Subject	Assignment	Due Date	√ (done)
English	Choose and read novel	by Oct 8	√
	Grammar Quiz on Chs 2-3	Oct 11	
	Book report on novel	Oct 11	
	Vocabulary exercise-30 words	Oct 15	
	Vocabulary quiz	Oct 17	
Math	Unit 3 review, p 86	Oct 8	√
	Test on Unit 3	Oct 9	
Science	Diagram on moon phases	Oct 8	
	Finish reading chapter 4	Oct 10	
Social Studies	Make political map of Europe	Oct 12	
	Travel brochure on France	Oct 19	
	French history timeline	Oct 29	
Spanish	1-paragraph autobiography	Oct 5	√
Art	Wire sculpture to match poem	Oct 18	

Get Your Assignments Organized

You can't do a very good job of an assignment if you don't have a clue about what it is. You can't possibly do the assignment well if you don't understand the things you are studying. So, if you want to get smarter—then get clear and organized about assignments. It takes seven simple steps to do this:

1. Listen to the assignment.

2. Write it down in an assignment notebook.
(Make sure you write down the due date.)

3. If you don't understand the assignment—ASK!
(Do not leave the classroom without knowing what it is you are supposed to do.)

4. If you don't understand the material well enough to do the assignment, talk to the teacher.
(Tell him or her that you need help getting it clear.)

5. Take the assignment book home.

6. Transfer assignments to your weekly or monthly schedule at home.

7. Look at your assignment book every day.

Get Ready Tip #6

Don't count on anyone else to listen to the assignment and get it down right. Get the assignment yourself. Find a reliable classmate to get assignments when you are absent—or contact the teacher directly.

Get Yourself Organized

Okay, so your schedule is on the wall—all neat and clear. Your study space is organized. Your study supplies are organized. You have written down all your assignments, and made all of your lists. Great! But do you feel rushed, frenzied, or hassled? Take some time to think about the behaviors that will help YOU feel as organized as your stuff and your schedule.

Before you leave school . . .

STOP — Take a few calm, unrushed minutes to think about what books and supplies you will need at home for studying. ALWAYS take your assignment notebook home.

When you get home . . .

FIRST — Put your school bag in the same spot every day, out of the way of the bustle of your family's activities.

STOP — After relaxing, or after dinner, take a few calm, unrushed minutes to look over your schedule and review what needs to be done. Review your list for the day. Plan your evening study time and set priorities. Don't wait until it is late or you are very tired.

Before you go to bed . . .

STOP — Take a few calm, unrushed minutes to look over your assignment notebook and to-do list for the next day one more time. Make sure everything is completed.

THEN — Put everything you need for the next day IN your book bag. Don't wait until morning. Make sure you have all the right books and notebooks in the bag. Make sure your finished work is all in the bag. Also, pack other stuff (for gym, sports, etc.) at the same time. Consistently put everything in one place, so you don't have to rush around looking for it.

In the morning . . .

STOP — Take a few calm, unrushed minutes to review the day one more time.

THEN — Eat a good breakfast.

Max finally finished his essay. He typed it and fixed all the errors. He scanned in great photos of whales and created a smashing graphic cover. It's done on time! He remembered to bring his lunch and soccer uniform. He brought the DVD he promised to share with his friend Tom.

Guess what Max forgot to bring to school today!

OH NO!

Get Ready Tip #7
It doesn't do much good to get your homework done if you don't turn it in.

Get Healthy

If you are sick, tired, droopy, angry, nervous, weak, or miserable, it is very hard to be a good student. It is hard to even use or show what you already know. Your physical and mental health is a basic MUST for doing as well as you would like to in school. So, don't ignore your health. Pay attention to how you feel. No one else can do that for you.

Get plenty of rest.

If you are tired, nothing else works very well in your life. You can't think, or concentrate, or pay attention, learn, remember, or study. Try to get 7 or 8 hours of sleep every night. Get plenty of rest on weekends. If you have lots of studying ahead of you, take a short nap after school.

Eat well.

You can't learn or function well on an empty stomach. And all that junk food (soda, sweets, chips, snacks) actually will make you more tired. Plus, it crowds the healthy foods out of your diet—the foods your brain needs to think well and your body needs to get through the day with energy. So eat a balanced diet with lean meat, whole grains, vegetables, fruit, and dairy products. Oh, and drink a lot of water—8 glasses a day is good.

Exercise.

Everything in your body works better when it gets a chance to move. Make sure your life does not get too sedentary. Do something every day to get exercise—walk, play a sport, play a game, or run. It is a good idea to get some exercise before you sit down to study, too. Exercise helps you relax, unwind, and de-stress. It is good for stimulating your brain.

Relax and relieve stress.

Your body and your mind need rest. Do something every day to relax. Take breaks during your study time and do anything that helps you unwind. You might try these: stretch, take a hot bath, take a nice long shower, laugh, listen to calming music, write in a journal. Pay attention to signs of anxiety and stress. Are you nervous, worried, angry, sad? If you're burdened with worries, anger, or problems, talk to someone—a good friend, a teacher or parent, or another trusted adult.

I got plenty of sleep last night. After school I did yoga exercises for relaxation. When I finish my snack, I'll be in great shape to start studying for my history test.

Here is some good advice for getting set to improve your study habits. Check up on yourself to see how you do with each of these tips. Then, set goals where you need to improve.

. . . in school:

1. Pay attention.

Get everything you can out of each class. Listen. Stay awake. Your assignments will be easier if you have really been present in the class.

2. Take notes.

Write down main points. If you hear it AND write it, you'll be likely to remember it.
(See pages 56–57 for note-taking advice.)

3. Ask questions.

It's the teacher's job to see that you understand the material. It's your job to ask if you don't.

4. Use your time in class.

Get as much as possible of the next day's assignment finished before you leave the class.

5. Write down assignments.

Do not leave class until you understand the assignment and have it written down clearly.

6. Turn in your homework.

If you turn in every homework assignment, you are a long way toward doing well in a class—even if you struggle with tests.

Better Grades & Higher Test Scores / READING & LANGUAGE gr. 4–6
Copyright ©2005 by Incentive Publications, Inc., Nashville, TN.

Get Ready: Study Habits

7. Gather your supplies.

Before you sit down to study, get all the stuff together that you will need: assignment book, notebook, notes, textbook, study guides, paper, pencils, etc. Think ahead so that you have supplies for long-term projects. Bring those home from school or shop for them well in advance.

8. Avoid distractions.

Think of all the things that keep you from concentrating. Figure out ways to remove those from your life during study time. Do your best to keep interruptions away from your study time. If you listen to music while studying, choose music that can be in the background of your mind. Loud music DOES interfere with concentration on homework.

9. Turn off the TV.

No matter how much you insist otherwise, you cannot study well with the TV on. Your homework will take longer and lose quality if you watch TV while you do it. Plan your TV time before or after study time.

10. Make phone calls later.

Plan a time for phone calls. Like TV watching, talking on the phone does not mix with focusing on studies. The best way to avoid this distraction is to study in a room with no phone. If you have a cell phone, turn it off during homework hours. Call your friends when your work is finished. Then, relax and enjoy the chatting time with your friends.

11. Hide the computer games.

Stay away from video games, computer games, e-mail, and Internet surfing. Plan time for these when studies are complete, or before you settle into serious study time.

12. Know where you are going.

Review your weekly schedule and your assignment notebook. Be sure about what needs to be done. Make a clear *To-Do* list for each day, so you will know what to study. Post notes on your wall, your refrigerator, or anywhere that will remind you about what things you need to get done!

13. Plan your time.

Think about the time you have to work each night. Make a timeline for yourself. Estimate how much time each task will take, and set some deadlines. This will keep you focused on the tasks.

14. Start early.

Start early in the evening. Don't wait until just before bedtime to get underway on any assignment. When it's possible, start the day before, or a few days before.

15. Do the hardest tasks first.

Do the hardest and most important tasks first. This keeps you from delaying the tough assignments. Also, you'll be doing the harder stuff when your mind is the most fresh. Study for tests and do hard problems early, when your brain is fresh. Do routine tasks later in the evening.

16. Break up long assignments.

Big projects, major papers, or test preparations can be overwhelming. Break each long task down into smaller ones, then take one small task at a time. This will make the long assignments less scary. You'll experience success more quickly. Never try to do a long assignment all in one sitting.

17. Take breaks.

Plan a break for your body and mind every 30 minutes. Get up, walk around, stretch, do something active or relaxing. However, avoid getting caught up in any long phone conversations or TV shows. You'll never get back to studying!

18. Cut out the excuses.

It is perfectly normal to want to avoid doing school work. Just about everybody has a whole list of habits for work avoidance. There are so many excuses people give for putting off work that a whole book could be filled with them. Excuses just take up your energy. The time you spend arguing that you have a good reason for avoiding your homework is time you could use to get the work done. If you want to be a better student, you'll need to dump your own list of excuses.

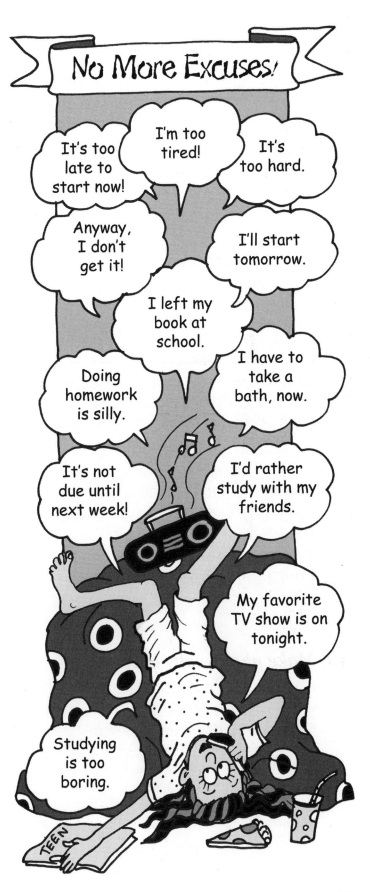

19. Ask for help.

You don't have to solve every problem alone or learn every skill by yourself. Don't count on someone noticing that you need help. Tell them. Use the adults and services around you to ask for help when you need it.

20. Plan ahead for long-range assignments.

Start early on long-range assignments, big projects, and test preparations. Don't wait until the night before something is due. You never know what will happen that last day. You could get sick. The electricity could go out. You could get stranded somewhere and not be able to get home. Get going on long tasks several days before the due date. Make a list of everything that needs to be done for a long-range assignment (including finding references and collecting supplies). Then, start from the due date and work backwards. Make a timeline or schedule that sets a time to do each of the tasks on the list.

21. Don't get behind.

Keeping up is good. Many students slip into failure, stress, and hopelessness because they get behind. The best way to avoid all of these is—NOT to get behind. This means DO your assignments on time.

If you do find yourself behind because of illness or something else unavoidable, *do something about it.* Don't get further and further into the pit! Talk to the teacher. Make a plan for catching up.

Getting behind is often caused by procrastination. Don't procrastinate. The more you do, the worse you feel, and the harder it is to catch up!

22. Get on top of problems.

Don't let small problems develop into big ones. If you are lost in a class, miss an assignment, don't understand an idea, or have done poorly on something—act quickly. Talk to the teacher, ask a parent to help, or find another student who has the information. Do **something** to correct the problem before it becomes overwhelming.

23. Reward yourself for accomplishments.

If you break down your assignments into manageable tasks, you will have more success more often. Congratulate and reward yourself for each task accomplished. Take a break, get some popcorn, go for a walk, brag about what you've done to someone. Think ahead about something you really want to do. Plan to fit that in when you finish a big assignment or when you finish a week that you've kept up with all your work. Every accomplishment is worth celebrating!

28

GET SET →

Get Tuned-Up with Thinking Skills

Your brain is capable of an amazing variety of accomplishments! There are different levels and kinds of thinking—all of them necessary to get you set for effective studying. Review these thinking skills.

Pay attention to what is possible for your mind. Then, use this information to freshen up your mental flexibility and put these skills to use as you learn and study.

Recall — To **recall** is to know and remember specific facts, names, processes, categories, ideas, generalizations, theories, or information. This thinking skill helps you remember such things as: *the formula for finding the area of a trapezoid, how to spell the words from your last science unit, the characteristics of a mollusk, the names of all the states, the capital of Egypt, the charge of an electron, or how to play a B-flat chord on the piano.*

Classify — To **classify** is to put things into categories. When you classify ideas, topics, or things, choose categories that fit the purpose and clearly define each category.

Albania, Algeria, Angola, Afghanistan, Andorra, Armenia, Austria, Azerbaijan, Australia

These are countries that begin with *A*. *(helpful category for alphabetizing)*
They are also countries that are in the eastern hemisphere. *(helpful category for a geography exercise)*

Generalize — To **generalize** is to make a broad statement about a topic based on observations or facts. A generalization should be based on plenty of evidence (facts, observations, and examples). Just one exception can prove a generalization false.

Safe Generalization — A safe generalization is one that is generally reliable.

Temperatures are generally lower at higher elevations.

Faulty generalization — A faulty generalization is invalid because there are exceptions.

Cats like to roam outside at night.

Broad generalization — A broad generalization suggests something is *always* or *never* true about *all* or *none* of the members of a group. Most broad generalizations are untrue.

All girls with red hair have bad tempers.

Stereotypes — A stereotype describes an individual member of a group or the whole group of people with a generalization. Stereotype generalizations are invalid because people in any group are individuals and have individual differences.

Children in large families don't get enough attention.

Teenagers are sloppy dressers.

French citizens are rude.

Elaborate — To **elaborate** is to provide details about a situation (to explain, compare, or give examples). When you elaborate, you might use phrases such as these: *so, because, however, but, an example of this is, on the other hand, as a result, in addition, moreover, for instance, such as, on the other hand, if you recall, furthermore, another reason is.*

> *The pizza was terrible because it was cold and soggy. To make matters worse, the sausage was rancid and the cheese smelled rotten. It tasted even lousier than the nachos.*

Infer — To **infer** is to make a logical guess based on information. Writers often give information and descriptions in stories and let the reader infer something about the characters or plot.

Someone reads a story in which the writer tells these things:
1. *Antonio's Pizza Shop lost money for the past year.*
2. *Many tables are empty at most times of the day.*
3. *More customers eat at Joe's Pizza Kitchen across the street.*

The reader infers that the Antonio's business is in trouble.

Antonio has a new cook. His spinach and garlic pizza looks and smells like seaweed. Angry customers walked out of the restaurant without paying. I infer that the pizza tastes as bad as it smells. I predict that the angry customers will not come back.

Sometimes it takes more than one thinking skill to make a prediction. In order to predict, you need to make inferences.

Predict — To **predict** is to make a statement about what will happen.

> *Because the pizza is so lousy, Antonio's Pizza Shop will lose customers.*

Distinguish Fact from Opinion — A **fact** is a statement that can be proven to be true.

An **opinion** is a statement that expresses personal attitudes or beliefs. Many opinions tell what a person believes or wishes should be so. It is not always easy to tell the difference between fact and opinion. Good thinkers will analyze statements carefully in order to keep from accepting opinions as fact.

Get Set Tip #1
Opinions often use the words **ought, should,** or **must.**

During playing time, each football team is allowed to have eleven players on the field. (Fact)

The players on the Rams' team are smarter than those on the Grizzlies' squad. (Opinion)

The Grizzlies should practice harder. (Opinion)

Next year, the Rams will win more games than the Grizzlies. (Opinion)

Recognize Cause and Effect — When one event occurs as the result of another event, there is a cause-effect relationship between the two.

Recognizing causes and effects takes skill. When reading, pay careful attention to words that give clues to cause and effect (the reason was, because, as a result, consequently).

Some effects have several causes. Some causes lead to several effects.

> *Because the cat was hungry, she howled at the door and scratched at the garbage can.*
> (cause)   (effect)   (effect)

> *The reason the cat was unhappy was that she was hungry.*
> (effect)   (cause)

Hypothesize — To **hypothesize** is to make an educated guess about a cause or effect.

A hypothesis is based on examples that support it but do not prove it. A hypothesis is something that can be—and should be—tested.

> *Very few of the people who own cats are allergic to animals.*

Extend — To **extend** is to connect ideas or things together, or to relate one thing to something different, or to apply one idea or understanding to another situation.

You are extending when. . .

. . . you read a poem about thunder and you listen more closely to the next thunderstorm.

. . . you learn the characteristics of insects, then find "bugs" that you realize are not insects.

Compare & Contrast — When you **compare** things, you describe the similarities.
When you **contrast** things, you describe their differences.

> *The poems are both odes. Both are written to a show the writer's passion about someone or something. "Ode to a Lost Friend" is written to a person. It is sober and sentimental. In contrast, "Ode to My Eraser" is written to an object. It is surprising and fun.*

Identify Bias — A **bias** is a one-sided attitude toward something. Biased thinking does not result from facts, but from feelings or attitudes.

Learn to look for bias; biased information may not be reliable, especially if it is presented as fact or nonfiction.

Example:

> I don't trust people who write letters to the editor. They are always cranks.

Draw Conclusions — A **conclusion** is a general statement that someone makes after analyzing examples and details.

A conclusion generally involves an explanation someone has developed through reasoning.

Maria and Lucy take a roller coaster ride together. About halfway through the ride, Maria notices that Lucy has stopped squealing and has become very quiet. When the ride ends, Lucy is hardly able to get off the ride. Maria sees that she is very pale and staggers when she walks. Maria concludes that Lucy is sick from the ride.

Analyze — To **analyze,** you must break something down into parts and determine how the parts are related to each other and how they are related to the whole.

For instance, you must analyze to . . .

   . . . *solve a math problem*

   . . . *outline a speech*

   . . . *edit a piece of writing for good word choice*

   . . . *divide an essay into paragraphs*

   . . . *examine an argument and decide if it is a good one*

Ah, ha! I get it, now. I need to **analyze** the facts and **synthesize** them into the perfect report.

Synthesize — To **synthesize,** you must combine ideas or elements to create a whole.

For instance, you must synthesize to . . .

   . . . *compose a poem from thoughts you have gathered*

   . . . *combine facts and dates into a timeline*

   . . . *coordinate schedules in your family*

   . . . *put effective diagrams, tables, and graphs into a report*

Evaluate — To evaluate is to make a judgment about something. Evaluations should be based on evidence. Evaluations include opinions, but these opinions should be supported or explained by examples, experiences, observations, and other forms of evidence.

When you evaluate an argument, a position, a piece of literature or other writing, an advertisement, a performance, or a media presentation, ask questions like these:

Are the conclusions reached based on good examples and facts?

Is this believable?

How effective is the argument?

Does it make sense?

Are the sources reliable?

Is the writer biased?

Logical Thinking *(or Reasoning)* — When you think **logically**, you take a statement or situation apart. You use **inductive reasoning** to examine the details that support a conclusion or **deductive reasoning** to examine a generalization that leads to specific details.

> *Dad was the first person to come home at the end of the day. If he found the door unlocked, and Ben was the last one to leave the house in the morning, then Ben did not lock the door.*

Identify Faulty Arguments — An **argument** is **faulty** when it is based on an error in logic. This means the information is misleading, or there are exceptions to the statement, or the statement is not supported by evidence.

> *Once you see that movie, you will want to become a scuba diver.*
>
> *Any business that does not display a flag has owners that are unpatriotic.*
>
> *Rich people are very happy.*

Who Let the Dogs Out?

Identify Propaganda — **Propaganda** is a form of communication intended to make listeners or readers agree with the ideas of a group. Unlike ordinary persuasive writing, propaganda often focuses on an appeal to emotions. Propaganda often uses faulty arguments, exaggeration, or information that distorts or confuses the truth.

To identify propaganda, look for faulty arguments, exaggeration, appeal to emotions, manipulation of facts, manipulation of emotions, or unsupported claims:

> *During Tom Gates' first term as governor, two convicted criminals committed murders while on parole. Do not re-elect Tom Gates, he's soft on crime.*

Learn to Think Divergently!

A divergent thinker is someone who lets his or her mind move away in
many different directions from an important core idea.

BE FLUENT

Generate lots of ideas about a topic.

I'm interested in learning about UFOs.

Have UFOs really visited Earth from outer space?

How long would it take a UFO to reach Earth from the next closest solar system if it traveled at the speed of light?

If aliens exist, would they be anything like me?

If UFOs have visited Earth, would our leaders tell us?

BE FLEXIBLE

Consider ideas that are different in kind or category from the main idea.

Everyone knows that aliens come from outer space. Or, do they?

You could say that a **germ** is an alien when it gets inside your body and makes you sick.

Some foreigners are called aliens.

Sometimes an idea is alien when you can't relate it to your life or experiences.

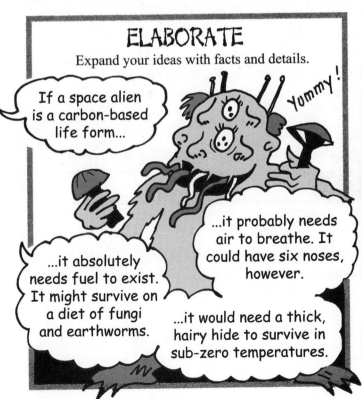

ELABORATE

Expand your ideas with facts and details.

If a space alien is a carbon-based life form...

Yummy!

...it probably needs air to breathe. It could have six noses, however.

...it absolutely needs fuel to exist. It might survive on a diet of fungi and earthworms.

...it would need a thick, hairy hide to survive in sub-zero temperatures.

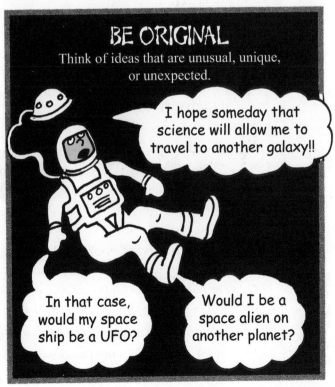

BE ORIGINAL

Think of ideas that are unusual, unique, or unexpected.

I hope someday that science will allow me to travel to another galaxy!!

In that case, would my space ship be a UFO?

Would I be a space alien on another planet?

Better Grades & Higher Test Scores / READING & LANGUAGE gr. 4–6
Copyright ©2005 by Incentive Publications, Inc., Nashville, TN.

Get Set: Thinking Skills

Get Brushed-Up on Information Skills

If you are going to get set to be a good student, you need sharp skills for finding and using information. You are fortunate to live in a time and place of almost unlimited resources for finding information. You can make use of those resources effectively only if you know what they are and what is in them.

Here is a quick review of some of the most common sources of information available for students. Get to know these references well.

Which Reference is Which?

Almanac: a yearly publication that gives information, basic facts, and statistics on many topics. Almanacs are organized with lists of information by topics. They have an alphabetical index. Much of the information is about current or recent years, but some of it is historical. Almanacs cover current events, famous people, sports, countries, geographic records, and many other categories. They usually have an index that lists information by categories.

Atlas: a book of maps. Atlases give geographical information in the forms of maps, tables, graphs, and lists. They include information about geography—including population, climate, weather, elevation, vegetation, regions, topics, topography, and much more. Some maps in atlases show political information such as countries and cities.

Bibliography: a list of books, articles, and other resources about a certain topic. Often a bibliography is found at the end of a book or article, giving a list of the sources used in the publication.

Biographical Dictionary or Reference: a book that gives a brief summary of the lives and accomplishments of famous persons. Entries are listed alphabetically. *Contemporary Authors, The Dictionary of American Biography*, and *Who's Who in America* are examples of this kind of reference.

Dictionary: a book that lists the standard words of a particular language alphabetically, and gives their meanings and pronunciations. Many dictionaries also provide other information about the word, such as its part of speech, uses, antonyms, and etymologies.

Special Dictionaries: dictionaries of words related to one subject only. There are many special dictionaries, listing such things as slang, scientific terms, historical terms, geographical features, biography, foreign words, or abbreviations.

Glossary: a listing of the important terms used in a specific book or article. A glossary is arranged alphabetically, and is generally located at the end of the book or article.

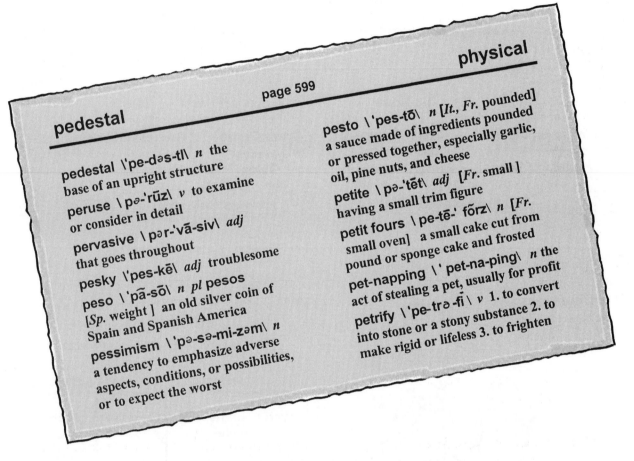

pedestal   page 599   **physical**

pedestal \'pe-dəs-tl\ *n* the base of an upright structure

peruse \pə-'rūz\ *v* to examine or consider in detail

pervasive \pər-'vā-siv\ *adj* that goes throughout

pesky \'pes-kē\ *adj* troublesome

peso \'pā-sō\ *n pl* pesos [*Sp.* weight] an old silver coin of Spain and Spanish America

pessimism \'pə-sə-mi-zəm\ *n* a tendency to emphasize adverse aspects, conditions, or possibilities, or to expect the worst

pesto \'pes-tō\ *n* [*It., Fr.* pounded] a sauce made of ingredients pounded or pressed together, especially garlic, oil, pine nuts, and cheese

petite \pə-'tēt\ *adj* [*Fr.* small] having a small trim figure

petit fours \pe-tē-' fōrz\ *n* [*Fr.* small oven] a small cake cut from pound or sponge cake and frosted

pet-napping \' pet-na-ping\ *n* the act of stealing a pet, usually for profit

petrify \'pe-trə-fi\ *v* 1. to convert into stone or a stony substance 2. to make rigid or lifeless 3. to frighten

Get Set Tip #2
Guide words are a great help in using dictionaries and glossaries. All the words on a page fall alphabetically between the two guide words. Brush up your skills with guide words.

Call me pessimistic, but I wouldn't spend a single peso on petrified petit fours smothered in pesto sauce.

From this dictionary page, you can tell that . . .

Pedestal, peso, and *pessimism* are nouns.

Persuade and *petrify* are verbs.

Pesky and *petite* are adjectives.

In *petite,* the accent is on the second syllable.

Petrify has a least three different meanings.

The plural of *peso* is *pesos.*

Petit fours and *petite* are words borrowed from the French language.

In French and Italian, *pesto* means *pounded.*

Encyclopedias: a set of books providing information on many branches of knowledge. Usually there are many volumes. Information is presented in the form of articles, and consists of a survey of the topic. The information is arranged alphabetically according to the topic or name of a person, place, or event. It is best to use key words to search for a topic in an encyclopedia.

The guide words at the top of encyclopedia pages are valuable tools to help you find topics. Any topic on page 92 would fall alphabetically between these two words. Topics circled below would be found on page 92.

A Biographical Encyclopedia

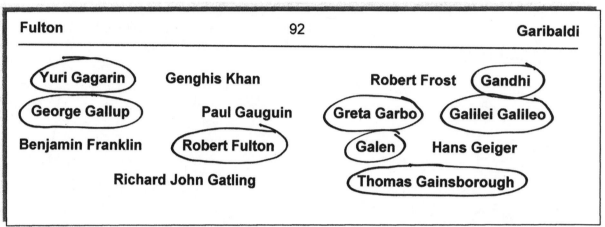

Fulton	92	Garibaldi

Yuri Gagarin   Genghis Khan   Robert Frost   Gandhi

George Gallup   Paul Gauguin   Greta Garbo   Galilei Galileo

Benjamin Franklin   Robert Fulton   Galen   Hans Geiger

Richard John Gatling   Thomas Gainsborough

Hmmm, I guess the entry for Ben Franklin is on page 91 . . .

Get Set Tip #3
Use key words to look for information in encyclopedias.

To find out about:	look under:	instead of:
mystery writer Agatha Christie's detectives	Christie	Agatha mystery detective
how Egyptians preserved mummies	mummy	Egypt preservation

Special Encyclopedias: There are many encyclopedias that contain information about one subject rather than about many subjects (as in regular encyclopedias). Individual volume encyclopedias or whole sets cover such topics as science, art, music, history, and sports. Don't miss this one: *The Encyclopedia of American Facts and Dates.*

Famous First Facts: a book that lists facts about firsts (first happenings, discoveries, and inventions) of many kinds in America, listed alphabetically. There is also an international version.

Gazetteer: a geographical dictionary, listing information about important places in the world. Subjects and places are listed alphabetically.

Guinness Book of World Records: a collection of information about the best and worst, most and least, biggest and smallest, longest and shortest, and other facts and records

Index: a list of information or items found in a book, magazine, set of books, set of magazines, or other publications. The index is generally located at the end of the resource. Information is listed alphabetically.

Sometimes a resource has an index that is a separate book. A specific magazine or journal sometimes has its own index, as do most encyclopedia sets. For instance, to find articles and information that appear in the _National Geographic_, you would consult a _National Geographic Index_ volume instead of looking in the back of each magazine. To find the volume and page location of information in a set of encyclopedias, you would consult the encyclopedia index accompanying the encyclopedia set. When a reference is on CD or online, a CD or online index accompanies the reference.

Internet: an extensive computer network that holds a huge amount of information from organizations and groups around the world as well as government agencies, libraries, schools, and universities, educational organizations, and businesses. Information can be located by browsing through categories and sites assembled by your Internet service provider and by searching the web with the help of a good search engine. The Internet can connect you to information on a vast number of topics related to all sorts of subject areas.

Get Set Tip #4
When you find a site that gives good information, add it to your list of favorites (or bookmark it) so you can get there quickly the next time.

Library Card Catalog: a file of cards that has three cards for every book in the library. These cards are filed separately. There is an author card, which is filed alphabetically by the author's last name; a subject card, which is filed alphabetically according to the subject of the book, and a title card, which is filed alphabetically according to the title of the book. In many libraries, card catalog information is now found on computers.

Library Computer Catalog: a computer file of author, title, and subject listings for all books (and other materials) in a library

Periodicals: publications that are issued at regular intervals, such as daily, weekly, monthly, quarterly, or annually. Magazines, newspapers, and scholarly journals are types of periodicals. Periodicals are an excellent source of current news and information.

Periodical Index: a book or computer database that lists the subjects and titles of articles in a particular magazine or newspaper, or a particular group of magazines or newspapers.

Newspapers: a valuable periodical published frequently, containing current information on national, international and local news. Newspapers also provide a wealth of information on sports, financial information, book reviews, editorial comments, reviews of film, theater and other entertainment events. Other features such as classified ads, comics, puzzles, TV-radio-movie listings, restaurant reviews, recipes, and horoscopes add to the list of information available in newspapers.

Quotation Indexes: listings of famous quotations and persons who said them, listed alphabetically by the first word of the quotation and by the last name of the speaker.

Table of Contents: an outline of the information contained in a book, listed in the order that the information occurs in the book. The Table of Contents is found at the beginning of the book.

Thesaurus: a reference book that groups synonyms or words with similar meanings. A thesaurus is sometimes organized by idea or theme with an alphabetical index. Other versions organize the words like a dictionary. Some thesaurus editions contain antonyms as well as synonyms.

Yearbook: a book that gives up-to-date information about recent events or findings, or that reviews events of a particular year. One such yearbook is the *World Book Yearbook of Facts.* Many encyclopedia sets publish a yearbook to update the set each year. This reduces the need to update the entire set to keep information current.

Don't forget about these other resources. They can add information that you could not easily find anywhere else.

Better Grades & Higher Test Scores / READING & LANGUAGE gr. 4–6
Copyright ©2005 by Incentive Publications, Inc., Nashville, TN.

Get Set: Information Skills

How the Library is Organized

When you are getting set to be a better student, you may need to brush up on your library skills. How well do you know your way around the library? Here is a review of your library's organization.

Every book in a library has a unique number called a *call number*. These numbers are used to organize the books. The call number is on the spine of each book. Most school and public libraries use the Dewey Decimal System as a classification system for *nonfiction* books.

How Nonfiction is Organized

The Dewey Decimal System has ten major subject area divisions. (See the chart below.) Nonfiction books are grouped by subject. Each subject and subdivision of the subject has a decimal number. Letters from the last name of the author also are a part of the call number.

The Dewey Decimal System

000-099	General Works References	400-499	Language	700-799	Fine Arts Sports
100-199	Philosophy	500-599	Pure Science Mathematics	800-899	Literature
200-299	Religion	600-688	Uses of Science Technology	900-999	History Biography Geography
300-399	Social Sciences				

How Biographies are Organized

Biographies are nonfiction books, so they are classified as a part of the Dewey Decimal System. Within the 900 section of the Dewey Decimal System, biographies and autobiographies are organized according to the name of the person who is the subject of the biography. These last names are organized alphabetically. The author's name is not a part of the organization.

Here is a sample of call numbers and organization of some biographies.

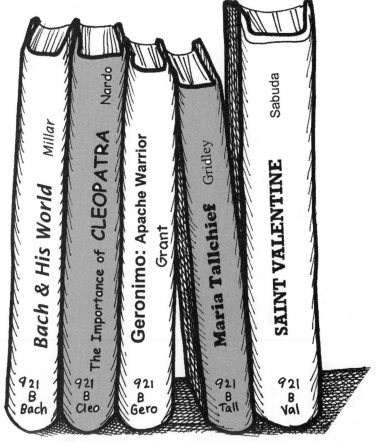

How Fiction is Organized

Fiction is organized according to the authors of the books. Fiction books are shelved alphabetically by the last name of the author. If there are authors with the same last names, then the first name comes into use as a part of the organization. If there is more than one book by an author, then the books are organized within that author's section by title, alphabetically.

(In titles beginning with articles such as a, an, or the, the article is dropped when alphabetizing.)

The call number consists of the letter **F** and some letters from the author's last name.

Better Grades & Higher Test Scores / READING & LANGUAGE gr. 4–6
Copyright ©2005 by Incentive Publications, Inc., Nashville, TN.

Get Set: Information Skills

Finding Information in the Library

A **library card catalog** contains three cards for each book in the library—a **subject** card, a **title** card, and an **author** card. The cards are alphabetized by subject, the first main word in the title, and the last name of the author.

When you look for a book in the library, look under the title or author if you know either of these. Otherwise, search for the subject you want to research.

Each card shows the call number so that you can locate the book. In addition, the card shows quite a bit of information about each book: author, title, illustrator, publisher, copyright date, number of pages, and if the book has illustrations.

SUBJECT CARDS

HORSES-STORIES

Fic
Hen   Henry, Marguerite
              King of the Wind
              Illus. by Wesley Dennis
          Rand McNally, 1948.
          172 p.   •   illlus.

CONSERVATION

574.5
Ban   Banks, Martin
              Conserving Rain Forests
          Steck-Vaughn, 1989.
          48 p.   •   illus.

AUTHOR CARDS

Fic
Hen   **Henry, Marguerite**
              King of the Wind
              Illus. by Wesley Dennis
          Rand McNally, 1948.
          172 p.   illlus.

574.5
Ban   **Banks, Martin**
              Conserving Rain Forests
          Steck-Vaughn, 1989.
          48 p.   illus.

TITLE CARDS

Fic
Hen   **King of the Wind**
          Henry, Marguerite
              Illus. by Wesley Dennis
          Rand McNally, 1948.
          172 p.   illlus.

574.5
Ban   **Conserving Rain Forests**
          Banks, Martin
          Steck-Vaughn, 1989.
          48 p.   illus.

Many libraries list all their materials on a computer system. The computer catalog holds the same information as the card catalog. You can search for a book on the computer system by doing a title search, an author search, or a subject search. You can type in a key word (or more than one word) to a title or subject search to find books that have that word in the title.

In many libraries, the computer screen also will tell you if the library has the book on the shelf or when it will be available.

SPORTS-ANECDOTES

796   **Not So Great Moments in Sports**
Pe   By Pellowski, Michael
        Illus. by Myron Miller
        N.Y.: Sterling Pub Co, 1994
        95 p.   illlus.

I want to do research on the life of Benjamin Franklin.

Do a subject search. Type in **Franklin.** *You'll get a list of books about this founding father.*

I want to find something about my favorite subject, black holes!

Do a subject search. Type in **black holes.** *If the list yields nothing, type in* **space.**

I'm looking for a collection of poems by Ogden Nash.

Do an author search. Type in **Nash, Ogden.** *You'll see a listing of his books.*

I'm looking for a book called, *Puddles, and Wings, and Grapevine Swings.*

Do a title search. Type in the whole title. You'll find the book if the library has it.

Whoops! I can't remember the title of the book I want, but it has the word "midnight" in it.

Do a title search. Type in the word **midnight.** *You'll get a list of books with* **midnight** *in the title. Scan the list to find the one you wanted.*

I want to find a book called *The Atlas of World History.*

Do a title search. Type in the whole title.

Finding Information on the Internet

It is a skill to use the Internet well for finding reliable information. It takes practice. Here is some good advice for smart use of the Internet.

Browse—Your Internet provider gathers pages on general topics. These give you quick access to information on several of the most popular topics, such as news, weather, health, travel, music, and sports. Most providers also offer quick links to kids' pages and reference materials.

Search—For a more advanced search, use a good search engine, such as google.com or yahoo.com. Try different engines until you find your favorite. To use a search engine, type in a key word (such as *snowboarding*). To make your search more specific, type in a phrase (such as *snowboarding records*) or more than one word connected by AND (*snowboarding* AND *Olympics*).

Good Questions to Ask about a WebSite

- Is the information useful?
- Is the website sponsored by a reliable organization?
- Does the site give sources for the facts?
- Is the material easy to understand and up to date?
- Does the author appear to be qualified?

Be choosy—Use your time wisely to get the best information by choosing reputable sites. Sites from the government, established companies or organizations, and universities are usually reliable (Examples: National Hockey League **www.nhl.com**; Field Museum **www.fmnh.org**; NASA **www.nasa.gov**; National Geographic for Kids **www.nationalgeographic.com/kids/**).

Be smart—Learn to evaluate the websites you visit. Don't waste time on sites that won't give information that is reliable or in-depth enough.

Be careful— Download information only from sites that seem reputable. If you are going to download software, it is safest to do it directly from the company that publishes the software. Be very careful what you download from individuals. Never open an e-mail or download a file unless you know the source of the document. Keep a good anti-virus program on your computer. Keep the program updated.

Be safe—NEVER give away any personal information on the Internet.

Internet Terms to Know

bookmark – a shortcut option that allows you to get to a site without typing in the address

BPS *(bits per second)* – how fast information moves from one place to another

browser – a software tool that is used to view sites on the Internet

chatting – "talking" with other people on the Internet (usually by typing)

chatrooms *(or chat groups)* – addresses online where many people can talk to each other

cookie – little bits of text or code that a web server leaves on your computer to track information about your personal preferences

cyberspace – refers to all the resources available on the Internet

domain name – the name that identifies an Internet site

download – to copy files or programs or information from Internet sites

e-mail *(electronic mail)* – mail that is sent over the Internet between persons

hacker – a person very skilled with computers and Internet use, who is therefore able to enter computer programs without authorization

HTML *(hyper-text mark-up language)* – the computer code used to create web pages

hyperlink – addresses, words, or graphics that are inserted into documents on the world wide web (A click on the link leads to another web page.)

That's a Good Question!

When should I NOT use the Internet to get information?

Answer:
Stay OFF the web when you can get the same information faster with a walk to your bookshelf!

hypertext – a word or group of words that form a hyperlink

ISP *(Internet service provider)* – a company that sells connections to the Internet

keyword – a word that you type into a search engine

login or logon – to connect to the Internet

logoff – to disconnect from the Internet

mailbox – a place where the ISP keeps e-mail for a user

net surfing – visiting sites on the Internet

offline – not connected to the Internet

online – connected to the Internet

post – place a message in a newsgroup or discussion group for others to read

search – to explore the Internet for information on a specific topic using a program *(search engine)* designed to search for specific words

server – a computer that provides an Internet service to clients

SPAM *(sending particularly annoying messages)* – junk e-mail or postings in discussion groups

upload – to send files or information from your computer to another computer, usually through a modem or higher-speed connection

URL *(universal resource locator)* – the address for an Internet location

Web page – a computer document written in HTML code, placed for Internet access

website – a collection of Web pages set up by a person, group, or organization

Listening for Information

Keep your ears wide open! You can gain a great amount of information if you know how to listen well—to a speech, lecture, explanation, tape, TV program, or reading. Here are some tips for smart listening. They can help you get involved in the listening process so that you take in more good information through your ears.

1. Appreciate the value.
You listen for information to get:

. . . *details*

. . . *instructions*

. . . *directions*

. . . *facts*

. . . *examples*

. . . *hazards*

You listen for understanding to:

. . . *be able to discuss what you heard*

. . . *be able to process what you heard*

. . . *be able to relate it to your own experience*

. . . *be able to test what you heard*

2. Recognize the obstacles.
These things get in the way of good listening:

. . . *tiredness*

. . . *surrounding noise*

. . . *uncomfortable setting*

. . . *personal concerns, thoughts, or worries*

. . . *wandering attention*

. . . *too many things to hear at once*

. . . *missing the beginning or end*

. . . *talking (yourself)*

. . . *speaker talks too fast*

. . . *speaker's presentation is boring*

3. Make a commitment to improve.
You can't always control all obstacles (such as the comfort of the setting or the quality of the speaker's presentation), but there are things you can control. Put these to work to gain more from your listening:

. . . *Get enough rest.*

. . . *Do your best to be comfortable while you listen.*

. . . *Cut out as many distractions as possible.*

. . . *Keep your mind focused on what is being said.*

. . . *Look directly at the speaker.*

. . . *Take notes.*

. . . *Relate the speaker's ideas to your own life.*

. . . *Don't miss the beginning or ending.*

. . . *Pay attention to opening and closing remarks.*

. . . *Pay attention to anything that is repeated.*

. . . *As soon as possible after listening, summarize what you have heard. Put the summary into writing.*

I hear you!

Get Set Tip #5
Stop talking!
(You can't listen while you talk.)

48

Get Set: Information Skills

Better Grades & Higher Test Scores / READING & LANGUAGE gr. 4–6
Copyright ©2005 by Incentive Publications, Inc., Nashville, TN.

Reading for Information

To find information in written passages, you need to make use of many different reading skills. Some information can be gained quickly by scanning or skimming a list, definition, description, or other passage. To get other kinds of information, you need to give a close reading, paying attention to each detail. Before you read a passage, get clear about the purpose of your reading. How much detail do you need to get?

A curious incident took place recently on a bus traveling in northern California. Forty people were enjoying a tour of scenic spots along the coast's Highway 101.

Suddenly one of them shouted and pointed out a window. "Oh, my goodness! Look at that! It's a monster!"

Other tourists gasped and shrieked. "It's Bigfoot!" one yelled.

Outside, a large hairy creature was loping along at the edge of the highway. As the bus driver slowed the bus, passengers rushed to the right side of the bus to look.

Just about everyone had an exclamation or question such as: "Where is it?" "Yes, it's definitely Bigfoot!" "I don't see anything!" "What in the world is that?" "There's no such thing as Bigfoot!" "It must be a hoax!" "It's just a bear."

Soon the creature disappeared into the trees. Though the bus stopped, the group decided not to follow the creature into the woods. They hurried to the nearest town and reported the sighting to the authorities. Then they went on their way, pondering what they had seen—arguing, hypothesizing, and wondering. Could it be that they had seen the elusive Bigfoot?

Skimming

By skimming the passage, the reader can quickly gain the main ideas of the passage:

A busload of tourists saw a big hairy creature along side the road.

Some of the spectators thought they were seeing Bigfoot.

Close Reading

With a closer, slower reading, the reader will discover such specific details as:

There were 40 tourists on the bus.

The people were on a sightseeing tour.

The trip followed Highway 101.

Some people thought it was Bigfoot.

Some viewers were skeptical.

Some people didn't see anything.

The bus stopped.

The tourists did not search for the creature.

They reported the sighting.

Get Serious about Study Skills

Let's face it—good learning and good grades don't happen without some sharp study skills. Take advantage of every opportunity you get to strengthen skills like the ones described on pages 50–66.

WHAT'S THE DIFFERENCE?

Welcome to Clown Night School

Tell me, Tootles, what's the difference between a **summary** and a **paraphrase**?

That's easy Slappy Sam! A **paraphrase** is a restatement of someone else's ideas in your own words.

A **summary** is a short statement of the main ideas of a speech or piece of writing.

A clown wouldn't be a clown without the makeup. Each clown tries to create a face with a particular look with makeup. This "look" is called the **working face**. A clown often keeps the same working face whenever she or he takes on the clown role.

The working face begins with a thick coat of white stage makeup. Next, the clown uses bright colors and bold lines to paint on eyebrows, lips, lines, and other markings. The lines and patches of color emphasize parts of the face, create certain expressions, or add features such as creases, tears, eyelashes, or blushing cheeks.

The final result is an interesting "working face" that becomes that clown's personal trademark.

▬ Summary ▬

Each clown creates a face with a look that is unique to that clown. This face is painted on to give a particular expression and special features. A clown's face is called his or her "working face."

▬ Paraphrase ▬

Makeup is a main ingredient in making a clown. Every clown paints a "working face" that is unique to that clown. A clown uses bold colors and lines to paint an expression on top of a thick layer of white makeup. The working face includes features such as lips, eyebrows, and wrinkles. The end result of the artwork is a face that catches the interest of the audience and makes that clown different from other clowns.

Heather Lock Times, April 28

Loch Ness Monster, Fact or Fiction?

> Who could **doubt** my existence?

Angus McFogg, of Thistletown Bog, has become the latest, self-proclaimed witness to a sighting of the infamous Loch Ness Monster. Angus it not able to verify his claim. He claims that he saw a long-necked monster raise its head in front of his boat last week. He was not able to get his camera in time to capture a picture. Other occupants on his boat did not see the spectacle.

Stories about the Loch Ness Monster have been told for hundreds of years. The earliest known sighting was in 565 A.D. by St. Columbia. Over the years, many people have claimed to have seen the monster in the waters of Loch Ness, Scotland. None have been able prove it. The best-known photos are blurry and do not show distinct features. There are many sensible theories about how the photos could have been faked.

Most scientists are skeptical about whether a creature, either fish or mammal, could survive undetected in the 800-foot deep waters of Loch Ness. Nevertheless, people from all walks of life continue to report seeing the famous creature affectionately known to the world as "Nessie."

Summary

There has been a new sighting of the Loch Ness Monster. Like the other sightings, this one could not be proven. Although many people have claimed to have seen a large sea creature in Loch Ness, Scotland, most scientists believe there is not enough evidence to prove Nessie exists.

Paraphrase

There has been a new sighting of the Loch Ness Monster. This sighting was by Angus McFogg. He had no proof of the sighting, since others on the boat did not see the creature and he was not able to get a picture.

For many years, people have claimed to have seen a large, monster-like sea creature in Loch Ness, Scotland. There is, however, no evidence to prove the monster's existence. The pictures that do exist are not clear, and could be fakes.

Due to lack of evidence and their understanding of the conditions of the loch, most scientists doubt that such a creature could exist. This doesn't stop many people from believing in the creature or from claiming to have seen it.

Outlining

An outline is a way to organize ideas or information into main ideas and subideas (or supporting details). If you want to get set to improve as a student, it's a good idea to polish your outlining skills. You will find outlining very helpful for many study situations.

Starting a Dive Training Business

I. Decide on details of the business
    A. Clarify business purpose
    B. Choose specialty and type of client
    C. Choose name and location
    D. Decide on number/kind of employees

II. Look into supplies and costs
    A. Look for supplies
        1. Office supplies and furniture
        2. Diving equipment
        3. Training materials
    B. Make a price/cost list
        1. Office supplies and furniture
        2. Equipment
        3. Staff, staff expenses
        4. Insurance

III. Learn about starting a business
    A. Do book and web research
    B. Visit other dive shops
        1. Getting clients
        2. Leading training sessions
        3. Problems and risks

IV. Develop a business plan
    A. Registering business
    B. Marketing
    C. Finances/budget
    D. Business space, utilities
    E. Equipment
    F. Staff
    G. Transportation

You can use an outline to
- organize ideas to prepare a speech
- organize ideas for a piece of writing
- plan a project
- record and review information from a textbook
- get ready to retell a story
- take notes in class
- take notes from a textbook assignment
- prepare to give or write a report
- to write a story
- to write a speech
- to study a passage

An outline can be formal or informal. It can contain single words, phrases, or sentences, depending on its purpose.

I'll use an outline to organize ideas for starting a diving business.

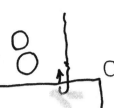

Choosing & Maintaining Scuba Gear

I. Introduction
   A. Importance of gear
   B. Basic gear needed
   C. Deciding to buy gear
      1. Estimated costs
      2. Getting advice

II. Choosing gear
   A. Mask
   B. Fins & booties
   C. Snorkel
   D. Suit
      1. Different kinds
      2. Fit
   E. Weight belt
   F. Regulator
   G. BC vest
   H. Dive watch or computer

III. Maintaining gear
   A. Regular soaking
   B. Regular inspection
   C. Repairs
      1. Repairing straps and buckles
      2. Repairing valves
      3. Repair kit
   D. Transporting gear properly
   E. Storing gear

IV. Avoiding loss of gear
   A. Recording and marking gear
   B. Organizing gear
   C. Tips for remembering gear
   D. Insuring gear

This outline shows the main ideas of my research about Scuba diving equipment. It will help me plan a speech on this topic.

Danger Below the Surface

Intro
- Divers set out to explore the shipwreck
- Had no idea what danger awaited them
- Unexpected discovery of treasure in the ship
- Describe the treasure (shiny objects)
- Divers' occupation with the treasure,
- Lack of awareness they had company
- Shock at discovering circling sharks

Looking for escape
- Signals about places
  to hide
- Signals to the boat

Sharks move in for attack
- Divers work a plan to trick the sharks
- The escape

Worried friends on the boat
- Seeing signs of sharks but no signs of divers
- Radio for help

Surprise return to surface
- Divers tell their story
- Divers learned a good lesson

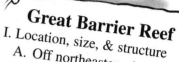

Great Barrier Reef

I. Location, size, & structure
  A. Off northeastern Australia
  B. Made of 2,800 coral reefs
    1. Ribbon reefs
    2. Platform reefs
    3. Fringing reefs
  C. World's largest system
  D. Largest structure of living
    organisms
  E. 1,240 miles long

II. Coral reefs
  A. Formed by polyps
  B. How corals grow
  C. Habitat for sea life

III. Life on the reef
  A. 400 types coral
  B. 1,500 species fish
  C. 4,000 species mollusks
  D. 500 species seaweed
  E. Birds, turtles, snakes

IV. Appeal/value of reef
  A. Beauty
  B. Tourism, diving
  C. Environmental health
  D. Wildlife habitat

V. Reef protection
  A. Pollution problems
  B. Bleaching problem
  C. Great Barrier Reef Marine
    Park Authority role
  D. World's largest marine
    protected area

Here I used a casual outline to organize the main ideas and details for an underwater story.

This outline organizes facts from my research on the Great Barrier Reef. Later, I'll expand these facts into a travel brochure on the reef.

Sharks and Divers, Main Ideas

Ch I. Number of attacks
— Four last year, numbers falling
— Better safety and treatment
— Some not reported; some countries hide reports

Ch II. Location of attacks
— Inshore of sandbars, between sandbars
— Steep drop-offs

Ch III. Kinds of attacks

A. Provoked attacks
— Touching sharks
— Humans feeding sharks or interfering with feeding

B. Unprovoked attacks
— Hit and Run attacks leave less severe injuries
— Occur in surf zone
— Shark bites or slashes victim and leaves
— Bump and bite attacks cause greater injuries
— Occur in deeper water
— Shark circles then bumps and attacks victim
— Sneak attacks cause severe injuries
— Occur without warning
— Shark attacks repeatedly

Ch IV. How to avoid attack
— Avoid splashing
— Never try to touch a shark
— Swim in a group
— Don't dive or swim at dawn, dusk, or night
— Remove shiny jewelry

I've used this rough outline as a way to note main ideas from a book about shark attacks on divers.

Taking Notes

A study skill of major importance is knowing how to take notes well and using them effectively. Good notes from classes and from reading are valuable resources to anyone who is trying to do well as a student. A lot of learning goes on while you are taking notes—you may not even realize it is happening!

Here is the basic process for taking notes:

1.
Write notes in formal or casual outline form.

2.
Listen for a main idea. Write it down.

3.
Indent and write examples that support each main idea.

4.
Use abbreviations or shortened forms for common words.

Here is what is happening when you take notes:

1. When you take notes, you naturally listen better. (You have to listen to get the information to write it down!)

2. When you listen for the purpose of taking notes, you naturally learn and understand the material better. Taking notes forces you to focus on what's being said or read.

3. When you sort through the information and decide what to write, you naturally think about the material and process it. This increases the chances that you will remember it.

4. The actual act of writing the notes fixes the information more firmly in your brain.

5. Having good notes in your notebook makes it possible for you to review and remember the information.

Tips for Wise Note Taking

from a speech or spoken lesson . . .

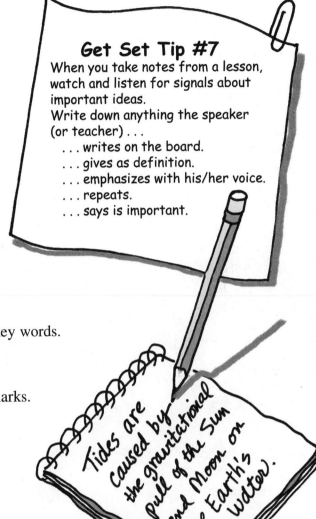

Get Set Tip #7
When you take notes from a lesson, watch and listen for signals about important ideas.
Write down anything the speaker (or teacher) . . .
. . . writes on the board.
. . . gives as definition.
. . . emphasizes with his/her voice.
. . . repeats.
. . . says is important.

- Have a notebook or a notebook section for each subject.

- When the talk begins, write the topic at the top of a clean page.

- Write the date and the subject at the top before the speech or lecture begins.

- Take notes on only one side of the paper.

- Use a sharp pencil or erasable pen.

- Write neatly so you can read it later.

- Leave big margins to the left of the outline. Use these spaces to star important items or write key words.

- Leave blank space after each main idea section.

- Pay close attention to the opening and closing remarks.

- Listen more than you write.

from a textbook assignment . . .

- Skim through one section at a time to get the general idea (a few paragraphs or use the textbook divisions). Then, go back and write down the main ideas.

- For each main idea, write a few supporting details or examples.

- Notice bold or emphasized words or phrases. Record these with their definitions.

- Read captions under pictures. Pay attention to facts, tables, charts, graphs and pictures, and the explanations that go along with them. Put information in your notes if it is very important.

- Don't write too little. You won't have all the main points or enough examples.

- Don't write too much. You won't have time or interest in reviewing the notes.

Preparing a Report

Reports—they're everywhere! Students are always being asked to do a report of some kind. When you hear the word, you might immediately think of a book report or a long written paper. But the world of reports is very broad. There are all kinds of reports. They can be papers, posters, demonstrations, speeches, audio or visual presentations, computer projects, or art projects—to name a few. They can be assigned for any subject area to cover just about any topic.

Whatever the subject or the type of report—they all have some things in common. First, you need some **raw material** (facts and information) as the basis for the report. To get that, you need to do some research. Then, for any report, you must **select and organize the information** so that it can be communicated (or reported!) Finally, a report is **presented.** This means you need to find a way to share with someone else what you learned about the topic.

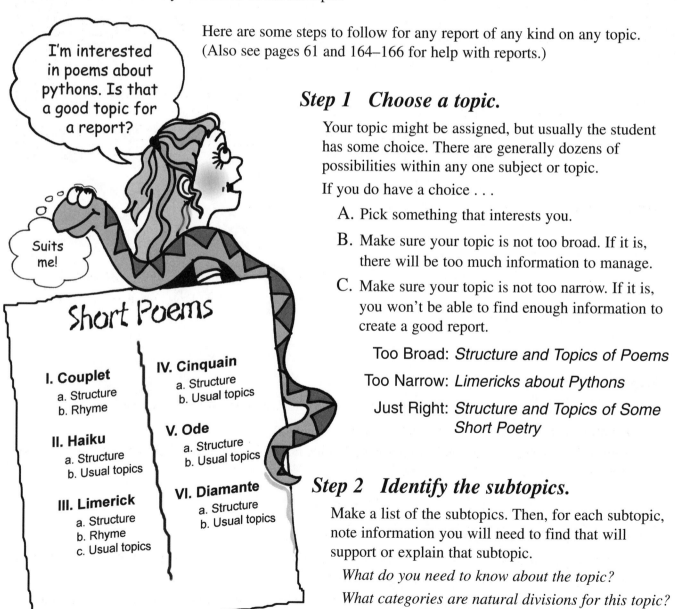

Here are some steps to follow for any report of any kind on any topic. (Also see pages 61 and 164–166 for help with reports.)

Step 1 Choose a topic.

Your topic might be assigned, but usually the student has some choice. There are generally dozens of possibilities within any one subject or topic.

If you do have a choice . . .

A. Pick something that interests you.

B. Make sure your topic is not too broad. If it is, there will be too much information to manage.

C. Make sure your topic is not too narrow. If it is, you won't be able to find enough information to create a good report.

Too Broad: *Structure and Topics of Poems*

Too Narrow: *Limericks about Pythons*

Just Right: *Structure and Topics of Some Short Poetry*

Step 2 Identify the subtopics.

Make a list of the subtopics. Then, for each subtopic, note information you will need to find that will support or explain that subtopic.

What do you need to know about the topic?

What categories are natural divisions for this topic?

You might use a rough outline for this step.

Step 3 Find information.

Use as many resources as you can to find solid information on your topic. Don't limit yourself to just one source or one kind of source. (See pages 36–41.)

As you observe, listen to, or read the sources, take notes. Write ideas, key words or phrases, and examples. Use a separate note card for each source and each major idea or fact you find.

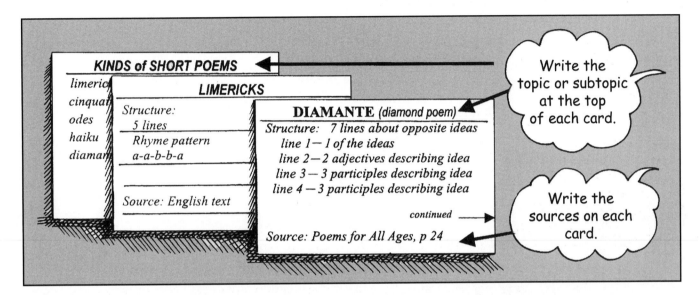

Step 4 Organize the information.

Organize the information by grouping your cards into subtopics and placing them in a logical sequence. Decide what fits where.

If you have too much information, or if some doesn't quite fit, this is the time to eliminate it.

If you have subtopics that are not well supported with examples or details, this is the time to do more research and collect more information.

Step 5 Decide on the format.

If you have been asked to write a paper or give a speech, then the format is already decided.

If you are free to choose a format or product, do this now.

How will you show what you have learned? Decide now! The steps you follow from this point on depend greatly on the format you choose. (See ideas on page 61.)

Step 6 Begin to put the report together.

If your report will be spoken or written, begin writing sentences and paragraphs, making sure each paragraph covers a subtopic with supporting details.

If your report follows a different format, you still need to decide how to communicate each idea and its supporting examples or details.

Step 7   Review and edit your work.

This is the time to look at your work. This is also a time to ask someone else to give a response. (Exactly how you review the work will depend on the format of the report.)

Ask questions such as these about the "rough draft" of your report, whatever form it takes:

Are the main ideas covered?

Is the information clear?

Is the information complete?

Does the manner of presentation make sense?

Does the report have a clear introduction and conclusion?

Is there a logical order for the presentation?

Is the material interesting? Is the presentation interesting?

If written, does the piece flow along well?

If written, are the mechanics and grammar correct?

After you and another person (or persons) have reviewed it, make revisions that are necessary.

Step 8   Put the final product together.

Whatever the format, this is the time to prepare the final product. Add extra materials at this time, too (drawings, diagrams, lists, charts, maps, graphs, timelines, tables, surveys).

Step 9   Present the report.

How will you share the information?

**Turn it in? Hang it up?
Sing it? Dance it? Show it?
Read it? Perform it?
Mail it? Publish it?**

This is the time to do it!

Get Set Tip #8
Avoid these common problems:
- Report topic too broad
- Report topic too narrow
- Missing some subtopics
- Not enough information on some subtopics
- Poor presentation of final report

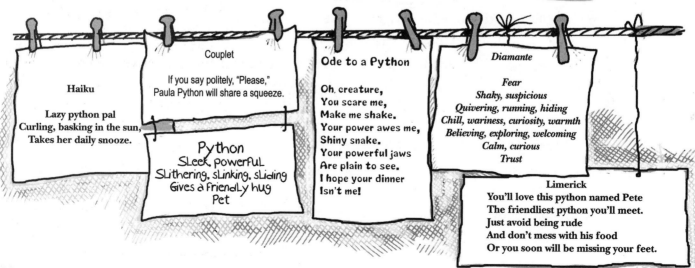

Haiku

Lazy python pal
Curling, basking in the sun,
Takes her daily snooze.

Couplet

If you say politely, "Please,"
Paula Python will share a squeeze.

Python
Sleek, powerful
Slithering, slinking, sliding
Gives a friendly hug
Pet

Ode to a Python

Oh, creature,
You scare me,
Make me shake.
Your power awes me,
Shiny snake.
Your powerful jaws
Are plain to see.
I hope your dinner
Isn't me!

Diamante

Fear
Shaky, suspicious
Quivering, running, hiding
Chill, wariness, curiosity, warmth
Believing, exploring, welcoming
Calm, curious
Trust

Limerick
You'll love this python named Pete
The friendliest python you'll meet.
Just avoid being rude
And don't mess with his food
Or you soon will be missing your feet.

Creative Reporting

When you think about a **report**, think about the many ways a report can be structured and shared. It might take a little creativity (or a lot), but nearly any body of information can be presented in a number of different or unexpected ways. Here are just a few options for preparing and giving a report.

Written or Spoken Reports

viewpoint (or different viewpoint)
cause-effect account
group of short poems
a book of crossword puzzles

letter
editorial
diary
narrative poem
photo essay
a protest
a dialogue
an argument

interview
questions

radio
broadcast

series of
riddles

clues to unravel a mystery
words & phrases cut from magazines
fictionalized account of an event
The Fact Book About_____
The Truth About_____

The ABC Book of_____
an event told as a news report
A Top 10 List of_____
10 Facts and 10 Fables About_____
A Day In the Life of_____

Myths About_____Debunked
20 Questions and Answers About_____
Strange and Amazing Facts About_____
Future Predictions About_____

Reports that Combine Writing & Art

- children's picture book
- advertisement
- an original CD
- travel brochure
- a map
- cartoons
- timeline
- game
- a book cover
- a music album cover
- an original song
- slide presentation
- instructive poster
- How-To Handbook
- A Guide Book to _____
- collage of pictures and words
- illustrated dictionary of terms

Other Reports

- a mime performance
- a painting or drawing
- a sculpture
- a dance
- a demonstration
- a model
- a scavenger hunt
- a drama

Better Grades & Higher Test Scores / READING & LANGUAGE gr. 4–6
Copyright ©2005 by Incentive Publications, Inc., Nashville, TN.

Get Set: Study Skills

How to Prepare for a Test

Good test preparation does not begin the night before the test.
The time to get ready for a test starts long before this night.
Here are some tips to help you get ready—weeks before the test and right up to test time.

1. **Start your test preparation at the beginning of the year—or at least as soon as the material is first taught in the class.**

   The purpose of a test is to give a picture of what you are learning in the class. That learning doesn't start 12 hours before the test. It starts when you start attending the class. Think of test preparation this way, and you will be less overwhelmed or anxious about an upcoming test. You will be much better prepared for a test *(even one that is days or weeks away)* if you . . .

   - pay attention in class
   - take good notes
   - keep your notes and class handouts organized
   - read all your assignments
   - do your homework regularly
   - make up any work you miss when you are absent
   - ask questions in class about anything you don't understand
   - review notes and handouts regularly

Get Set Tip #9
Don't wait until the last minute to study for a test.

This test would have been easier if I had paid more attention in class!

2. **Once you know the date of the test, make a study plan.**

   Look over your schedule and plan time to start organizing and reviewing material.

   Allow plenty of time to go through all the material.

   Your brain will retain more if you review it a few times and spread the studying out over several days.

3. **Get all the information you can about the test.**

   Record everything the teacher says about the test.

   Get clear about what material will be covered.

   If you can, find out about the format of the test.

   Make sure you get any study guides the teacher gives out.

   Make sure you listen well to any in-class reviews.

4. *Use your study time effectively.*

Dos & Don'ts

Do gather and organize all the notes, handouts, or study guides you have.

Do review your text, paying attention to bold words and statements.

Do review your notes. Use a highlighter to emphasize important points.

Do review any previous quizzes on the same material.

Do predict the questions that may be asked. Think about how to answer them.

Do make study guides and aids for yourself.

Do make a list of important points with brief reminders about each one.

Do make sets of cards with key vocabulary words, terms and definitions, main concepts, or other important bits of information.

Do ask someone (reliable) to quiz you on the main points and terms.

Don't spend your study time blankly staring at your notebook or mindlessly leafing through your textbook.

Don't study with someone else unless that person actually helps you learn material better.

Don't study in blocks of time so long that you get tired, bored, or distracted.

5. *Get yourself and your supplies ready.*

Do these things the night before the test (not too late):
- Gather all the supplies you need for taking the test (good pencils with erasers, erasable pens, scratch paper).
- Put these supplies in your school bag.
- Gather your study guides, notes, and text into your school bag.
- Get a good night of rest.

In the morning:
- Eat a healthy breakfast.
- Look over your study guides and note card reminders.
- Relax and be confident that your preparation will pay off.

Get Set: Study Skills

How to Take a Test

Before the test begins

- Try to get a little exercise before class to help you relax.
- Go to the bathroom and get a drink.
- Arrive at the class on time (or a bit early).
- Get settled into your seat; get your supplies out.
- If there is time, you might glance over your study guides while you wait.
- To relax, take some deep breaths; exhale slowly.

When you get the test

- Put your name on all pages.
- Before you write anything, scan over the test to see how long it is, what kinds of questions it has, and what it includes.
- Think about your time, and quickly plan how much time you can spend on each section.
- Read each set of directions twice.
- Circle key words in the directions.
- Answer all the short-answer questions. Do not leave any blanks.
- If you are not sure of an answer, make a smart guess.
- Do not change an answer unless you are absolutely sure it is wrong.

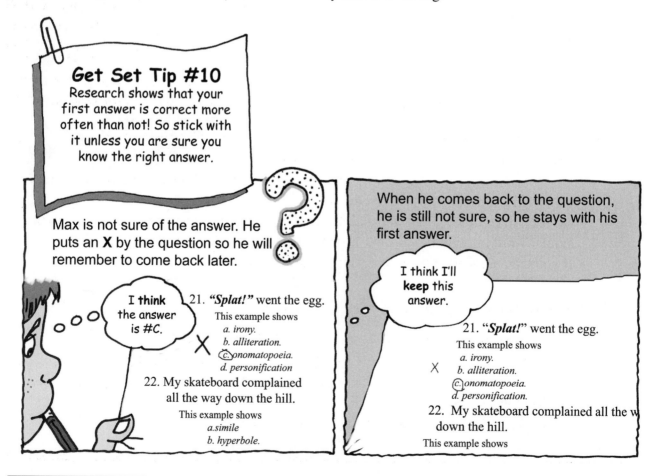

More Test-Taking Tips

Tips for Answering Multiple Choice Questions

Multiple choice questions give you several answers from which to choose.

- Read the question twice.
- Before you look at the choices, close your eyes and answer the question. Look for that answer.
- Read all the choices before you circle an answer.
- If you are not absolutely sure, cross out answers that are obviously incorrect.
- Choose the answer that is most complete or most accurate.
- If you are not absolutely sure, choose one of the answers that has not been ruled out.
- Do not change an answer unless you are absolutely sure of the correct answer.

Tips for Answering Matching Questions

Matching questions ask you to recognize facts or definitions in one column that correspond to facts, definitions, or descriptions in a second column.

- Read through both columns to familiarize yourself with the choices.
- Do the easy matches first.
- Cross off answers as you use them.
- Match the leftover items last.
- If you don't know the answer, make a smart guess.

> **Get Set Tip #11**
> On all questions, on any test—always read the directions through twice!

Tips for Answering Fill-in-the Blank Questions

Fill-in-the-blank questions ask you to write a word that completes the sentence.

- Read through each question. Answer it the best you can.
- If you don't know an answer, mark the question with an **X**. Go on to answer the questions you do know.
- Go back to the questions you marked with **X**. If you don't know the exact answer, write a similar word or definition. Come as close as you can to the correct answer.
- If you have no idea of the answer, make a smart guess.

Tips for Answering True-False Questions

True-false questions ask you to tell whether a statement is true or false.

- Watch for words like *most, some,* and *often.* Usually statements with these words are TRUE.
- Watch for words like *all, always, only, none, nobody,* and *never.* Usually statements with these words are FALSE.
- If any part of a statement is false, then the item is FALSE.

Even More Test-Taking Tips

Tips for Solving Analogies

An **analogy question** asks you to choose an answer by finding the relationship between a pair of words.

In an analogy, this symbol **:** means *is to*. This symbol **::** means *as*.

toes : foot :: fingers : _____

a. shoe   b. glove   c. hand   d. body

So the above analogy reads: ***toes*** are to ***foot*** as ***fingers*** are to _____

- First, you must establish the relationship between the first two words.
- Try to state a sentence that relates the words: *Toes are attached to a foot.*
- Second, find the word that shows the same relationship between the second pair.
- Try to finish a similar sentence about the other word: *Fingers are attached to a ___.*

Tips for Answering Reading Comprehension Tests

Reading comprehension tests ask you to read a piece of writing and answer questions about it.

- Read through the questions before you read the passage.
- Keep the questions in mind as you read the passage.
- Read each question carefully.
- Skim back through the passage to look for key words that are related to the question.
- Reread that section carefully.
- Eliminate any answers that cannot be correct.
- Choose the correct answer.

Tips for Answering Essay Questions

Essay questions ask you to write a short answer (usually a few paragraphs) about a subject.

- Make sure you are clear about what the question is asking.
- Think ahead to your answer. Sketch out a rough outline of the main points you will make and details supporting each point.
- Write an introduction that briefly states a summarized version of your answer.
- Write a body that states the main ideas clearly.
- Reinforce each main idea with details and examples.
- Write a summarizing sentence that restates the main idea.

GET SHARP —→

in

GRAMMAR, USAGE, MECHANICS, and SPELLING

Nouns

A *noun* is a word that names a person, place, thing, or idea.

common noun — any noun that does not name a specific person, place, thing, or idea
    persons: *sister, mayor, gorillas, pianist, doctor, dancer, electrician*
    places: *desert, school, attic, bedroom, street, cities, corner, park, church, malls*
    things: *enchiladas, mumps, snorkel, doughnut, razor, jacket, nosebleed, headache*
    ideas: *truth, jealousy, freedom, honesty, maturity, confusion, evil*

proper noun — the name of a specific person, place, thing, or idea
    Grandpa Giggles, Lake Huron, Golden Gate Bridge, Times Square, Mickey Mouse

concrete noun — names a thing that can be touched or seen
    guitar, pizza, keyboard, alligator, sidewalk, fork, volleyball, sidewalk, dentists

abstract noun — names something you can think about but cannot see or touch
    superiority, love, poverty, sadness, pride, fear, democracy, friendship

compound noun — made up of two or more words, two words, or hyphenated words
    baseball, jellybean, high school, coffeepot, father-in-law, sixth-graders

collective noun — names a collection of persons, animals, places, or things
    team, tribe, herd, flock, jury, committee, United Nations, orchestra, bunch, gang

singular noun — names one person, place, thing, or idea
    fingernail, box, veto, goose, knife, country, foot, tooth, alto, jealousy

plural noun — names more than one person, place, thing, or idea
    fingernails, boxes, vetoes, geese, knives, countries, feet, altos, jealousies

DID YOU KNOW?

Nouns have gender, you know!

No way!

It's true!

female - bridesmaid, aunt, doe, actress, hostess
male - rooster, brother, bull, fireman, actor
idefinite - gorilla, president, dentist, lamb, conductor

Nouns are grouped into one of three cases. The case of a noun tells how it is related to the other words in the sentence. Here's how to tell which case is which.

CRACKING THE CASE(s)

nominative case — A noun is in the nominative case when it is used as the subject of the verb.

*Yesterday, a rare **document** disappeared from a locked safe.*

*Right after the disappearance, top **detectives** came running.*

*How did the **thief** manage to get away with the document?*

possessive case — A noun is in the possessive case when it shows possession or ownership.

*How many people knew the **safe's** combination?*

*So far, the **document's** true value has been kept a secret.*

*News reporters were anxious to hear the **detectives'** theories.*

objective case — A noun is in the objective case when it is used as the direct object, the indirect object, or the object of the preposition.

*Sergeant Sharp interviewed three **suspects**. (direct object)*

*Chef la Lunch brought the **investigators** lunch. (indirect object)*

*The chef presented the biggest crepe to the chief **inspector**. (object of a preposition)*

Be positive about appositives!

An appositive is a noun placed next to another noun or pronoun to add information about it. An appositive may be a noun alone, or it may have other words that modify it.

*Wilma Wiley, **the renowned document thief**, could not be located.*

*No one knows the whereabouts of her cagey partner, **Twila**.*

*The detectives got a lucky break, **an anonymous tip**.*

*The lead detective, **Sergeant Sharp**, was optimistic about solving the case.*

Get Sharp Tip #1
Commas are used to set most appositives off from the rest of the sentence. If the appositive is essential to the meaning of the sentence, commas are not needed.
(Sergeant Smart was the one who followed up on all the leads.)

13 *Rules for Forming Plural Nouns*

1. Add **s** to the singular form of most nouns.

2. Add **s** to most nouns that *end in o preceded by a vowel.*
radios, rodeos, stereos, studios

3. Add **s** to most musical terms that *end in o.*
pianos, altos, sopranos, cellos, banjos

4. Add **s** to most nouns that *end in y preceded by a vowel.*
keys, monkeys, donkeys, valleys

5. Add **s** to proper nouns that *end in y.*
O'Gradys, Savoys, Barrys

6. Add **s** to most nouns that *end in f or fe where the final f sound is still heard in the plural.*
safes, hoofs, chiefs, beliefs

7. Add **s** to the end of nouns that *end in ful.*
pailfuls, tankfuls, tablespoonfuls

8. Add **s** to the most important word in a *compound word or hyphenated word.*
commanders in chief, Secretaries of State, sisters-in-law, great-aunts

9. Add **es** to nouns which *end in ch, sh, s, x, and z.*
churches, lunches, bushes, foxes, buses, messes, buzzes

10. Add **es** to many nouns that *end in o preceded by a consonant.*
echoes, heroes, tomatoes, tornadoes, volcanoes

11. Add **es** to most nouns that *end in y preceded by a consonant. (Change the y to i.)*
flies, pennies, diaries, cities, fairies

12. Add **es** to nouns that *end in f or fe where the final sound becomes a v sound.(Change the f to v.)* *wives, knives, leaves, calves*

13. Add **'s** to *symbols, letters, figures, and words described as words.*
D's, 9's, +'s, x's, $'s
*She counted the **hello's** in the dialogue.*
*You included seven **then's** in your paragraph.*

4 Rule Breakers for Plural Nouns

1. Some plurals are formed by irregular spelling changes.
women, teeth, geese, mice, children, cacti, oxen

2. Some nouns have the same singular and plural forms.
deer, sheep, buffalo, antelope

3. Some nouns sound like plurals but have a singular meaning.
mathematics, series, mumps, physics

4. Some nouns only have a plural form.
species, scissors, slacks, clothes, measles

banana of one gorilla........→
two bananas for one gorilla........→
a banana for gorillas to share........→
bananas for several gorillas........→

THE SQUEEZE MACHINE

........→gorilla's banana
........→gorilla's bananas
........→gorillas' banana
........→gorillas' bananas

5 Rules for Forming Possessive Nouns

1. Add **'s** to make most singular nouns into the possessive form.
tadpole's legs, leopard's spots, Joe's job, soprano's voice

2. Add **only an apostrophe** to change plural nouns ending in *s* into the possessive form.
giraffes' necks, potatoes' eyes, foxes' teeth, sharks' skeletons

3. Add **'s** to make most other plural nouns into the possessive form.
women's rights, geese's feathers, mice's whiskers, children's giggles

4. Add **'s** to make most compound nouns into the possessive form.
mother-in-law's opinion, jellybean's color, crackerjack's flavor

5. Add **'s** to the last noun in a series to show shared possession.
Bob, Billy, Brenda, Brad, and Betsy's team

Pronouns

A *pronoun* is a word that is used in place of a noun.

Ask Professor Know-it-all
She knows a lot!

What is a personal pronoun?

Answer: a pronoun that refers to people or things
Examples: I, you, he, she, it, we, they, his, hers, her, its, me, myself, us, yours

What is a subject pronoun?

Answer: a pronoun used as the subject of a sentence or in place of a predicate noun
Examples: I, we, it, they, she, he, you

What is an object pronoun?

Answer: a pronoun used as a direct object, indirect object, or object of a preposition
Examples: them, me, her, him, us, you, it

personal pronoun — refers to people or things
    singular personal pronouns – *She does great gymnastics tricks.*
    plural personal pronouns – *Do **they** eat pizza every night?*
    first person pronoun – *I can catch that train!*
    second person pronoun – *When did **you** learn to sing like that?*
    third person pronoun – *Roxy sends **them** her favorite music.*

subject pronoun — used as the subject of the verb
    We have never been to Antarctica.
    *Did **they** tell mom about our travel plans?*

object pronoun — used as a direct or indirect object, or object of a preposition
    *The crowd cheered **us**.* (direct object)
    *Give **her** a round of applause.* (indirect object)
    *Did the judge award first prize to **them**?* (object of preposition)

possessive pronoun — shows possession or ownership
    *The fanciest skateboard is **mine**.*

reflexive pronoun — throws the action back upon the subject of a sentence
    *Cici bought **herself** a new skateboard today.*

intensive pronoun — calls special attention to a noun or pronoun, giving it special emphasis
    *Georgie **himself** painted the designs on the board.*

relative pronoun — relates to another noun or pronoun in the sentence
    Some skateboarders prefer boards that are longer.

indefinite pronoun — does not specifically name its antecedent
    Everybody thinks these athletes are awesome.

interrogative pronoun — asks a question
    Who scheduled the performance for tomorrow?
    Whose is this?

demonstrative pronoun — points out a noun
    This was a fascinating competition.
    *Weren't **those** the best tricks ever?*

Which Pronouns are Which?

personal pronouns first person: second person: third person:	*I, me, mine, my, we, our, ours, us* *you, your, yours* *he, his, him, she, her, hers, it, its, it, they, their, theirs, them*
singular pronouns	*I, you, he, she, it, my, mine, me, your, yours, his, him, her, hers, its*
plural pronouns	*we, you, they, our, ours, your, yours, their, theirs, us, them*
subject pronouns	*I, you, he, she, it, we, you, they, who, whoever*
object pronouns	*me, you, him, her, it, us, you, them, whom, whomever*
possessive pronouns	*my, mine, your, yours, his, her, hers, its, our, ours, their, theirs, your, yours*
relative pronouns	*who, whose, whom, which, what, that, whoever, whosoever, whatever, whatsoever, whichever*
intensive & reflexive pronouns	*myself, yourself, yourselves, ourselves, himself, herself, itself, themselves*
interrogative pronouns	*who, whose, what, which, whoever, whatever, whom*
demonstrative pronouns	*this, that, these, those*
indefinite pronouns	*all, another, any, anybody, anything, anyone, both, each, either, everybody, everyone, everything, few, many, much, most, neither, none, nobody, no one, nothing, one, other, some, somebody, someone, several, something, such*

Who owns this silly hat? Is it yours or mine?

It's hers! Give the hat to its owner.

Get Sharp Tip # 2
Unlike possessive nouns, possessive pronouns NEVER have apostrophes.

73

Get Sharp: Grammar Guide

Verbs

A *verb* is a word that expresses action or existence.

action verb — a word that expresses physical or mental action

> Charlie **slipped** and **tumbled** down the steep rock. (physical)
>
> He **regretted** choosing this trail. (mental)

being verb — a word that describes a state of being (tells what the subject *is* or *feels*).

> After the day's hike, Charlie **felt** sick. He **seemed** dazed. **Is** he ready for another hike?

linking verb — links a subject to a noun or adjective in the predicate

> The campfire **is** a welcome sight. It **kept** burning all day.

singular verb — a verb with a singular subject

> Which campsite **provides** campers with the best view?

I scream in a very **active voice**, especially when I see a bear!

HELP!

plural verb — a verb with a plural subject

> All three campers **huddle** by the fire.

points of view — form of the verb matching the person of the subject

> **first person verb** — *I* **scream.** *We* **scream.**
>
> **second person verb** — *You* **scream.**
>
> **third person verb** — *He* **screams.**
> *She* **screams.**
> *They* **scream.**

active voice — verb form used when the subject **performs** the action

> Gravity **pulls** her heavy backpack towards the ground.

passive voice — verb form used when the subject **receives** the action

> The backpack **is pulled** down by gravity.

transitive verb — a verb that **transfers** its action to an object

> Five campers **climbed** Mount Grizzly twice. (Mount Grizzly is the direct object.)
>
> The mountain **gave** the climbers a challenge. (Climbers is the indirect object; challenge is the direct **object**.)
>
> All of them **were covered** with bruises. (Bruises is the object of the preposition *with*.)

intransitive verb — a verb that completes its action **without an object**

> After the climb, the hikers **looked** exhausted.
>
> They **yawned** endlessly.

verb phrase – more than one word used to make up a verb; one or more helping verbs and a main verb

> **main verb** – in a verb phrase, the verb that expresses action or feeling
> **helping verb** – the verb that helps complete the meaning of the main verb
>> Soon the new trail **will open**. (*open* is the main verb; *will* is the helping verb)

principal verb parts – Every verb has four principal parts. These are used to form all the verb tenses.
> base form, (present) — ***scream*** present participle — ***(is) screaming***
>> past — ***screamed*** past participle — ***(have, has) screamed***

verb tenses – the form of the verb used to designate the time of the action or state
> **present tense** — expresses action that happens now or continually: *We **scream**.*
> **past tense** — expresses action that already happened: *We **screamed**.*
> **future tense** — expresses action that will take place: *We **will scream**.*
> **present perfect tense** — expresses action which began in the past but continues to the present: *We **have screamed**.*
> **past perfect tense** — expresses action which began in the past and was completed in the past: *We **had screamed**.*
> **future perfect tense** — expresses action which will begin in the future and will be completed by a specific time in the future: *We **will have screamed**.*

irregular verbs — verbs that do not follow the usual rules for forming tenses

verbal – word formed from a verb, but used as a noun, adjective, or adverb
> **gerund** — a verb form that ends in *ing* and is used as a noun
>> ***Screaming*** *makes your throat sore.*
>> *Most of us were tired of **squealing**.*
> **participle** — a verb form used as an adjective
>> *The **frightened** hikers escaped from the bear.*
>> *The **chattering** girls startled the bear.*
> **infinitive** — a verb form usually introduced by *to*, and used as a noun, adjective, or adverb
>> ***To finish*** *the climb by dark was their goal.*
>> *The first one **to get** to camp starts the fire.*

progressive form – verb form that shows that the action is continuing (*The progressive form may be found in all six tenses.*)
> *We **are screaming** now.*
> *We **were screaming** yesterday.*
> *We **will be screaming** tomorrow.*
> *We **have been screaming** all day.*
> *We **had been screaming** all day yesterday.*
> *We **will have been screaming** for hours.*

Forming Verb Tenses for Regular Verbs

To form the PRESENT TENSE . . . use the base form of the verb.
dread, swallow, complain, close, carry, worry, enjoy, eat, save

To form the PRESENT PARTICIPLE . . . add *ing* to the base form of the verb.
(Sometimes you will need to drop a final *e* or change *y* to *i* before adding *ing*.)
dreading, swallowing, complaining, closing, carrying, worrying

To form the PAST TENSE . . . add *d* or *ed* to the base form of the verb.
(Sometimes you will need to change a final *y* to *i* before adding *ed*.)
dreaded, swallowed, complained, closed, carried, worried

To form the FUTURE TENSE . . . use *will* with the base form of the verb.
*We **will swallow**. They **will complain**. He **will worry**.*
    OR . . . use time words, such as *tomorrow, later,* or *next week* with the base form.
***Tomorrow** we **leave** at noon. **Later** we **get** home. **Next week** we **enjoy** our pictures.*

To form the PRESENT PERFECT TENSE . . . use *have* or *has* with the past form.
*We **have dreaded** this for a long time. He **has complained** about the hike often.*

To form the PAST PERFECT TENSE . . . use *had* with the past form.
*We **had anticipated** this trip for weeks. Charlie **had worried** about that steep drop.*

To form the future PERFECT TENSE . . . use *will have* or *shall have* with the past form.
*Amie **will have been** here six times. We **shall have enjoyed** ourselves immensely!*

For progressive forms . . . combine the present participle of the verb with a form of the helping verb **be**. The form of **be** shows the tense.

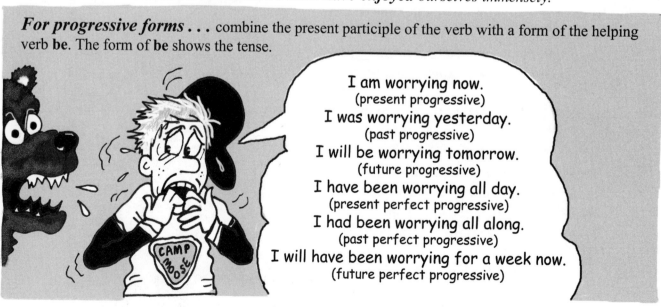

I am worrying now.
(present progressive)
I was worrying yesterday.
(past progressive)
I will be worrying tomorrow.
(future progressive)
I have been worrying all day.
(present perfect progressive)
I had been worrying all along.
(past perfect progressive)
I will have been worrying for a week now.
(future perfect progressive)

Get Sharp: Grammar Guide

Better Grades & Higher Test Scores / READING & LANGUAGE gr. 4–6
Copyright ©2005 by Incentive Publications, Inc., Nashville, TN.

Forming Verb Tenses for Irregular Verbs

Here are some verbs that do NOT follow the rules for forming tenses. They are called *irregular verbs*. These are just a few irregular verbs. There are many more.

present	present perfect	past	past perfect	future	future perfect
am, be	has been, have been	was, were	had been	will be, shall be	will have been, shall have been
begin	has begun	began	had begun	will begin	will have begun
blow	has blown	blew	had blown	will blow	will have blown
bring	has brought	brought	had brought	will bring	will have brought
catch	has caught	caught	had caught	will catch	will have caught
choose	has chosen	chose	had chosen	will choose	will have chosen
come	has come	came	had come	will come	will have come
do	has done	did	had done	will do	will have done
drink	has drunk	drank	had drunk	will drink	will have drunk
eat	has eaten	ate	had eaten	will eat	will have eaten
fight	has fought	fought	had fought	will fight	will have fought
fly	has flown	flew	had flown	will fly	will have flown
give	has given	gave	had given	will give	will have given
go	has gone	went	had gone	will go	will have gone
grow	has grown	grew	had grown	will grow	will have grown
know	has known	knew	had known	will know	will have known
lie	has lain	lay	had lain	will lie	will have lain
raise	has risen	rose	had risen	will raise	will have risen
ring	has rung	rang	had rung	will ring	will have rung
see	has seen	saw	had seen	will see	will have seen
sing	has sung	sang	had sung	will sing	will have sung
speak	has spoken	spoke	had spoken	will speak	will have spoken
swim	has swum	swam	had swum	will swim	will have swum
take	has taken	took	had taken	will take	will have taken
throw	has thrown	threw	had thrown	will throw	will have thrown

swim
has swum
swam
had swum
will swim
will have swum

I will swim a lot at camp.

Better Grades & Higher Test Scores / READING & LANGUAGE gr. 4–6
Copyright ©2005 by Incentive Publications, Inc., Nashville, TN.

Get Sharp: Grammar Guide

Transitive:

"I **took** an unexpected trip over Danger Drop Waterfalls," bragged Gramps.

(The verb *took* transfers action to *trip*; the object *trip* receives the action.)

Intransitive:

"The fun **vanished** when my canoe crashed," he sighed.

(The verb *vanished* completes its action without an object.)

A *direct object* is someone or something that receives the action of a verb.

It answers the question **whom?** or **what?**

*The Danger Drop scared **Gramps** out of his wits!* (*Gramps* is the direct object.)

*His friends shouted **warnings** and took **pictures**.* (*Warnings* and *pictures* are direct objects.)

*Afterwards, he gave **pictures** to all of his friends.* (*Pictures* is the direct object.)

An *indirect object* comes between the verb and the direct object.

It answers the questions **to whom?** or **for whom?** or **to what?** or **for what?**

*Before the canoe trip started, Gramps loaned **Charlie** his camera.*
    (*Charlie* is the indirect object. *Camera* is the direct object.)

*The sign gave **riders** clear warnings about the dangerous water.*
    (*Riders* is the indirect object. *Warnings* is the direct object.)

*Gramps gave his **canoe** a good inspection before he started the trip.*
    (*Canoe* is the indirect object. *Inspection* is the direct object.)

Verbs that Link

A *linking verb* connects the subject of a sentence with a noun or adjective in the predicate.

Roasted hot dogs around the campfire **taste** *great!*

The marshmallows quickly **turned** *black.*

Suddenly, the campers **smelled** *smoke.*

Link to What??

A linking verb can connect the subject *to a* **predicate noun** that identifies the subject.

Danny Trail **is** *the* **ranger** *of the state park.*

A linking verb can connect the subject *to a* **predicate adjective** that describes the subject.

In his uniform, Danny always **looks** *official.*

Common Linking Verbs

am	was	seem	turn
are	appear	sound	feel
taste	smell	grow	become
were	turn	look	is

Common Helping Verbs

am	were	can	would
is	been	could	did
are	had	will	may
be	has	do	might
was	have	does	should

Verbs that Help

A *helping verb* helps the main verb express action or helps complete the meaning of the verb.

Charlie **has** *been wanting to drive the motorboat on Bear Lake.*

He **might** *get a chance today, if he's lucky.*

He **can** *put his boat into the water at Grizzly Landing.*

Better Grades & Higher Test Scores / READING & LANGUAGE gr. 4–6
Copyright ©2005 by Incentive Publications, Inc., Nashville, TN.

Get Sharp: Grammar Guide

Adjectives

An **_adjective_** is a word that modifies, or describes, a noun or pronoun.

An adjective can modify a noun.
  Look at those **scrumptious** raspberries.

OR, an adjective can modify a pronoun.
  They are **delectable**.

A **predicate adjective** follows a linking verb, but always describes the subject.
  The berries are **fat** and **flavorful**.

* An adjective can tell **how many**. _I ate **one hundred seventy-seven** berries._
 most, several, few, little, many, some, much, or any number

* An adjective can tell **what kind**. _Then came the **horrendous** stomachache._
 unhappy, colorful, extraordinary, worst, chocolate, three-hour

* An adjective can tell **which one**. _**That** snack was a big mistake._
 those, his, these, the, Amy's, which, other, her, their, our, whichever

Special Adjectives

simple — a one-word adjective

yellow, exotic, boisterous, suspicious, ninety, outrageous, spicy, rubbery, tiny

compound — made up of more than one word *(sometimes hyphenated)*

subzero, seafaring, knee-high, underground, mile-high, long-term

common — any adjective that is not proper; not capitalized

frilly, disgusting, spectacular, seventeen, crooked, thrilling, young

proper — formed from a proper noun; always capitalized

German, Californian, Roman, European, American

predicate — an adjective that follows a linking verb
and describes the subject of the sentence
*That story sounds **suspicious**.*

an herb
a shocking story
the last taco
a big mystery
an ugly wart

articles — a special group of adjectives made up of *a, an,* and *the*

A and *an* are indefinite articles because
they refer to one of a general group.

A is used before words beginning with consonant sounds.

An is used before words beginning with vowel sounds.

The is a definite article because it identifies a specific person, place, thing, or idea.

demonstratives — an adjective that
points out a specific noun:
these, those, this, that.

*(These words are adjectives
only when followed by a noun.)*

This gumdrop is tastier than that one.
Those toenails are cracked.
These rattlesnakes are asleep.

Better Grades & Higher Test Scores / READING & LANGUAGE gr. 4–6
Copyright ©2005 by Incentive Publications, Inc., Nashville, TN.

Get Sharp: Grammar Guide

Adverbs

An *adverb* is a word that modifies, or describes, a verb, adjective, or other adverb.

An adverb can modify a **verb**. *It is a good idea to handle spiders* **cautiously**.

An adverb can modify an **adjective**. ***Very*** *dangerous spiders should be avoided.*

An adverb can modify another **adverb**. *Poisonous spiders* **almost** *always terrify me.*

- An adverb can tell **how**. *Lucy considered* **thoughtfully** *before touching the spider.*
  easily, grumpily, loosely, miserably, happily, repeatedly, well, firmly

- An adverb can tell **when**. ***Yesterday***, *she insisted she would never go near a snake.*
  soon, later, tomorrow, early, immediately, often, never, usually, forever, annually

- An adverb can tell **where**. *This tarantula has lived* **here** *for years.*
  here, there, everywhere, outside, inside, upstairs, below, anywhere, around

- An adverb can tell **to what extent**. *She was* **terribly** *anxious to show her bravery by handling the spider.*
  almost, extremely, least, really, terribly, very, quite, more, rather, slightly

Get Sharp Tip #3
Consider the placement of adverbs in your sentences. The position may affect the meaning.

EEEEK!

Only *Lucy handled the tarantula.*
Lucy **only** *handled the tarantula.*

Scarcely *Lucy had been around black widows.*
Lucy had **scarcely** *been around black widows.*

After, *the hairy spider escaped dinner.*
The hairy spider escaped **after** *dinner.*

Some adverbs that end in **ly**	Some adverbs that do not end in **ly**	Some adverbs used to modify adjectives and other adverbs
early	afterward	somewhat
loudly	almost	almost
frequently	already	partly
softly	always	barely
angrily	never	rather
noisily	anywhere	extremely
immediately	now	really
easily	backward	totally
usually	often	hardly
carelessly	below	so
casually	seldom	too
critically	before	rarely
lonely	sometimes	unusually
hotly	beneath	quite
rarely	outside	just
eagerly	somewhere	usually
annoyingly	nowhere	very
purposely	better	terribly
overtly	early	particularly
tremendously	soon	especially
openly	ever	nearly
smartly	then	
hungrily	least	
harshly	long	
sweetly	farther	
grumpily	tomorrow	
arguably	fast	
secondly	there	
tensely	forever	
shortly	too	
eventually	further	
totally	well	
unlikely	here	
supremely	worse	
peculiarly	inside	
desperately	worst	
accurately		
absentmindedly		

I'm almost always terribly frightened of spiders, especially when a particulary hairy one is crawling up my totally bare arm!

Adjectives that Compare

Adjectives can be used to *compare* one or more persons or things.

A ***comparative adjective*** compares one person or thing with another.

A ***superlative adjective*** compares one person or thing with several others.

For most one-syllable adjectives (and some two-syllable adjectives),
form the comparative by adding ***er*** and the superlative by adding ***est***.

For most adjectives of two or more syllables, form the comparative by adding ***more***
and the superlative by adding ***most***.

The words ***less*** and ***least*** are used before all adjectives to form the negative
comparative and superlative forms.

Base Form	Comparative	Superlative
wild	wilder	wildest
fine	finer	finest
big	bigger	biggest
witty	wittier	wittiest
splendid	more splendid	most splendid
complicated	more complicated	most complicated
able	less able	least able

Rule Breakers

The comparative and superlative forms of some adjectives are
irregular. You'll have to learn these forms without the rules.

Base Form	Comparative	Superlative
good	better	best
bad	worse	worst
well	better	best
many	more	most
little	less	least
much	more	most
far	farther *or* further	farthest *or* furthest

84

Adverbs that Compare

Adverbs can be used to *compare* one or more actions.

A *comparative adverb* compares one action with another.

A *superlative adverb* compares one action with several others.

For most short adverbs, form the comparative by adding *er* and the superlative by adding *est*.

For most long adverbs (and a few short ones) form the comparative by adding *more* and the superlative by adding *most*.

The words *less* and *least* are used before all adverbs to form the negative comparative and superlative forms.

Base Form	Comparative	Superlative
soon	sooner	soonest
long	longer	longest
early	earlier	earliest
foolishly	more foolishly	most foolishly
deeply	more deeply	most deeply
smoothly	less smoothly	least smoothly
awkwardly	less awkwardly	least awkwardly

far

farther

farthest

Rule Breakers

The comparative and superlative forms of some adverbs are *irregular.* You'll have to learn these forms without the rules.

Base Form	Comparative	Superlative
badly	worse	worst
well	better	best
little	less	least
much	more	most
far (distance)	farther	farthest
far (degree)	further	furthest

Better Grades & Higher Test Scores / READING & LANGUAGE gr. 4–6
Copyright ©2005 by Incentive Publications, Inc., Nashville, TN.

Get Sharp: Grammar Guide

Prepositions

A *preposition* is a word that shows a relationship between a noun or a pronoun and another word in the sentence.

Common Prepositions

above	because of	for	off	subsequent to
about	before	from	on	through
according to	behind	in	on account of	throughout
across	below	in addition to	on top of	till
after	beneath	in back of	out	to
against	beside	in front of	out of	toward
along	besides	in place of	outside	under
alongside	between	in spite of	outside of	underneath
amid	beyond	inside	over	until
among	but	inside of	over to	unto
apart from	by	instead of	past	up
around	despite	into	prior to	upon
aside from	down	like	round	with
as	during	near	save	within
at	except	of	since	without

In a sentence, a preposition is always followed by an **object**.
*Aviatrix Gracie finally flew **through** the clouds.(Clouds* is the object of *through.)*

The preposition, its object, and any modifiers form a **prepositional phrase**.
*She chose to be a pilot **instead of a microbiologist.***

Caution!
When the object of a preposition is a pronoun, remember to use the object form of pronouns ONLY.
me   him
you   her
us   them

Caution!
Some words that form prepositions can also be adverbs. Remember!
A word is a preposition ONLY when it has an object.

Preposition: She stayed **inside** the airplane.
Adverb: She stayed **inside**.

Get Sharp: Grammar Guide

Better Grades & Higher Test Scores / READING & LANGUAGE gr. 4–6

Conjunctions

A **conjunction** connects individual words or groups of words.

A **coordinate conjunction** connects a word to a word, a phrase to a phrase, or a clause to a clause. The words, phrases, or clauses joined by a coordinate conjunction must be equal or of the same type.

> *Weather **and** mechanical problems delayed Gracie's takeoff.*
>
> *The flight may proceed tomorrow **but** will not go today.*

Common coordinate conjunctions: *and   or   not   yet   nor   but   for   so*

A **subordinate conjunction** connects, and shows a relationship between, two clauses that are **not** equally important. It connects a dependent clause to an independent clause.

> *Gracie will begin her flight tomorrow **provided that** the weather has improved.*
> (The second clause, *the weather has improved*, is the dependent clause.)

Common subordinate conjunctions:

as	*after*	*although*	*as if*	*as long as*	*as soon as*
if	*before*	*even though*	*when*	*since*	*provided that*
till	*because*	*so that*	*unless*	*until*	*whenever*
than	*where*	*while*	*whatever*	*in order that*	

Correlative conjunctions are coordinate conjunctions used in pairs.
Neither the pilot **nor** the airport officials have any control over the weather.

Common correlative conjunctions:

either . . . or	neither . . . nor	not only . . . but also	both . . . and
whether . . . or	just . . . as	just . . . so	

Get Sharp Tip #4
Punctuation for an interjection is usually an exclamation point. It usually separates the interjection from the rest of the sentence.

Interjections

An **interjection** is a word or short phrase included in a sentence to communicate surprise or other strong emotion.

> *Hooray! Gracie is finally ready take off for New Zealand!*
>
> *Oh, no! There's trouble with the engine!*
>
> *Whew! Everything's okay!*
>
> *There she goes! Good luck, Gracie!*

Get Sharp: Grammar Guide

Phrases

A *phrase* is a group of related words that is missing a subject, a predicate, or both.

an out-of-control roller coaster

wearing a desperate grin

on top of the world

dropping through thin air

a full-throated scream

after the incident with the bumper car

gripped by a sudden fear

seventeen stomach-churning turns

bothered by wildly whipping hair

a narrow escape

Prepositional Phrases

A *prepositional phrase* . . . a preposition and its object *(along with any modifiers)*
   beneath the steel tracks
   inside her troubled stomach
   around a sharp corner

*The passenger **in the front seat** gets the best view. (prepositional phrase used as an adjective)*

*Will the coaster jerk to a stop **before Maggie gets sick**? (prepositional phrase used as an adverb)*

Gerund Phrases

A *gerund phrase* . . . contains the *ing* form of a verb used as noun
   serious squealing
   watching the world speed by
   enjoying every last minute

Leaning the right direction *is essential to not getting sick. (gerund phrase used as subject of the sentence)*

One forbidden activity **is standing** *in the roller coaster car. (gerund phrase used as a predicate noun)*

*Maggie felt proud for **enduring the ride twice**. (gerund phrase used as object of the preposition* **for***)*

Infinitive Phrases

An *infinitive phrase* . . . **includes the combination of the word** *to* **and the base form of a verb.**

> *to explore the caves*
> *to forget about the time*
> *to escape from danger*

To stand up on a roller coaster *is foolish.* (*infinitive phrase used as a noun—the subject of the sentence*)

Joe wanted **to explore the ride again.** (*infinitive phrase used as the direct object of the verb* wanted)

Is this the right ticket **to buy**? (*infinitive phrase used as an adjective—tells which* ticket)

Anne ducked **to avoid getting too wet on the ride.** (*infinitive phrase used as an adverb telling why she* ducked.)

Participial Phrases

A *participial phrase* . . . **contains a verb's present, past, or perfect participle used as an adjective.**

> *a crocodile biting riders on the "Swamp Cruise"*
> *a rider on the "Swamp Cruise" bit by a crocodile*
> *a rider barely bitten by a crocodile*

We heard of a crocodile **biting a rider.** (*present participial phrase describes the* crocodile)

The rider **bit by the crocodile** *was not badly injured.* (*past participle phrase describing the* rider)

Sam Smith, **bitten by the crocodile,** *managed to get treatment quickly.*
(*perfect participle phrase describing* Sam Smith)

DID YOU KNOW?

Some phrases are essential. Some are not.

An *essential phrase* is necessary to the basic meaning of the sentence.
The man **who runs the ferris wheel** *is my uncle.*

A *nonessential phrase* is **not** necessary to the basic meaning.
My uncle, **who runs the ferris wheel**, *is a retired teacher.*

An essential phrase needs no commas.

A nonessential phrase is set off with commas.

Get Sharp: Grammar Guide

Clauses

A *clause* is a group of related words with a subject and a predicate.

Noun Clauses

A *noun clause* . . . a subordinate *(or dependent)* clause that functions as a noun

That she was running out of air *worried the diver. (clause used as the subject of the sentence)*

She calculated **it would take five minutes to surface.** *(clause used as a direct object of the verb* calculated)

Alert **whoever is on the boat** *that she may be in trouble. (clause used as an indirect object of the verb* alert)

I worry about **the possibility that she can't make it.** *(clause used as the object of the preposition* about)

Adjective Clauses

An *adjective clause* . . . a subordinate *(or dependent)* clause used as an adjective to describe any noun or pronoun

(**NOTE:** An adjective clause **always** begins with *who, whom, which, whose,* or *that*.)

Is the octopus, **which is lurking behind the plants,** *headed this way? (clause modifies the noun* octopus)

It's the biggest lobster **that I've seen so far.** *(clause modifies the noun* lobster)

Oh, it's you **who borrowed my new fins!** *(clause modifies the pronoun* you)

Better Grades & Higher Test Scores / READING & LANGUAGE gr. 4–6
Copyright ©2005 by Incentive Publications, Inc., Nashville, TN.

Adverb Clauses

An *adverb clause* . . . **a subordinate** *(or dependent)* **clause used as an adverb**

(*NOTE:* An adverb clause **always** begins with a subordinate conjunction such as *although, after, as, as if, before, because, if, since, so that, unless, until, where, when, which,* or *that*).

Because the visibility was poor, I decided to head for the boat. *(clause tells* **why** *for the verb* decided*)*
I'll leave the camera in the boat ***until we return later for lunch.*** *(clause tells* **when** *for the verb* leave*)*
Meet me by the cave ***where we saw the giant squid.*** *(clause tells* **where** *for the verb* meet*)*
I took precautions ***as if my life depended on them.*** *(clause tells* **how** *for the verb* depended*)*

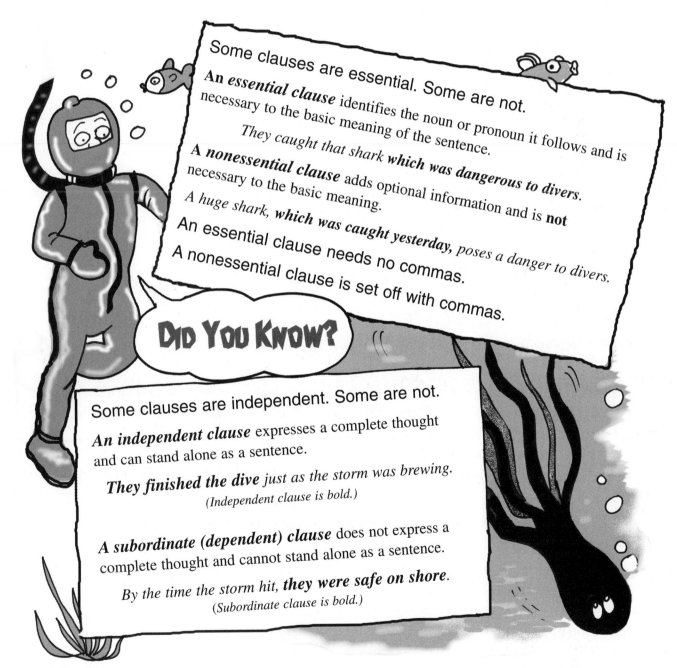

Some clauses are essential. Some are not.

An *essential clause* identifies the noun or pronoun it follows and is necessary to the basic meaning of the sentence.

They caught that shark ***which was dangerous to divers.***

A *nonessential clause* adds optional information and is **not** necessary to the basic meaning.

A huge shark, ***which was caught yesterday,*** *poses a danger to divers.*

An essential clause needs no commas.
A nonessential clause is set off with commas.

DID YOU KNOW?

Some clauses are independent. Some are not.

An *independent clause* expresses a complete thought and can stand alone as a sentence.

They finished the dive *just as the storm was brewing.*
(Independent clause is bold.)

A *subordinate (dependent) clause* does not express a complete thought and cannot stand alone as a sentence.

By the time the storm hit, ***they were safe on shore***.
(Subordinate clause is bold.)

Better Grades & Higher Test Scores / READING & LANGUAGE gr. 4–6
Copyright ©2005 by Incentive Publications, Inc., Nashville, TN.

Get Sharp: Grammar Guide

10 Sentence Parts to Remember

1. SUBJECT — the part of a sentence that is doing something or about which something is said

Seven lion tamers bravely faced seven ferocious lions.

2. SIMPLE SUBJECT — the subject without the words that describe or modify it

*Seven lion **tamers** bravely faced seven ferocious lions.*

3. COMPLETE SUBJECT — the simple subject and all the words that modify it

***Seven lion tamers** bravely faced seven ferocious lions.*

4. COMPOUND SUBJECT — made up of two or more simple subjects

***Seven lions and four tigers** surrounded the brave lion tamers.*

5. PREDICATE — the part of the sentence that says something about the subject

*Seven lion tamers **bravely faced seven ferocious lions.***

6. SIMPLE PREDICATE — the predicate (verb) without the words that describe or modify it

*Seven lion tamers bravely **faced** seven ferocious lions.*

7. COMPLETE PREDICATE — the simple predicate and all words that modify it

*Seven lion tamers **bravely faced seven ferocious lions.***

8. COMPOUND PREDICATE — composed of two or more simple predicates

*Seven lion tamers **charmed seven ferocious lions** and **entertained four feisty tigers.***

9. PHRASE — a group of related words that lacks either a subject or a predicate (or both)

Outside the ring, *the lions paced impatiently. (2 phrases)*

Were the lions **in a hurry** to get some dinner? *(3 different phrases)*

Which tigers *were growling* **during the performance**? *(3 different phrases)*

10. CLAUSE — a group of words that has a subject and verb

While some of the tigers are rather tame, *others are terribly fierce. (2 clauses)*

The whip, which the lion tamer used often, **made a sharp cracking sound.** *(2 clauses)*

That clown who is teasing the tigers; *he's not afraid at all. (2 clauses)*

Better Grades & Higher Test Scores / READING & LANGUAGE gr. 4–6

8 Kinds of Sentences to Remember

1. SIMPLE SENTENCE — a sentence with only one independent clause (complete thought). It may contain one or more phrases, but no dependent clauses.

Has she ever walked a tightrope before?

2. COMPOUND SENTENCE — a sentence made up of two or more simple sentences. A coordinate conjunction, punctuation, or both must join these simple sentences.

Zoey can ride an elephant and she can swing from a trapeze.

3. COMPLEX SENTENCE — contains one independent clause and one or more dependent clauses

Besides her acrobatic skills, Zoey has great skills walking the tightrope.

4. COMPOUND-COMPLEX SENTENCE — contains two or more independent clauses and one or more dependent clauses

When she was a little girl, Zoey pretended that she was working for a circus.

5. DECLARATIVE SENTENCE — makes a statement

Unfortunately the high wire walker has slipped from the wire.

6. INTERROGATIVE SENTENCE — asks a question

Was there a net below to catch him when he fell?

7. IMPERATIVE SENTENCE — makes a command
(often has an understood subject—**you**)

Don't plan to have a safe life if you walk on high wires.

8. EXCLAMATORY SENTENCE — communicates strong emotion or surprise

What an astounding performance!

4 Basic Sentence Patterns to Remember

#1 Subject + Verb
Storms raged.
Did storms rage?
Wind blew and water rose.
Wind and waves increased.

#2 Subject + Verb + Direct Object(s)
Waves pounded the coast.
Water damaged the beaches and highways.
Wind and waves destroyed beaches and battered businesses.

#3 Subject + Verb + Indirect Object + Direct Object
Water gave beaches a beating.
Did the storm cause the town damage?
The storm brought the area misery.

#4 Subject + Verb + Predicate Noun or Adjective
The wind was a monster.
Which storm was the hurricane?
The wind sounded deafening and terrifying.
That storm seemed worse.

Get Sharp #5
Any of the parts of each pattern may be compound.

Complicated Sentences

Some Compound Sentences

Was that a hurricane warning or was it a hurricane watch?

Cars flew through the air and power lines crashed to the ground.

The tree snapped, a branch fell, and the roof flew away.

Some Complex Sentences

Although we were watching, we never saw the tornado coming.

Since we were hiding in the basement, we didn't hear the roar until it was almost upon us.

After the tornado passed, we found a tractor stuck in a treetop.

Some Compound-Complex Sentences

My stomach sinks, and my heart beats wildly whenever I hear that roaring sound.

When tornado season arrives, we put flashlights in the basement and we stock up on food.

After floods subside and before hurricanes start, the weather is fine and we're happy.

Subject-Verb Agreement

Subject-Verb agreement is as easy as 1-2-3!
1. Single subjects require singular verbs.
2. Plural subjects require plural verbs.
3. Pronouns used as subjects must also agree in number with the verb.

Ask Professor Know-it-all
She knows a lot!

What about subjects that already end in **s**? Are they singular or plural?

Answer: Some are singular and need a singular verb:
news
physics
United States
Los Angeles

What about scissors?

Answer: It's plural, like these:
jeans   pants
tweezers   pliers
sunglasses   measles

Thanks, Professor!

---

*Band **members** **arrive** at noon to record.*
*On this album, Suzie's **drums** **accompany** every song.*
***She** **plays** expertly.*
*Seven **technicians**, skilled with sound, **travel** with the band.*
*This **band**, with its great vocalists, **appeals** to all age groups.*
*Two **songs** from their last album **have won** major awards.*
***Fans**, eager to buy the record, **wait** for the store to open.*

Special Cases: Compound Subjects

Compound subjects joined by *and* or by *both . . . and* require a plural verb.
> *Both **Mara** and the other **vocalist** **have** laryngitis.*
> ***Traveling** and late **nights** **are** hard on a singer's health.*

When compound subjects *refer to the same person or thing*, a singular verb is required.
> *The **drummer** and **leader** of the band **is** Angela.*

When compound subjects are joined by *or, either . . . or*, or *neither . . . nor*, the verb agrees with the subject closest to it.
> *Neither **illness** nor **holidays** **interrupt** the schedule.*
> *Did the **guitars** or the **guitar player** **miss** the plane?*
> *Either the **sound** or the **lights** **were broken** tonight.*

Better Grades & Higher Test Scores / READING & LANGUAGE gr. 4–6
Copyright ©2005 by Incentive Publications, Inc., Nashville, TN.

Special Cases: Names and Titles

A title or a name takes a singular verb form, even though it may look plural.

> ***Warner and Wagoner Guitars* sponsors** *the band.*

> **Is *Indiana*** *home to three band members?*

> *The **Garden Arena* was** *the site for last night's concert.*

> ***Star Wars* remains** *the favorite movie of the drummer.*

Special Cases: Collective Nouns

When a collective noun names a group acting as a unit, it takes a singular verb.

> *What a fine sound the **orchestra* is producing**!*

> *The whole **family* claps** *wildly for their son, the lead singer.*

> *One **group* expresses** *shock at the band's outfits.*

When a collective noun refers to the individuals in a group, it takes a plural verb.

> *The **orchestra* are tuning** *their instruments.*

> ***Why are* the family* spread** *throughout the arena?*

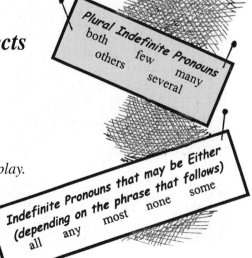

Collective Nouns
group
team
orchestra
flock
family
collection
club
audience
committee
herd
Senate
legislature
jury
Congress

Special Cases: Nouns of Amount

When thought of as a single unit, nouns of amount take a single verb.

> ***Eight months* seems** *a long time to be on a tour.*

> **Is *twenty dollars*** *the cost of a ticket to the concert?*

When thought of as separate units, nouns of amount take a plural verb.

> *The **eight months* pass** *quickly when you travel every day.*

Nouns of Amount
dollars   hours
grams   tons
pounds   halves
quarters inches
years   feet
decades gallons

Singular Indefinite Pronouns
another   much
anybody   neither
anyone   nobody
anything   no one
each   nothing
either   one
everybody   somebody
everyone   someone
everything   something

Special Cases: Indefinite Pronouns as Subjects

Indefinite pronouns do not refer to a specific person, place, or thing. They can be singular or plural.

> *Can **anybody** of any age* purchase *a concert ticket?*

> *No, **everyone* is** *not right for this audience.*

> ***Something** great* happens* *for fans when this band begins to play.*

> *Before the concert, **several* hang** *around the door.*

> ***Few* are allowed** *back stage.*

> ***None** of the fans* have** *access to the dressing rooms.*

> ***Most** of the concert* sounds** *very loud.*

Plural Indefinite Pronouns
both   few
others   many
              several

Indefinite Pronouns that may be Either
(depending on the phrase that follows)
all   any   most   none   some

Pronoun Particulars

Hey, Dude! My **guitar** is way out of tune. That's why **it** sounds so bad!

Remember this about pronouns:

1. **A pronoun must have a clear antecedent** *(noun to which it refers).*

    *When did the bass **player** finally arrive? Why was **he** late?*
        *(**Player** is the clear antecedent of **he**.)*

    *Both the bass player and the drummer missed the bus. That's why **she** was late.*
        (The antecedent is unclear—Is it player or drummer or neither?)

2. **A pronoun must agree with its antecedent** *(in person, gender, and number)***.**
    ***Brad** said **he** ordered tickets for himself and four friends.* (third person, masculine gender)
    ***Angela** has played the drums since **she** was three years old.* (third person, feminine gender)
    *Aren't **they** the **musicians** who had the best-selling record?* (plural subject and pronoun)
    *Only one **album** sold less than a million copies; **it** was their first.*(singular subject and pronoun)

3. **An indefinite pronoun used as a subject must agree with the verb.**
    ***Somebody** **needs** to replace the broken guitar strings.*
    ***Nothing** ever **interferes** with the afternoon rehearsal.*
    ***Each** of the band members **memorizes** his or her parts.*
    ***Several** more strings **broke** that day.*
    ***Others** **think** this music is too loud, also.*
    *Few **fans** were **disappointed** in the music **they** **heard**.*

4. **The interrogative pronoun who (or whoever) is used as a subject of a sentence. Whom (or whomever) is used as an object.**
    ***Whoever** loves loud music will love this band!* (subject)
    ***Who** got us these great seats?* (subject)
    *To **whom** was that last song dedicated?* (object)
    *The seats are open for **whomever** gets there first.* (object)

More pronoun particulars

5. Use subject pronouns as subjects or predicate pronouns.
(Never use an object pronoun as a subject.)

Correct: *Did **they** sell over five thousand tickets today?*
             *It was **she** who gave away those expensive tickets.*
             *Weren't **we** lucky to get those front row seats?*

Incorrect: *It was **him** who got a back stage pass.*
             ***Them** are the ones who snuck into the dressing room.*
             *Didn't **us** get the best seats?*

6. Use object pronouns as direct objects or indirect objects.
(Never use a subject pronoun as an object.)

Correct: *How lucky Dylan was to get autographs from all of **them**!*
             *Every band member gave **him** a free CD.*
             *Who was that dancing with **you** in the aisle?*

Incorrect: *Next week, Sara will start taking drum lessons from **I**.*
             *Who taught **they** to dance?*
             *Did the Cooley brothers get up to dance along with **she**?*

7. In a compound subject, use subject pronouns.

Correct: ***She and he** dance together all the time.*
             *When will **they and Sam** ever get up to dance?*
             *Unfortunately, our **friends and we** are terrible dancers.*

Incorrect: ***Him and her** have been taking dance lessons for years.*
             *When **B.J. and us** started dancing, everyone laughed.*
             *Couldn't **them and me** start our own band?*

8. In a compound object, use object pronouns.

Correct: *For the best pictures, only entrust the camera to **them or me**.*
             *Please give **him and us** copies of the picture of Alonzo dancing.*
             *When the concert was over, no one was more exhausted than **her or him**.*

Incorrect: *Okay, who took that terrible picture of **she and I**?*
             *These concert tickets cost our **parents and we** over a hundred dollars.*
             *Luckily, the evening was free for the **girls and they**.*

Compound subjects need a plural verb.

Axel and I certainly **need** a trip to the repair shop!

Usage Dos & Don'ts

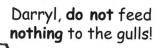 **DON'T** USE A DOUBLE NEGATIVE ➡  **DO** USE ONLY ONE NEGATIVE IN A SENTENCE

Incorrect Usage:

No fishing is never allowed here.
No camping is allowed neither.
Scarcely nobody swims here.
Hardly no one goes boating here.
You shouldn't take no starfish home.

Correct Usage:

No fishing is ever allowed on the beach.
No camping is allowed either.
Scarcely anybody swims here.
Hardly anyone goes boating here.
You should take no starfish home.

Darryl, **do not** feed **nothing** to the gulls!

What do you mean, Doreen? I did **not** feed **anything** to the seagulls.

 DON'T USE A DOUBLE SUBJECT. ➡ **DO** USE EITHER A NOUN OR PRONOUN TO NAME THE SUBJECT OF THE SENTENCE

Incorrect Usage:

Max he got a terrible sunburn.
It's a shame that Alex he got seasick.

Correct Usage:

Max got a terrible sunburn.
It's a shame that Alex got seasick.

DON'T USE *of* WITH *would,* ➡ **DO** USE *have* WITH *would, could,* *could,* OR *should.* OR *should.*

Incorrect Usage:

You would of screamed, too.
Rex could of been badly injured.

Correct Usage:

You would have screamed, too.
Rex could have been badly injured.

DON'T USE *here* OR *there* WITH A DEMONSTRATIVE PRONOUN. ➡ **DO** USE DEMONSTRATIVE PRONOUNS WITHOUT *here* OR *there*.

Incorrect Usage:

This here fish is a reef shark.

That there guy is bothering the shark.

Will those there sharks attack us?

Correct Usage:

This fish is a reef shark.

That guy is bothering the shark.

Will those sharks attack us?

DON'T SPLIT INFINITIVES ➡ **DO** TRY TO KEEP THE *to* NEXT TO THE VERB IN AN INFINITIVE.

Incorrect Usage:

She tends to easily burn in the sun.

Can you all remember to not swim alone?

Correct Usage:

She tends to burn easily in the sun.

Can you all remember not to swim alone?

DON'T USE *where* AFTER *at*. ➡ **DO** USE *where* WITHOUT *at*.

Incorrect Usage:

Where is the lifeguard at?

Do you know where your sunscreen is at?

Correct Usage:

Where is the lifeguard?

Do you know where your sunscreen is?

DON'T DANGLE PARTICIPLES. THE MEANING WILL BECOME UNCLEAR. ➡ **DO** KEEP THE PARTICIPLE CLOSE TO THE WORD IT MODIFIES.

Incorrect Usage:

Sam caught a marlin fishing from the yacht.

We heard about the beached whale eating lunch in front of the TV.

Correct Usage:

Fishing from the yacht, Sam caught a marlin.

While eating lunch in front of the TV, we heard about the beached whale.

Usage Mix-Ups

anyway and anyways

Anyway does not need an *s* at the end. There is no such word as *anyways*!
The same is true for **anywhere, everywhere, nowhere** and **somewhere**.

      Correct: *Anyway, I can't possibly ride on an elephant.*

                   This elephant is going nowhere.

                   Did you drop your camera somewhere?

      Incorrect: *I can't see elephants anywheres!*

                   Yes, I guess I dropped my camera somewheres during the trip.

beside and besides

Beside means "next to" or "at the side of." **Besides** means "in addition to."

      Correct: *Is that a zebra beside the stream?*

                   What did the zebra eat besides your lunch?

      Incorrect: *Beside eating my lunch, the zebra feasted on a hearty meal of gazelle.*

                   I saw three zebras resting besides the stream.

between and among

Between is used to show a relationship or comparison between two persons or things, or to compare more than two items within the same group.

Among is used to show a relationship in which more than two persons or things belong to the same group.

set and sit

Set means "to place" or "to put." Forms of *set* are usually followed by a direct object.

Sit means "to place oneself in a seated position."

 Forms of *sit* are not followed by a direct object.

 (Forms of *set* are *set, setting, set, set.* Forms of *sit* are *sit, sitting, sat, sat.*)

Correct:	*The zookeeper set the food bucket too close to the cheetah.*
	Which panther is sitting closest to the fence?
	The gorilla has sat by that fence since dinner.
	A rumor has it that she sits there waiting to snatch visitors' fingers.
Incorrect:	*Don't sit that food bucket near the cheetah!*
	Robert set himself down right next to the gorilla.
	Why are you setting so close to the panther's mouth?
	I'm sure I sat my hamburger right here on the fence.

raise and rise

Raise means "to lift" or "to grow." Forms of *raise* are usually followed by a direct object.

Rise means "to move upward" or "get up." Forms of *rise* are not followed by a direct object.

 (Forms of *raise* are *raise, raising, raised, raised.* Forms of *rise* are *rise, rising, rose, risen.*)

let and leave

Let means "to allow to." *Leave* means "to go away."

Correct:	*Let me help you get loose from the lion's jaws.*
	Which lion will let you pet him?
	Don't you wish that lion would leave you alone?
Incorrect:	*I'll let this cage door open so you can visit the lions.*
	Did your mom leave you go into the lion's cage?
	Leave me do that by myself.

lay and lie

Lay means "to put" or "to place." Forms of *lay* are usually followed by a direct object.

Lie means "to recline" or "to be positioned." Forms of *lie* are not followed by a direct object.

(Forms of *lay* are *lay, laying, laid, laid.* Forms of *lie* are *lie, lying, lay, lain.*)

can and may

Can is in indication of ability.

May is a request or granting of permission.

    Correct: *Can a hippo eat peanut butter sandwiches without getting sick?*
                  May I give the hippo my peanut butter sandwich?

    Incorrect: *Zookeeper, can I play with the gorillas?*
                  The gorillas are so agile that they may swing from the bars.

good and well

Good is an adjective. Use it before nouns and with linking verbs to modify a subject.

Well is an adverb. Use it to modify action verbs. *Well* is also used as an adjective to mean "in good health."

    Correct: *I hope I can do a good job at my interview for the zookeeper's job.*
                  You certainly did well performing as a gorilla.

    Incorrect: *You look well in that gorilla suit.*
                  It's well that you got the job as a zookeeper.
                  Didn't I do good at pretending to be a gorilla?

how come and why

How come is not good usage for asking a question. In formal writing and speech, use **why** instead.

    Correct: *Why did you choose to spend the night in the python cage?*

    Incorrect: *How come you stayed overnight with the pythons?*

bad and badly

Bad is an adjective. Use it before nouns and with linking verbs to modify a subject.

Badly is an adverb. Use it to modify action verbs.

Correct:	*The bad bear ate all the berries. Then, he felt bad about eating all the berries.*
	The bear behaved badly when he ate all the berries.
Incorrect:	*The bear felt badly about the berries.*
	The bear behaved bad yesterday.

sure and surely

Sure is an adjective. Use it before nouns and with linking verbs to modify a subject.

Surely is an adverb. Use it to modify verbs, adjectives, and other adverbs.

Correct:	*Dr. Shirley surely is smart.*
	Surely it's time to give vaccinations to the animals.
	It's sure hot in this zoo infirmary.
Incorrect:	*The gorillas sure are looking sick.*
	Are you surely the giraffes aren't sick, too?

quick and quickly

Quick is an adjective. Use it before nouns and with linking verbs to modify a subject.

Quickly is an adverb. Use it to modify verbs.

Correct:	*Could the vet find a quick cure for Bruno's ailment?*
	How quickly will the medicine work?
Incorrect:	*Bruno got sick very quick after he ate the hiker's backpack.*
	That's the quickliest I've ever seen a bear get sick.

real and really

Real is an adjective. Use it before nouns and with linking verbs to modify a subject.

Don't use *real* as a substitute for the adverbs *really* or *very*.

Really is an adverb. Use it to modify action verbs, adjectives, or other adverbs.

Capitalize

. . . all proper nouns and proper adjectives

A **proper noun** is the name of a particular person, place, thing, or idea.
Sancho, Chicago, Long Island Sound, George Washington Bridge, Valentine's Day

A **proper adjective** is an adjective formed from a proper noun.
Italian food, French fries, American flag, Brazilian rivers, Caribbean beaches

. . . the names of people and the initials or abbreviations that stand for those names

Angela Algae, Homer S. Heartbreak, Aunt Blabby, Mr. Ragoo, Sir Munchalot

october **15**
dear Friend amy,

I no that i Am having some Trouble with My capitalization.
at home, mother and uncle john keep Trying to help Me with this
Big problem. at School, the Teacher gives me Rules to Learn.
Mostly, I can't remember Any of them. do you ever Have This
much trouble with Anything? maybe When you come to Visit For
thanksgiving in november, you Can help. Until then, I'LL just
Struggle aLong.

Your friend,
SAmmy

. . . names of countries, cities, states, counties, and towns

Japan, San Francisco, Peru, Afghanistan, St. Louis, Jackson County, Columbus, Ohio

. . . geographical names

Missouri River, Grand Canyon, Lake Michigan, Gopher Gulch, Rio Grande River

. . . words that indicate particular sections of a country or area

Western U.S., Northern France, Southern Pacific, Middle East, Southeast Asia

. . . the names of languages, races, and nationalities (and proper adjectives formed from them)

Turkish, Caucasian, Russian, Columbian, Africans, Latin, Arabian, French

. . . the names of religions (*and proper adjectives formed from them*)

Islam, Judaism, Christianity, Buddhism, Buddhist, Catholic

. . . titles used with names of persons and abbreviations standing for those titles

Mrs. Tuttle, Sir Francis Femur, Corporal Clang, Prince Charming, James Johnson, Jr.

. . . words such as mother, father, aunt, and uncle (*when these words are used as names*)

Aunt Suzy, Uncle Snoozy, Father Time, Mother Nature, Mother Teresa

. . . the first and last words of a title, and every word in between except articles (a, an, the), short prepositions, and short conjunctions

The Legend of the Green-Footed Gorilla and Her Hidden Treasure
What You Don't Know About the Bermuda Triangle
Never Believe News from a Plastic Radio

. . . abbreviations of titles

Mrs., Dr., Pvt., Mr., Sgt., Pres., St.

. . . abbreviations of organizations

FBI, NASA, N.Y.P.D., NATO

. . . the names of days of the week and months of the year

April, September, Wednesday, Friday

. . . the names of holidays and special days

Halloween, Easter, Fourth of July, Bastille Day

. . . names of historical events, documents and periods of time

Civil War, Declaration of Independence, Ice Age, Renaissance

. . . the names of organizations, associations, or a team and its members

Olympians, Chamber of Commerce, Fighting Irish, Justice Department

. . . names of businesses

Fantastic Toys, Inc., Popcorn Unlimited., Old Typewriters, Inc., J.C. Penney Co.

. . . official names of products

Kleenex, Coca-Cola, Clorox, Windex

. . . names of subjects taught in school when they name courses

Geometry, Physics, Geography, Physical Education

. . . the first word of every sentence and of a direct quotation

Never put worms in the food processor! She asked, "Why not?"

Punctuate

Punctuate with a comma ,

. . . between words, phrases, or clauses in a series (at least three items)
Alphonso saw zebras, lions, giraffes, hippos, and elephants.

SAFARI, ANYONE?

On April 15, Alphonso took food, water, a good hat, a camera, and binoculars as he headed off on a safari.

Later that day, behaving carelessly, he disturbed a sleeping lion.

OOPS !

Oh, how he wished he had followed the advice of Archie, the park ranger!

. . . to separate digits in a number to distinguish hundreds, thousands, etc.
200,000,000 or 17,041,107 or 55,555

. . . to distinguish items in an address or date
September 15, 1818

. . . to set off the exact words of a speaker from the rest of the sentence
"Remain inside the Land Rover," shouted the guide.

. . . to separate a noun of direct address from the rest of the sentence
Stay away from that elephant, Alphonso.

. . . between two independent clauses joined by such words as: but, or, nor, for, yet, and so
He brought no compass, nor did he bring a sleeping bag.

. . . to separate an adverb clause or long modifying phrase from the independent clause following it
Besides being hot and grumpy, Alphonso was afraid of the zebras.

. . . to separate an interjection or weak exclamation from the rest of the sentence
Oh, how he wished he had brought better food!

. . . to set off a word, phrase, or clause that interrupts the main thought of a sentence
The last person to see Alphonso, other than the giraffe, was Sam.

. . . to separate an explanatory phrase from the rest of the sentence
His greatest weakness, a non-existent sense of direction, led to the mistaken wrong turn.

. . . to separate an appositive
Jon B. Schurr, a rescue worker, went searching for Alfonso.

. . . to enclose a title, name, or initials that follow a person's last name
Dr. Sally Sure, M.D., was ready with her first aid kit.

. . . to separate two or more adjectives that equally modify the same noun
A weary, frightened Alfonso was finally found by the ranger.

Punctuate with a period .

. . . to end a sentence that makes a statement or gives a command that is not an exclamation

I wonder if that giraffe ever gets a sore throat..
Keep an eye on your lunch when the animals are around.

. . . after each part of an abbreviation (unless the abbreviation is an acronym)

Mr., Dr., Co., Sept. p.s., Mt.

. . . as a decimal point and to separate dollars and cents

$9,999.99

. . . after an initial

J.R. Rumble, Nancy B. Fancy, C. I. A.

Punctuate with a question mark ?

**. . . at the end of a direct question
(an interrogative sentence)**

Can't you see that the hippos do not want to be disturbed?

Don't step in that lion trap!

Punctuate with an exclamation point !

. . . to express strong feeling (May be placed after
a word, phrase, or exclamatory sentence.)

Stop! Don't step in that trap!

(Note: Never use more than one exclamation point
at the end of a word, phrase, or sentence.)

Punctuate with an ellipsis *(three periods)* • • •

. . . to show that one or more words are left out of a quotation

"You should have known . . . I tried to warn you about it," said Sam.

. . . when the final words are left out of a sentence (Place the ellipsis after the period.)

It was not her last encounter with an elephant. . .

Punctuate with parentheses ( )

**. . . around words included in a sentence to add information or help
make an idea clearer**

After that incident (the one on the safari), Alphonso was more wary of traps.

Punctuate with a semicolon **;**

. . . **to join two independent clauses that are not connected with a coordinate conjunction**
> *He could never believe in something like Bigfoot; that changed last night.*

. . . **to join two independent clauses when the clauses are connected only by a conjunctive adverb** (*also, as a result, for example, however, therefore*)
> *It could be an ordinary animal; but no ordinary animal has footprints like this.*

. . . **to separate groups of words or phrases that already contain commas**
> *He heard grunts, screams, and moans; then a rumble, a crash, an ear-splitting shriek.*

It's Mother-in-Law Bake-Off Day!

It is a good-smelling,

lip-smacking,

finger-licking,

prize-winning day!

Punctuate with a colon **:**

. . . **after the salutation of a business letter**
> *Dear Professor Parsons:*

. . . **between the parts of a number that indicate time**
> *11:13 p.m.*

. . . **to formally introduce a sentence, question, or quotation**
> *So my question is this: What did you really see out there in the woods last night?*

. . . **to introduce a list**
> *You'd believe me if I said I saw any of these: a cougar, a bear, a moose, or an elk.*

Punctuate with a hyphen —

. . . **to make some compound words:** *brother-in-law, passer-by, forget-me-not*

. . . **to join the words in compound numbers from 21–99:** *sixty-two, twenty-nine*

. . . **between the numbers in a fraction expressed in words:** *three-fourths, one-half*

. . . **to join a capital letter to a noun or participle:** *V-shaped, U-turn*

. . . **to form new words beginning with the prefixes** *self, ex, all,* **and** *great: self-taught, great-aunt*

. . . **to join two or more words in a compound modifier:** *well-groomed, high-energy*

Punctuate with a dash ——

. . . **to indicate a sudden break or change in the sentence**
> *I really did come face to face with Bigfoot—not that I could ever convince you.*

. . . **to emphasize a word, series of words, phrase, or clause**
> *The smell—a powerful odor like none other I've ever encountered—was overwhelming.*

110

Punctuate with italics (<u>or underlining</u>)

**. . . titles of magazines, newspapers, pamphlets, books, plays, films, radio and
television programs, book-length poems, record albums, and the names of
ships and aircraft**

Did you borrow my copy of *Three Dogs on a Surfboard*?
I read about lice in *The Journal of Yucky Ailments*.

. . . foreign words not commonly used in everyday English:

Let's eat some *petit fours*.

. . . scientific names:

I've been bitten by a *Crocodylus acutus*.

. . . any word, number, or letter that is being discussed or used in a special way

The meaning of the word *maelstrom* is "a whirlpool or swirling chaos."

Punctuate with an apostrophe ,

. . . to replace letters that are omitted in a contraction

we're, it's, I'll, you've, can't, they'd, won't

. . . to form the plural of a letter, number, or sign:

3's, z's, #'s

. . . form the possessive form of a singular noun

boy's surfboard, mosquito's bite, man's sunburn

. . . to form the possessive form of a plural noun

boys' surfboards, mosquitoes' bites, mice's tails

. . . with an expression indicating time:

three o'clock

Get Sharp Tip #6
Don't put apostrophes
in words that don't
need them.

All of our pizza's
have anchovie's.

I'll have a slice
of pizza, but hold
the apostrophes
(and the anchovies)!

Punctuate with quotation marks " "

**. . . titles of songs, poems, short stories, lectures, courses, episodes of radio or
television programs, chapters of books, and articles found in magazines,
newspapers, or encyclopedias**

"*The Mystery of the Big Footprints*" is an article about the Sasquatch.
Our whole class was mesmerized by Annie's poem, "The Night I Saw Bigfoot."

**. . . to set apart a word that is being discussed, to indicate that a word is slang, or
to point out that the word is being used in a special way**

This gives a whole new meaning to the word "monster."
Toni went "ballistic" when she heard the low growl behind her.

. . . before and after direct quotations (See examples on page 113.)

Bigfoot Territory

A Hiker's Notebook

by Ike D. Trail

Friday, 13th, Somewhere in the Northwest

Most of my fellow hikers were skeptical about the existence of Bigfoot in this area.

1. "There's nothing to worry about, since there is no such thing as Bigfoot," said Jen, my hiking partner.

2. I answered: "I'm not so sure."

3. "Many people tell stories about seeing Bigfoot," I added.

4. "That's all they are—stories," Jen shouted back, "Just fairy tales!"

5. "Anyway, let's get out of here," I begged.

6. Then I added, "Don't you smell something strange?"

7. Jen was unshakable; "No stupid legend will scare me away!" she insisted.

8. I heard her mumble under her breath, "Bigfoot is a silly superstition!"

9. "Heeeeellllppppppp!" she screamed as she ran away, terrified.

10. "Is this what Jen thinks now: 'Bigfoot does not exist'?"

Punctuating Quotations

. . . Place quotation marks around **exact words** quoted *(all examples above)*.

. . . Periods and commas are **always** placed **inside** quotation marks *(1-5)*.

. . . An exclamation point or question mark is placed:
   inside the quotation marks when it punctuates the quotation *(4, 6-9)*;
   outside when it punctuates the main sentence *(10)*.

. . . Semicolons or colons are placed **outside** quotation marks *(2, 7)*.

14 Spelling Rules to Remember

1... Write *i* before *e* except after *c*, or when sounded like **long a** (as in *neighbor* or *weigh*).

Examples: *achieve, quotient, piece, believe, grief, convenient, shriek, hygiene, receive, deceive, conceit, freight, sleigh, neighbor, reign, weigh*

Rule breakers: *their, conscience, science, weird, neither, leisure, foreign, heir, height, seize, counterfeit, either, sovereign, financier*

2... The spelling of a base word does not change when you add a prefix.

Examples: *misunderstood, disregard, extraordinary, transatlantic, reinvestigate*

3... When a one-syllable word ends in a consonant preceded by one vowel, double the final consonant before adding a suffix that begins with a vowel.

Examples: *napping, hitting, shopped, reddish, fretted, muddy, robber, beggar*

4... When a multi-syllable word ends in a consonant preceded by one vowel, and the accent is on the last syllable, double the final consonant before adding a suffix that begins with a vowel.

Examples: *forgettable, beginning, regretted*

5... When a word ends in silent *e*, drop the *e* before adding a suffix which begins with a vowel.

Examples: *usable, vacation, rated, stating, liking, roper, hoping*
Do not drop the *e* when the suffix begins with a consonant.

Examples: *useful, statement, likeness, hopeless, spiteful, noiseless, lonely*

Rule breakers: *truly, argument, ninth,*

6... If the letter before a final *y* is a vowel, do not change the *y* when adding a suffix.

Examples: *keyless, payable, joyous, playful, prayed, boyish*

7... If the letter before a final *y* is a consonant, change the *y* to *i* before adding any suffix except *ing*. The *y* never changes when adding *ing*.

Examples: *carried, laziness, pliers, fried, pitiless, business, fanciful, worrying, frying*

8 . . . The ending pronounced *shun* is generally spelled *tion*.

 Examples: *equation, conversation, motion, ration, vacation, education*

 Rule breakers: *confusion, musician, cushion, decision, transfusion*

9 . . . If the letter before a final *y* is a vowel, do not change the *y* when adding a suffix.

 Examples: *sprayed, keys, joyful, rays, monkeying, boyhood*

10 . . . When a prefix ends with the same letter that begins the main word,
 include both letters.
 When a suffix begins with the same letter that ends the main word,
 include both letters.

 Examples: *misstep, illogical, illegal, immobile, accidentally, meanness, tailless*

11 . . . When the letters *c* and *g* have a soft sound they are followed by *i, e,* or *y*.

 Examples: *pencil, circus, celery, certain, cereal, cycle, saucy, gigantic, rigid, gesture,
 legend, gently, gyrate, edgy*

12 . . . When the letters *c* and *g* have a hard sound they are followed by *a, o,* or *u*.

 Examples: *cannot, cactus, organize, cougar, cupcake, cuckoo, copper, gallop,
 gastronomical, gorilla, ego, legume, gulp, gusto*

13 . . . Suffixes that follow the *soft c or g* always begin with *i* or *e*.

 Examples: *magician, contagious, negligence*

14 . . . The letter *q* is always followed by the letter *u* in the English language.

 Examples:

Quarrel in the Quicksand
A critique by Monique Quincy

The newest adventure movie begins in a **qu**iet a**qu**arium and **qu**ickly moves to a mos**qu**ito-infested **qu**agmire. By this time the hero, **Qu**ince **Qu**ark, has ac**qu**ired a girlfriend and a major **qu**arrel with the villain, Enri**qu**e Mc**Qu**ire (with his **qu**artet of human-like insects). They battle in the **qu**icksand of an unknown e**qu**atorial swamp. The viewer is fre**qu**ently re**qu**ired to overlook **qu**ite obvious stretches of reality and get used to **qu**estions that have no answers. But, in the end, the awesome e**qu**ipment and **qu**ick thinking allows good to con**qu**er evil. The viewer are left to savor the s**qu**ashing of the bad guys and in**qu**ire how soon the se**qu**el will be released.

Better Grades & Higher Test Scores / READING & LANGUAGE gr. 4–6
Copyright ©2005 by Incentive Publications, Inc., Nashville, TN.

Get Sharp: Spelling Guide

Words with Tricky Sounds

Here's a quick guide to those confusing letters that make different sounds in different places. To be a good speller, you need to get these straight!

Phil the Magician

He performs clever and scintillating tricks to a mixed chorus of laughter and applause!

F The *f* sound can be spelled with *f* (*funny, fantastic, friend, gift, bereft*) or with *ph* (*phone, physical, phrase, graph*), or with *gh* (*laughter*).

G The **hard g** sound can be spelled with *g* (*gutter, gumball, leg, aggravate*) or with *gh* (*ghost, ghetto, ghastly*).

J The *j* sound can be spelled with *j* (*jelly, jolly, jester, eject*) or with *g* (*giant, gym, edge, legend*).

K The *k* sound can be spelled with *k* (*kickball, kitchen, liking, okay*), with *c* (*catalog, clever, Eric, Canada*), or with *ch* (*chorus, chemist*).

N The *n* sound can be spelled with *n* (*nifty, ninety, blend, banana*), with *kn* (*knee, knot, knob*), with *gn* (*gnat, gnome*), or with *pn* (*pneumonia*).

R The *r* sound can be spelled with *r* (*riddle, rascal, argue, thrill, eager*), with *rh* (*rhinoceros, rhyme*), or with *wr* (*write, wriggle, wrong*).

S The *s* sound can be spelled with *s* (*sassy, sassafras, Sacramento*), with *c* (*celery, city, sincere*), with *sc* (*scissors, scene, scintillating*), or with *psy* (*psychiatry, psychic*).

T The *t* sound can be spelled with *t* (*tickle, tackle, tattoo, snippet*) or with *pt* (*pterodactyl*).

W The *w* sound can be spelled with *w* (*witch, wizard, wish, away*) or with *wh* (*whine, whistle*).

Z The *z* sound can be spelled with *z* (*zero, zoo, kazoo, zap*) or with *x* (*xylophone*).

KR The *kr* sound can be spelled with *kr* (*krypton*), with *cr* (*cranky, creepy, excruciating*), or with *chr* (*Christmas*).

SH The *sh* sound can be spelled with *sh* (*wash, shallow, shiver, shirk*), with *ch* (*chef, chateau*), or with *s* (*sugar, sure*).

SK The *sk* sound can be spelled with *sk* (*skinny, skate, whisk*), with *sc* (*scrape, scared*), with *sch* (*scheme, school*), or with *squ* (*squirt, squall, squeeze*).

Better Grades & Higher Test Scores / READING & LANGUAGE gr. 4–6
Copyright ©2005 by Incentive Publications, Inc., Nashville, TN.

Words with Missing Sounds

Some letters don't make any sound at all!

Pay attention to these words with silent letters. Learn their spelling well.

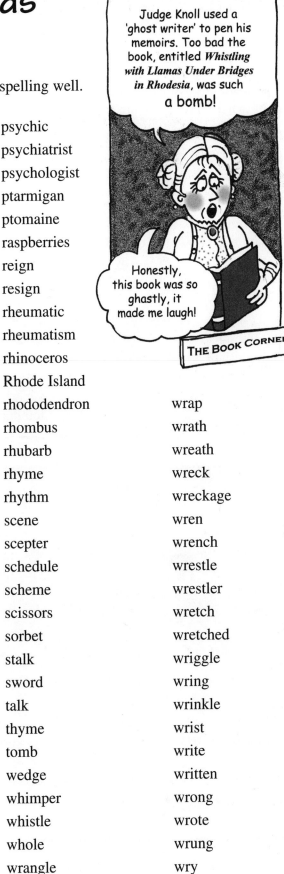

Judge Knoll used a 'ghost writer' to pen his memoirs. Too bad the book, entitled *Whistling with Llamas Under Bridges in Rhodesia*, was such a bomb!

Honestly, this book was so ghastly, it made me laugh!

THE BOOK CORNER

ache	heirloom	psychic	
answer	herb	psychiatrist	
badge	honest	psychologist	
ballet	hymn	ptarmigan	
balmy	judge	ptomaine	
bomb	knack	raspberries	
bridge	knave	reign	
budge	knead	resign	
calm	knee	rheumatic	
castle	kneel	rheumatism	
chalk	knew	rhinoceros	
character	knickers	Rhode Island	
chlorine	knife	rhododendron	wrap
chord	knight	rhombus	wrath
chorus	knives	rhubarb	wreath
cough	knit	rhyme	wreck
crumb	knock	rhythm	wreckage
czar	knoll	scene	wren
dough	knot	scepter	wrench
dumb	know	schedule	wrestle
edge	knowledge	scheme	wrestler
fudge	known	scissors	wretch
ghetto	knuckle	sorbet	wretched
ghastly	lamb	stalk	wriggle
ghost	laugh	sword	wring
gnarled	ledge	talk	wrinkle
gnash	llama	thyme	wrist
gnat	light	tomb	write
gnaw	muscle	wedge	written
gnome	pledge	whimper	wrong
gourmet	pneumonia	whistle	wrote
heir	psalm	whole	wrung
heiress	pseudonym	wrangle	wry

Better Grades & Higher Test Scores / READING & LANGUAGE gr. 4–6
Copyright ©2005 by Incentive Publications, Inc., Nashville, TN.

Get Sharp: Spelling Guide

Words with Tricky Endings

The English language has endings galore! And so many of them sound or look very much alike.

These different endings can wreak havoc on your spelling, unless you know which ending is which for use on what word! Here are some of the tricky ones.

... end with *ant*

applicant	mutant
assistant	observant
attendant	occupant
defiant	participant
distant	pheasant
elegant	pleasant
elephant	redundant
hydrant	restaurant
ignorant	significant
important	vigilant
migrant	vacant

... end with *ent*

absorbent
adolescent
accident
ambivalent
apparent
belligerent
benevolent
fluent
negligent
president
resident
superintendent
temperament

... end with *ate*

accumulate	graduate
calculate	hesitate
candidate	hibernate
celebrate	imitate
chocolate	incubate
devastate	irrigate
decorate	liberate
delegate	operate
duplicate	rotate
educate	saturate
estimate	separate

... end with *al*

brutal	hysterical	rural
classical	legal	spiral
commercial	practical	technical
electrical	oral	theatrical
fatal	recital	tropical
frugal	residential	typical

... end with *el*

cancel
channel
level
model
pummel
shrivel
unravel
vessel

... end with *le*

bundle
candle
clavicle
gargle
icicle
terrible
visible
wrestle

... end with *ile*

fragile
fertile
futile
hostile
infantile
juvenile
reptile
senile

... end with *ize*

apologize
criticize
equalize
familiarize
fantasize
hypothesize
optimize
realize
utilize

... end with *ise*

exercise
promise
supervise
surprise
televise

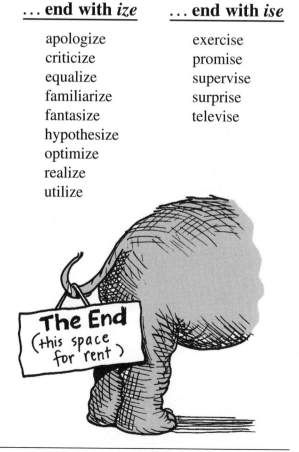

The End
(this space for rent)

... end with *tion*

addition
dictation
portion
prevention
revolution
tradition

... end with *sion*

confusion
decision
erosion
explosion
invasion
transfusion

... end with *ion*

cushion
fashion

... end with *cian*

magician
musician

Elephants never forget! Suffixes that follow the soft **c** or soft **g** always begin with **i** or **e**.

Adolescent elephants are elegant

... end with *uous*

arduous
conspicuous

... end with *ious*

contagious
malicious

... end with *eous*

advantageous
courteous
gorgeous
igneous
outrageous

... end with *ius*

genius

... end with *ous*

adventurous
anonymous
dangerous
frivolous
glamorous
jealous
marvelous
tremendous
wondrous

... end with *able*

abominable
admirable
allowable
commendable
conquerable
enjoyable
lovable
payable
perishable
reliable
understandable
washable

... end with *ible*

edible
eligible
accessible
admissible
gullible
impossible
invisible
legible
reversible
sensible
tangible
terrible

... end with *ance*

abundance
acceptance
acquaintance
allowance
appearance
assurance
attendance
elegance
importance
insurance
nuisance
reliance

... end with *ence*

absence
abstinence
affluence
influence
consequence
dependence
evidence
independence
negligence
occurrence
sequence

119

Confusing Words

accept *or* except?

accept *(receive)*; except *(excluding)*

> That zoo doesn't **accept** rattlesnakes.
>
> They have all poisonous snakes **except** rattlers.

adopt *or* adept?

adopt *(take on or take in)*; adept *(skilled)*

> Maria just **adopted** twelve cobras.
>
> It's good she's so **adept** at handling snakes.

advice *or* advise?

advice *(recommendation)*; advise *(to give advice)*

> When you were **advised** to stay away from that snake, why didn't you take the **advice**?

affect *or* effect?

affect *(to influence)*; effect *(a result)*

> Julia's mother's warnings did not **affect** her in the least.
>
> Even the sign saying, "Piranhas are Deadly" had no **effect** on her behavior.

angle *or* angel?

angle *(geometric figure)*; angel *(heavenly being)*

> Do you think **angels** have to do geometry—things like measuring **angles** and naming triangles?

attitude *or* altitude?

attitude *(demeanor)*; altitude *(height)*

> You have a sour **attitude** about mountain climbing! Is it because you get sick at high **altitudes**?

carton *or* cartoon?

carton *(container)*; cartoon *(funny picture)*

> I heard you got a good job drawing **cartoons** on **cartons** of caramel corn.

Better Grades & Higher Test Scores / READING & LANGUAGE gr. 4–6

celery or salary?

celery *(chewy, stringy vegetable)*; **salary** *(money paid for work)*
*Don't eat **celery** just before you ask your boss for a raise in your **salary**.*

college or collage?

college *(school of higher education)*; **collage** *(many items combined into a work of art)*
*A **collage** of rock music stars is not likely to be appropriate for your **college** application.*

coma or comma?

coma *(state of unconsciousness)*; **comma** *(mark of punctuation)*
*After a month in a **coma**, Moe was happy that he could tell a **comma** from a semicolon.*

desert or dessert?

desert *(a very dry place)*; **dessert** *(a tasty, sweet, after-dinner food)*
*When I was lost in the **desert**, I had repeated dreams about cold, creamy **desserts**.*

dairy or diary?

dairy *(a place where milk products are processed)*; **diary** *(a written record of one's life)*
*We stumbled upon a secret **diary** hidden in a bottle in the **dairy**.*

incredible or inedible?

incredible *(unbelievable)*; **inedible** *(not fit for eating)*
*Wasn't it **incredible** how Amy lunched on such **inedible** things as shoelaces?*

lose or loose?

lose *(be without something you had)*; **loose** *(not tight)*
*If you wear your pants so **loose**, you just might **lose** them!*

though, through, or thorough?

though *(however)*; **through** *(within something)*; **thorough** *(complete)*
*Matt was **thoroughly** clean even **though** he rode his bike right **through** the mud puddle.*

which or witch?

which *(a question pronoun used to identify what one)*; **witch** *(a character with magical powers)*
*One **witch** wandered through poison ivy. One did not. **Which witch** has the itch?*

Other Troublesome Words

Italian words taste the best.

Some of the most troublesome words for spellers are borrowed from different languages. Other words that often stump spellers are very short words or very long words. Here is the correct spelling for some of the most common of those tricky words—all at one quick glance.

MENU

Borrowed Food Words

banana
crepe
tortilla
barbecue
omelet
petit fours
spaghetti
doughnut
macaroni
molasses
vanilla
lasagna
enchilada
crepes
bologna
sauerkraut
éclair
fricassee
paella
enchilada
soufflé
crème caramel
hors d'oeuvres
gourmet

Borrowed Words

acrobat
algebra
antique
blitz
bourgeois
buoy
carousel
chauffeur
comet
cul-de-sac

diamond
dynamite
elite
eureka
fiancée
juvenile
guru
ink
khaki
kindergarten

lasso
magazine
mosquito
mandarin
octopus
pajama
piano
pirate
résumé
sarong

shampoo
status quo
tambourine
tornado
tourniquet
tsar
tycoon
veranda
yacht

little Words

about
all
almost
already
any
awful
busy
buy
candle
circle
color
cough
could
does
drawer
early
easy

enough
enter
entry
ever
every
fifth
first
fought
forget
four
forty
friend
gym
half
here
hope
hurried

island
just
knives
laugh
length
listen
many
mine
might
much
must
often
open
people
please
really
refer

safety
should
since
though
thought
toward
truly
tough
used
very
week
when
which
while
whole
won't
would

Better Grades & Higher Test Scores / READING & LANGUAGE gr. 4–6
Copyright ©2005 by Incentive Publications, Inc., Nashville, TN.

BIG Words

abominable

abracadabra   *ambidextrous*   arteriosclerosis

biodegradable   brontosaurus

circumstantial   delicatessen   ELECTROMAGNETIC

EXAGGERATION   hieroglyphics

hippopotamus

MAGNANIMOUS   obstreperous   ORTHODONTIST

(parenthetical)   PARLIAMENTARIAN

Pennsylvania   perpendicular   pharmaceutical

philanthropic   phosphorescence   plagiarism

polysyllabic   precipitation   sarsaparilla

simultaneously   *unambiguous*   VETERINARIAN

xenophobia   xylophone

Some paleontologists say that prehistoric dinosaur fossils from such diverse creatures as the brontosaurus and the pterodactyl are often found in the eroding sedimentary rock layers that date back to the Cambrian Era.

Get Sharp: Spelling Guide

Commonly Misspelled Words *(Spelled correctly!)*

Tom Foolery cautions you: "Learn these words. They are often spelled wrong."

absence
about
accident
acre
account
accurate
accuse
ache
achieve
address
adolescent
advertise
again
aisle
allowance
almost
already
always
amateur
ambulance
among
amuse
ancient
angel

angle
anniversary
anonymous
answer
Antarctica
anxious
any
apologize
architect
argument
arithmetic
attendance
attention
August

balloon
banana
beauty
beautiful
because
been
beginning
believe
benefit
bicycle
biscuit
blizzard
blue

bookkeeper
brake
break
breakfast
breath (n.)
breathe (v.)
brief
broccoli
built
bureau
burglar
business
busy

cafeteria
calendar
canal
cancel
candle
cannot
canoe
capacity
carburetor
carton
cashier
caught
cauliflower
cemetery
certain
character
chief
chocolate
choose
chorus
cinnamon
citizen
climb
cocoa
collar
college
color
Columbus
coming
committee

cough
could
counterfeit
country
courage
courtesy

damage
dangerous
dear
deceive
defense
deficient
definitely
delicious
dependence
desert
desperate
diamond
dictionary
difference
dinosaur
doctor
dollar

easy
education
efficiency
elegant
elephant
embarrass
emergency
empty
enough
escape
esophagus
every
exaggerate
exciting
excuse
exercise
exhaust
explain
extraordinary

Get Sharp: Spelling Guide
Better Grades & Higher Test Scores / READING & LANGUAGE gr. 4–6

familiar
fatigue
February
fifth
foreign
forget
forty
fountain
fourth
fragile
frequent
friend
frighten
frugal

gauge
genius
ghost
gnaw
gorgeous
graduate
grammar
grief
guarantee
guess

half
Halloween
having
heaven
heard
height
here
hippopotamus
history
hoarse
honest
hour
hypothesis

icicle
ignorance
immature
immediately
improvement
incident
independence

busness?
busyness?
business?
buissnes?
buisiness?

infection
influence
initial
innocent
interrupt
interview
irregular
island
instead

jealous
jeopardy
journal
journey
juice
just
justice

kitchen
knead
knew
knife
knives
knock
know

laboratory
laid
language
laundry
laugh
lawyer
league
legislature
library
librarian

license
lieutenant
lightning
likable
likeness
limousine
Lincoln
literature
location
lonely
loose
lose
lovely

machinery
magic
magnify
making
manageable
many
marriage
maneuver
marshmallow
Mediterranean
meant
measurement
medal
medium
memorize
miscellaneous
minute
mischief
molecule
mortgage
mosquito
movement
much

national
naughty
necessary
negligence
neighbor
neither
nervous
niece
noodle

noticeable
nuclear
nuisance
numb

obey
occasionally
occur
occurrence
odor
official
often
once
opaque
opportunity
opposite
ordinary
original
ought
outrageous

Pacific
pajamas
paradise
particle
paid
parallel
parliament
peculiar
people

surprize?
suprize?
suprise?
surprise?
supprise?

perform
physician
picnic
piece
pilot

Better Grades & Higher Test Scores / READING & LANGUAGE gr. 4–6
Copyright ©2005 by Incentive Publications, Inc., Nashville, TN.

Get Sharp: Spelling Guide

pleasant
pleasure
pledge
police
politics
potatoes
practice
presence
privilege
promise
protein

quantity
quaint
quarrel
quarter
question
quiet
quite
quotient

raise
realize
really
receive
recent
recognize
rehearse
reign
remedy
require
reservoir
resign
restaurant
rhythm
ridiculous

said
Saturday
scared
schedule
scene
seems
seize
separate
sheik
shoes

shriek
similar
since
sincere
sleigh
society
sophomore
spaghetti
stalk
straight
stomach
success
sugar
sure
sword

tattoo
taught
technique
terrible
terrific
thorough
though
through
tired
tomorrow
tonight
tongue
trespassing
triangle
trouble
truly
Tuesday
toward
twelfth
typical

uncomplicated
unconscious
uniform
unique
united
universe
unusual
useable
used
usually

vacuum
vegetable
vacation
vehicle
very
villain
virtue
virus
visible
voice

waist
waste
weather
Wednesday
week
weigh
weird
where
whether
which
whoever
whole
women
won't
would
wreath
write
writhe
writing
wrote

xenogenesis
xenolith
xylophone

yellow
yacht
yesterday
your
you're

zealous
zephyr
zinnia
zoology

Don't be fooled! These may look right, but they are not!

nesessary
freind
hieght
bananna   doller
beleive   lonly
Febuary
aplolgise   choclat
calender
beautaful   lovly
attendence
wierd   exercize
seperate
tommorrow
lisence
resturant   excape
cafateria
paralell
literture

GET SHARP →

in

WRITING and SPEAKING

What to Write?

There are so many possibilities for writing. Think beyond paragraphs, stories, and essays. Here are some of the many forms that writing can take. Try them all!

A-B-C books

adventures
advertisements
advice columns
allegories
analogies
anecdotes
announcements

I am not just fooling around when I talk about all the writing possibilities!

answers
anthems
appeals
apologies
arguments
assumptions
autobiographies
awards

ballads

beauty tips
bedtime stories
beginnings
billboards
biographies
blurbs
books
book jackets
book reviews
brochures
bulletins
bumper stickers

calendar quips

campaign speeches
captions
cartoons
CD covers
cereal boxes
certificates
characterizations
children's books
cinquains
clichés
clues
codes
colloquialisms
comedies
comic strips
commercials
comparisons
complaints

consumer reports
contracts
contrasts
conundrums
conversations
couplets
critiques
crossword puzzles
cumulative stories

debates

definitions
descriptions
dialogues
diamantes
diaries
diets
directions
directories
documents
doubletalk
dramas
dream scripts

editorials

e-mails
encyclopedia entries
epics
epigrams
epilogues
epitaphs
endings
essays
evaluations
exaggerations
exclamations
excuses
explanations

fables

fairy tales
fantasies

feature articles
folklore
free verse

gags

game rules
good news/bad news
gossip
graffiti
greeting cards
grocery lists

haiku

headlines
health tips
horoscopes
how-to booklets
how-NOT-to booklets
hymns

improvisations

indexes
inquiries
interviews
introductions
invitations

jingles

job applications
job descriptions
jokes
journals
jump rope rhymes

lectures

legends
letters
limericks
lists
love notes
luscious words
lyrics

magazines

malapropisms
marquee notices
memories
memos
menus
metaphors
minutes
monologues
movie reviews
mysteries
myths

narrations

news articles
news flashes
newspapers
nonsense
notes
novels
nursery rhymes

obituaries

observations
odes
opinions

palindromes

pamphlets
parables
paraphrases
parodies
party tips
persuasive letters
petitions
phrases
plays
poems
post cards
post scripts
posters
prayers
predictions
problems
problem solutions

product descriptions
programs
profound sayings
prologues
propaganda
proposals
protest letters
proverbs
puns
puzzle clues
puzzle answers

quatrains

questions
questionnaires
quips
quizzes
quotations

raps

reactions
real estate notices
rebuttals
recipes
remedies
reports
requests
requiems
restaurant reviews
resumes
reviews
rhymes
riddles

sale notices

sales pitches
satires
sayings
schedules
science fiction
secrets
self-portraits
sentences
sequels
serialized stories

sermons
signs
silly sayings
skywriting messages
slogans
soliloquies
songs
sonnets
speeches
spoofs
spooky stories
spoonerisms
sports accounts
stories
summaries
superstitions

tall tales

telegrams
telephone directory
test items
textbooks
thank you notes
theater programs
travel posters
titles
tongue twisters
travel brochures
tributes
trivia
TV commercials
TV guides
TV scripts

understatements

vignettes

vitas

want ads

wanted posters
warnings
weather forecasts
weather reports
web pages

wills
wise sayings
wishes
words

yarns

yellow pages

Well, maybe I am fooling around just a little bit.

Get Sharp Tip #7
Choose a genre that fits the purpose of the writing.

Writing Modes

There are dozens of forms for writing (as you've seen on pages 128–129). In general, these fall into a few larger categories of writing, called **modes**. Different modes are used for different purposes.

Here are the different modes of writing. When you want to accomplish one of these purposes, it is your choice what form (genre) to use!

Get Sharp Tip # 8
A piece of writing (such as a poem) can fit into more than one category. It might be narrative, as well as descriptive and imaginary!

Expository — writing that explains or informs

Narrative — writing that tells a story about events that happened (real or imaginary or some of each)

Imaginative — writing that includes made-up details (not real)

Persuasive — writing that tries to convince a reader of something

Descriptive — writing that gives details about how some thing (or person or place) looks, acts, smells, tastes, sounds, or feels

Personal-Expressive — writing that shares the writer's personal reflection or perspective on a topic

Andrea, did you know that the writing **genre** (form) depends somewhat on the purpose of the writing? However, there is no **one** genre that must be used for a particular purpose. For example:

To convince someone of something (persuasive writing), you might write an essay. Or, you might write a letter or poem. But you could also use these same forms (essays, letter, poem) to inform about something (expository writing).

I want to convince everyone that table tennis is the world's greatest sport. I think I'll write a persuasive essay.

Which Writing Mode?

- a recipe for tuna-artichoke ice cream — *expository, imaginative, descriptive*

- a poster advertising talking backpacks — *persuasive, descriptive*

- safety rules on a snowboard hill — *expository*

- directions for taking a wheelchair on the subway — *expository*

- a reflection by a hit-and-run victim — *personal-expressive, narrative*

- an editorial denouncing the new city sidewalk plan — *persuasive, expository*

- the diary of a sword-swallower — *personal-expressive, descriptive, narrative*

- a science fiction story about an underwater city — *imaginative, descriptive, narrative*

- a news article about a tidal wave — *expository, descriptive, narrative*

- an encyclopedia entry explaining the water cycle — *expository*

- a tall tale about cows that ran a farm — *imaginative, descriptive, narrative*

- an opinion about the attractiveness of nose rings — *persuasive, descriptive*

- a short story about Japanese-speaking ladybugs — *imaginative, descriptive, narrative*

- a travel brochure for a resort in Australia — *persuasive, descriptive*

- the autobiography of an Olympic diver — *personal-expressive, narrative, descriptive*

Prose & Poetry

WHAT'S THE DIFFERENCE?

What's the difference between **prose** and **poetry**? My editor says I can write either one for my piece in the school newspaper.

Well, G.G., **prose** is writing that is done in an ordinary form using sentences and paragraphs.

And **poetry** is written in lines or stanzas (groups of lines). These may or may not contain complete sentences.

Poetry is often shorter than prose.

The words and lines in poetry are usually arranged to have more rhythm than prose lines.

SPECIAL FEATURES

SPORTS WRITER

ARTS

Sometimes there is rhyme in a poem.

poetry

I ate the last piece of pie you were saving for yourself.
And I know strawberry-rhubarb is your favorite.
I'm really sorry.
It was delicious.
And it was just calling out to me from the fridge.

prose

Dear Diary,
I know I should not have done this, but I could not help it. I came home from soccer practice, tired and hungry. When I opened the refrigerator to look for something to eat, right there in front of me was a big, beautiful piece of strawberry-rhubarb pie. I was sure my mom was saving it for herself, since it is her very favorite food. But, it seemed to call out my name, so I ate it. I will have to apologize to Mom.
Will

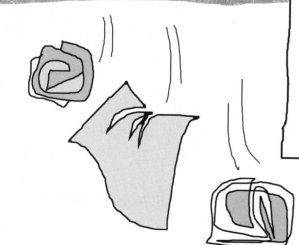

More About Poetry

These are some special characteristics often found in poetry. Many (except for rhyme) are found in prose, too. But poetry makes consistent use of these.

- Poetry takes an especially imaginative look at something.
- Poetry adds life to an idea, or makes something extraordinary out of an ordinary event.
- Poetry has a strong appeal to the senses and the emotions.
- The sounds of poetry are pleasing to hear. Poetry makes use of rhyme, rhythm, repetition, alliteration, assonance, and onomatopoeia. (See pages 138–141.)
- Poetry makes special use of figurative language (techniques such as similes, metaphors, puns, imagery, idioms, personification). (See pages 138–141.)

Some Poetry Forms

ballad — a poem that tells a story, usually written in quatrains (4-line stanzas)

blank verse — unrhymed poetry with a meter (repetition of accented and unaccented syllables). The lines are generally 10 syllables in length, with an accent on every other syllable, beginning with the second syllable.

> *My toaster greedily grabs the slices,*
> *Gobbles them down, deep down inside.*
> *I dare not try to take them from her.*
> *Her hot temper makes sure of that.*

cinquain — 5-line poem usually following this form:
    Line 1 (one word — title)
    Line 2 (two words — descriptive of title)
    Line 3 (three words — action about the title)
    Line 4 (four words — a feeling about the title)
    Line 5 (one word — repeat of title, or a synonym)

couplet — two lines of verse that rhyme

> *"What, no homework back today, Tom Wade?"*
> *No, Ma'am . . . so you'll have less papers to grade.*

elegy — a poem that expresses sadness about someone's death

Somehow, I ended up writing an ode for a ping-pong-playing frog!

To a Frog

To you, my green and slippery friend
Your talents never seem to end.
Though your feet are webbed
You never fall.
You nimbly leap,
To hit every ball.

epic — a long story poem, usually telling the adventures of some hero

Probably the most famous epic poem is *The Odyssey,* a book-length poem by Homer. It follows the adventures of Odysseus, a Greek hero, over a period of many years.

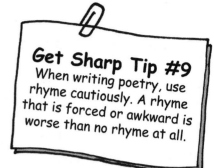

Get Sharp Tip #9
When writing poetry, use rhyme cautiously. A rhyme that is forced or awkward is worse than no rhyme at all.

free verse — unrhymed poetry that has no meter

I dreamed the clouds were dragons.
Billows of fluff, not fire,
Came toward me.
I needed not my sword.

haiku — a kind of Japanese poetry that gives an impression of something in nature

It has 3 lines. The first line has 5 syllables; the second has 7 syllables; the third line has 5 syllables.

Softly swirling cream
Chocolate, melting in my mouth
Trickling down my throat.

A daring young hunter named Nan
Said, "Trap a big tiger I can."
Though she followed her map
And set a good trap,
The tiger outsmarted her plan.

Heh, heh!

limerick — a 5-line humorous poem with a particular rhyme and rhythm scheme

Lines 1, 2, and 5 rhyme with each other, and each has three accented syllables.

Lines 3 and 4 rhyme, and each has two accented syllables.

lyric — a short poem giving a personal feeling or perspective

ode — a long lyric poem

quatrain — a 4-line poem, usually with *aabb, abab,* or *abcb* rhyme pattern

Mix a pepper milkshake,
Take a hearty drink.
You'll wind up with heartburn
Quicker than you think.

sonnet — a 14-line poem that gives a poet's personal feelings

A sonnet has a very specific line length, meter, and rhyme scheme.

What Makes Writing Effective?

Read a lot of stuff!
Translation: Read good writing in many different forms. Notice what the writer does to accomplish the things shown in the "effective writing" list.

Check out how other writers write.
Translation: Carefully review the list of writing skills. (See pages 136-137 and 146-147.) Notice how other writers use them. As you write, practice using them.

Get to know writing devices.
Translation: Review the list of devices writers use to make their writing more interesting and effective. (See pages 138-141.) Include these in your writing.

Know what you're doing.
Translation: Follow a process when you write. include all the steps. (See pages 142-143.)

WHEN IN DOUBT — PHONE A FRIEND

My four best friends give a lot of advice.

You are constantly reading what other people write. As a part of your life as a student, you are repeatedly being asked to write something. In school, your writing is often evaluated in some way. Even if it isn't, you want to write something that is good, makes sense, or has some effect. So, how can you tell if writing is "good"? Here are some characteristics of writing that *works*.

Effective writing. . .

. . . makes sense

. . . reads smoothly

. . . keeps the reader's attention

. . . says what the writer wants to say

. . . accomplishes the purpose the writer intends

. . . speaks to the audience the writer intends

. . . uses words that are interesting and powerful

. . . pleases, satisfies, informs, or challenges the reader

. . . arranges ideas and details in a way that gets the point across

. . . has, says, or does something unique to that piece of writing

. . . is not cluttered with irrelevant words or ideas

. . . is not cluttered with repetitive words or ideas

. . . does not rely on over-used words or clichés

. . . is not confused by errors in spelling and mechanics

Writing Skills

Use this as a checklist while you write. Put the skills to use in your own writing.

I. WORD USE

_____Choose precise words for accurate meaning and interest.

_____Choose fresh, original, and varied words and phrases.

_____Recognize and avoid over-used words or clichés.

_____Recognize and choose active rather than inactive words and phrases.

_____Select words that help to create the mood you want to set.

_____Include figurative language; use it in fresh ways.

_____Choose the right words for the purpose and audience.

_____Arrange words within sentences to make the meaning clear.

_____Arrange words in sentences to give an interesting rhythm and smooth flow.

_____Avoid repetitive or unnecessary words or phrases.

_____Recognize and choose words and phrases that produce strong sensory images.

II. SENTENCE CONSTRUCTION

_____Create sentences that have a sensible and natural flow.

_____Include sentences with varied length, structure, sound, and rhythm.

_____Write sentences that communicate meaning clearly.

_____Structure sentences to focus attention on main ideas and important details.

_____Write sentences that sound pleasing when read aloud.

_____Only include sentences that contribute to the meaning and purpose.

_____Provide smooth transitions between sentences.

_____Use dialogue correctly and appropriately in written pieces.

III. CONTENT & ORGANIZATION

_____Create written pieces that show clear understanding of the particular writing task.

_____Create written pieces that show completeness and clear organization.

_____State main ideas and purposes clearly.

_____Use sufficient and relevant details and examples to support a main idea.

_____Combine ideas and details in a way that flows smoothly.

_____Combine ideas and details in a way that develops meaning clearly.

_____Combine ideas and details in a sensible sequence.

_____Contribute ideas that have freshness.

_____Create strong titles for written pieces.

_____Create strong, attention-getting beginnings.

_____Create strong, effective endings or conclusions.

IV. USE OF FORMS & TECHNIQUES

_____Produce a variety of kinds of writing: expository, descriptive, persuasive, narrative, imaginative, and personal-expressive writing.

_____Develop experience writing a variety of forms and genres.

_____Effectively use a variety of writing techniques and literary devices. (See pages 138–141.)

_____Develop a consistent and appropriate point of view for the passage.

_____Adapt form, style, and content appropriately for appeal to a specific audience.

_____Adapt form, style, and content appropriately for the purpose of the writing.

_____Include dialogue in the text where effective and appropriate.

_____Engage the audience and convey personal commitment (voice) to the writing.

V. EDITING & REVISING

_____Recognize and replace overused, ordinary, or inactive words and phrases.

_____Revise sentences for clarity, rhythm, and flow.

_____Rearrange ideas or lines for proper sequence, better meaning, or better flow.

_____Eliminate excess or repetitive words or ideas in sentences.

_____Eliminate repetitive or unrelated ideas in passages.

_____Replace awkward transitions.

_____Vary lengths of sentences for smoothness or effectiveness in conveying meaning.

_____Improve weak beginnings or endings.

_____Replace weak or imprecise titles.

_____Strengthen a passage by adding dialogue, or by changing existing text to dialogue.

_____Revise writing for accuracy in capitalization and punctuation (including quotations).

_____Revise writing for spelling accuracy.

_____Revise writing for correct use of grammatical construction.

Get Sharp Tip #10
Don't try to polish all your writing skills at once! Work on one (or a few) at a time.

VI. USE OF THE WRITING PROCESS

_____Show ability to participate in each part of the writing process.

_____Take part in motivational activities that stimulate ideas.

_____Actively and fluently collect ideas, words, and phrases for writing.

_____Organize a rough draft using collected ideas.

_____Examine own writing for technique, effectiveness, and organization.

_____Examine and respond to others' writing appropriately and constructively.

_____Use responses and observations to make revisions in own writing.

_____Review your own writing carefully for correct conventions.

_____Prepare a polished, finished piece after examining for revision needs.

_____Take part in sharing, presenting, or publishing finished products.

Writing Techniques & Devices

Here are some of the things writers use or do to make writing effective. They can make your own writing better. Include them when they fit your form and purpose.

assonance — **repeated vowel sounds in a line, phrase, or sentence**

Assonance occurs within words. It gives rhythm to phrases and is pleasing to hear.
Example: *That rat just sat on my hat.*

alliteration — **repeated consonant sounds in a line, phrase, or sentence**

Alliteration usually appears at the beginning of words. It sets a rhythm or mood to sentences or phrases. It is fun and pleasing to the ear.
Example: *Bewildered, bruised, and battered, Bill hobbled home with his broken bicycle. It's a bad day for bumbling Bill.*

characterization — **the way the writer explains the characters in the story**

Characterization tells readers about a character's personality, appearance, motivations, or behaviors.

consonance — **repeated consonant sounds in a line, phrase, or sentence**

Consonance is different from alliteration in that consonance is the repetition of a consonant sound anywhere in the words of a line, not just at the beginning. Like alliteration, it adds to the mood and rhythm of the line. It is fun and pleasing to the ear.
Example: *Katie kicks her chronic hiccups.*

figurative language — **a way of using language that expands the literal meaning of the words and gives them a new or more interesting twist**

Metaphors, similes, puns, and idioms are examples of figurative language.

Hurried and hassled, Hannah hustled home ahead of the hurricane. Would she withstand the whip-lashing winds and the waves of watery weather?

Speaking figuratively, it's raining cats and dogs!

foreshadowing — some suggestions within the text or story that give the reader hints about something that may happen later in the story

This technique increases suspense and leads the reader to anticipate events to come.

hyperbole — extreme exaggeration used to increase the effect of a statement

This serves to add humor and imagination to particular types of writing, such as tall tales. It also adds emphasis to a point the speaker or writer is trying to make.

Example: It was so cold that my words froze before they reached her ears.

imagery — details that appeal to the senses

Imagery makes the experience more real!
Example: A shrill, piercing scream split the still night sky.

irony — a discrepancy between what is said and what is meant, or between what appears to be true and what is really true

Example: The man dressed in rags was the richest man in the country.

metaphor — a comparison between two things that are not ordinarily alike

Like other figurative language, metaphors make writing fresh, interesting, moving, humorous, or touching.

Examples:

Her wrinkles were deep as canyons.

Writing a poem is opening a can of yourself.

Your bedroom is like the Bermuda Triangle.

mood — the feeling in a piece of writing

Mood is set by a combination of the words and sounds, the setting, the imagery, and the details. Mood may give a feeling of cold, mystery, hurriedness, softness, fear, darkness, hopelessness, etc.

onomatapoeia - use of a word whose sound makes you think of its meaning
The use of onomatopoeia adds auditory appeal to the writing.

POP

HISS

sizzle

crackle

BOOM

fireworks split the night sky

personification — giving human characteristics to a nonliving object

Personification compares two unlike things by attributing human thoughts, feelings, appearances, actions, or attitudes to an object or animal.

Examples:

Sneaky fog slinks around corners, using its gray paintbrush to cover the city.

When he swam past a submarine, the shark commented to his wife, "That looks like a tin full of people."

point of view — lets the reader know who is telling the story

The story may be told by a character in the story, a narrator who is in the story, or a narrator who is not in the story. Within the story, a character may tell the story about himself or herself (first person). Some stories have a series of narrators, speaking in first or second person.

pun — a play on words

A pun is a word or a phrase used in a way that gives a funny twist to the words.

Examples:

Going to the dentist is a fulfilling experience.

Mother says it's a drain on our budget to hire a plumber.

The surgeon was such a joker that he had me in stitches.

Could a spelling bee hold a conversation with a talking dog?

An elephant doesn't need a moving van. She just packs up her trunk and goes.

rhyme — repeating of sounds

Rhyme may occur at the ends of lines or within the lines.

Example of ending rhyme:
*There once was a guy from LaCrosse
Whose teeth were allergic to floss.*

Example of internal rhyme:
Wearing galoshes, they sloshed through mushy, gushy mud.

satire — writing that makes fun of the shortcomings of people, systems, or institutions for the purpose of enlightening readers or bringing about a change

Satires are often written about governmental systems or persons of power and influence. They can range from light fun-making to harsh, bitter mockery.

simile — a comparison between two unlike things, using the word *like* or *as* to connect them

Like other figures of speech, similes make writing fresh, interesting, moving, humorous, or touching. They surprise and delight the reader, and make the description more real.

Examples:

My big brother demolishes his food as fast as a garbage disposal.

Homework is like hiccups—hard to get rid of.

theme — the main meaning or idea of a piece of writing

It includes the topic and a viewpoint or opinion about the topic.

Example: *On page 132, the poem and the prose selection both are written on the same theme. The theme is someone apologizing for something without being truly sorry about the act that was done.*

tone — the approach a writer takes toward the topic

The tone may be playful, hostile, humorous, serious, argumentative, suspicious, etc.

Your Tone Affects My Mood!

Dear Editor:
What right does the city have to tell us what we can do on our own property? This is America! I should be able to plant any kind of tree that I choose in my yard. Mark my words. There will be an uprising among the citizens of Ashville if this ruling is not reversed! Impeach the mayor!
J. I. Rayte

All the soft, silky sounds in this poem help to set a quiet, reflective **mood.**

The **tone** is more about the author and his or her attitude toward what he or she is writing. Of course, the writer's tone affects word choice, and helps to set the mood for the reader.

The **mood** is more about the reader. It's the feeling the reader gets from the writing. The words and sounds, the setting, the images, and the details all combine to set a mood.

The Writing Process

Stage 1 Romancing

This is the reason for writing! It is the spark that gets ideas brewing. It can be . . .

a group experience	*a thought*
an individual experience	*a feeling*
a piece of literature	*a question*
an unexpected happening	*a memory*
a life event	*a discussion*

Many things can romance you into writing. Whatever it is, the romance stage serves to inspire ideas, impressions, emotions, opinions, questions, beliefs, explorations, or mysteries. It brings those possibilities and imaginings that are tucked away in your mind up to the surface, and gets you ready to write. Don't skip this stage. When writers can't write, or can't think of anything—they haven't spent enough time on this!

Stage 2 Collecting

This is a wonderfully creative stage of the writing process. It's the time you gather words, phrases, fragments, thoughts, ideas, facts, questions, and observations—the process of brainstorming about and broadening of the original idea. Allow plenty of time for collecting. Write down everything.

Stage 3 Organizing

This is the when you take a close look at all those impressions you have collected and start thinking about what fits together. This is the time to ask yourself . . .

- *What goes with this idea?*
- *Which ideas should be grouped together?*
- *Where would this fit into the whole picture?*
- *What do these ideas or phrases have in common?*

Then, use some method to visually connect the pieces together. Your organizational tool may be a chart, web, storyboard, outline, a series of boxes, a diagram, a list, or a series of note cards. It can be anything that groups your usable ideas together in a way that will help you connect them in your writing.

Stage 4 Drafting

Okay, now it's time to write! Start putting those words together into phrases, those phrases together into lines or sentences, those sentences together into paragraphs.

Stage 5 Reviewing

This is the author's chance to get the writing out into the light and see how it looks and hear how it sounds—before sharing it with anyone else.
Ask questions of yourself, such as . . .

Does it make sense?

Do I like it?

Are the ideas in the right order?

Will the beginning attract readers?

Does it say what I intended?

Is it smooth and clear?

Are any words or pieces missing?

Is the ending memorable?

Stage 6 Sharing for praises and questions

Ask someone else to review and respond to your writing. The response can be in the form of praise, compliments, questions, or suggestions. Ask someone who will take time to read it seriously, and who will give you responses that can actually help you improve your writing.

Stage 7 Revising

In this stage, you get to make use of the response from another reader and from your own review (Stage 5). Revise, replace, add, delete, rearrange, and otherwise strengthen your writing.

Stage 8 Checking mechanics

Now it's time to inspect your latest draft for spelling, correct grammar, mechanical and structural errors or weaknesses—and to fix them! A teacher or parent may give you some help here.

Stage 9 Polishing

All the changes have been made. Now is the time to create a final, accurate copy. This might be typed, written, dictated, or recorded some other way.

Stage 10 Showing off

Now that the writing is polished, it is time to share it. There are dozens and dozens of possibilities for this. Find some way to publish, display, or otherwise showcase your final product.

Helping Students with Writing

Advice to Parents & Teachers

Saturate students with literature. Writing flourishes in an environment that is loaded with lots of literature (of all kinds). Hearing good writing motivates students to write. It sparks ideas and lets them see how many things there are to write about.

Sensitize students to everyday experiences. Let them know that they can write about anything—simple or earth-shattering, mundane or outrageous, sad or funny, serious or frivolous, public or private. Help them find words for telling about virtually any person, place, feeling, experience, or event.

Instigate meaningful writing activities. Ask students to write only about topics that are relevant to them and their lives. They will have more to say and they will write better if they feel a connection to the topic.

Think short! It is easier for the student to handle the writing process when working on short pieces of writing. Long stories are difficult to revise and polish. There are many short forms of writing that can be used to teach and practice the writing process.

Offer choice. Allow writers as much choice as possible. Writers are always more eager to write when they "own" the topic (when they have chosen a topic that is personally appealing).

Write together—often. When a student is introduced to a new form, when a writer seems stuck, when a topic is difficult, when a writer is reluctant or insecure—write together (as a group). Besides being fun and satisfying, collaborative writing refreshes and reinforces the process. It lets students experience immediate success with fewer struggles.

Emphasize the process. Dwell on the various stages. Talk a lot about each step. Do each step together. Discuss what makes each step important. Remember that the process is more important than a particular final product.

Avoid overworking every piece of writing. Don't pressure students to go through the entire writing process every time they write. If you do, they will quit writing! Remember this: every stage of the writing process is important in itself. Students will have a real writing experience even if they only get through stage 1, 2, or 5.

Allow plenty of time for writing. Give students plenty of time to work through all parts of the process. Good writing cannot be rushed.

Top Ten

Writing Tips
to Share with Young Writers

1. Collect more ideas than you need. Write down lots of thoughts, phrases, and words. The ones you don't need can always be dropped later.

2. Use all your senses when you brainstorm ideas. Think about feelings, sights, sounds, smells, tastes, experiences, places, and people.

3. Use interesting, strong action words.

4. Use fresh, original adjectives and adverbs. (But don't use too many.)

5. Use a variety of sentences—different structures, lengths, and beginnings.

6. Don't get bogged down trying to write everything correctly. You can fix spelling, punctuation, and grammar later.

7. Remember the reader. Would someone want to read or hear this all the way through?

8. Put yourself into your writing. Let your personality and passions show.

9. Read your written work aloud (if only to yourself). Does it sound smooth, sensible, and pleasing? Does it make sense?

10. Find a way to share what you write.

NOTE TO ADULTS:
YOU WRITE, TOO!
WHEN YOU WRITE AT THE SAME TIME YOUR CHILD OR STUDENT IS WRITING, EVERYTHING CHANGES. MODEL THE USE OF THE PROCESS FOR THE STUDENTS. SHARE WHAT YOU WRITE IN ITS VARIOUS STAGES. ASK FOR THEIR INPUT.

Now that you're back in school, Mom, let me give you some writing tips . . .

WRITING PROCESS SCORING GUIDE

TRAIT	SCORE OF 5	SCORE OF 3	SCORE OF 1
CONTENT	• The writing is very clear and focused. • The main ideas and purpose stand out clearly. • Main ideas are well-supported with details and examples. • All details are relevant to the main idea. • The ideas have some freshness and insight. • The ideas fit the purpose and audience well. • The paper is interesting and holds the reader's attention.	• The writing is mostly clear and focused. • The main ideas and purpose are mostly clear. • Details and examples are used but may be somewhat limited or repetitive. • Most details are relevant to the main idea. • Some details may be off the topic. • Some ideas and details are fresh; others are ordinary. • The paper is interesting to some degree. • The ideas and content are less than precisely right for the audience and purpose.	• The writing lacks clarity and focus. • It is hard to identify the main idea. • The purpose of the writing is not evident. • Details are few, not relevant, or repetitive. • Ideas or details have little sparkle or appeal to hold the reader's attention. • The paper has not developed an idea well.
WORD CHOICE	• Writer has used strong, specific, colorful, effective, and varied words. • Words are used well to convey the ideas. • Words are well chosen to fit the content, audience, and purpose. • Writer has chosen fresh, unusual words, and/or has used words/phrases in an unusual way. • Writer has made use of figurative language, and words/phrases that create images.	• Writer has used some specific and effective words. • A good use of colorful, unusual words is attempted, but limited or overdone. • The words succeed at conveying main ideas. • The writer uses words in fresh ways sometimes, but not consistently. • The word choice is mostly suited to the content, audience, and purpose.	• There is a limited use of specific, effective, or colorful words. • Some words chosen are imprecise, misused, or repetitive. • The words do not suit the content, purpose, or audience well. • The words do not succeed at conveying the main ideas.
SENTENCES	• Sentences have a pleasing and natural flow. • When read aloud, sentences and ideas flow along smoothly from one to another. • Transitions between sentences are smooth and natural. • Sentences have varied length, structure, sound, and rhythm. • The structure of sentences focuses reader's attention on the main idea and key details. • The sentence sound and variety make the reading enjoyable. • If the writer uses dialogue, it is used correctly and effectively.	• Most of the sentences have a natural flow. • When read aloud, some sentences have a "less than fluid" sound. • Some or all transitions are awkward or repetitive. • There is some variety in sentence length, structure, sound, and rhythm; but some patterns are repetitive. • The sentences convey the main idea and details, but without much craftsmanship. • If the writer uses dialogue, it is somewhat less than fluid or effective.	• Most sentences are not fluid. • When read aloud, the writing sounds awkward or uneven. Some of the paper is confusing to read. • Transitions are not effective. • There is little variety in sentence length, structure, sound, or rhythm. • There may be incomplete or run-on sentences. • The sentence structure gets in the way of conveying content, purpose, and meaning.

A score of 4 may be given for papers that fall between 3 and 5 on a trait. A score of 2 may be given for papers that fall between 1 and 3.

146

Get Sharp: Writing Guide

Better Grades & Higher Test Scores / READING & LANGUAGE gr. 4–6
Copyright ©2005 by Incentive Publications, Inc., Nashville, TN.

WRITING PROCESS SCORING GUIDE

TRAIT	SCORE OF 5	SCORE OF 3	SCORE OF 1
ORGANIZATION	• The organization of the piece allows the main ideas and key details to be conveyed well. • The piece has a compelling beginning that catches the attention of the reader. • Ideas are developed in a clear, interesting sequence. • The piece moves along from one idea, sentence, or paragraph to another in a manner that is smooth and useful to develop the meaning. • The piece has a compelling ending that ties up the idea well and leaves the reader feeling pleased.	• Organization is recognizable, but weak or inconsistent in some places. • For the most part, the organization of the piece allows the main ideas and key details to be conveyed. • The structure seems somewhat ordinary, lacking flavor or originality. • The piece has a beginning that is not particularly inviting to the reader or not well-developed. • Some of the sequencing is confusing. • The piece does not always move along smoothly or clearly from one idea, sentence, or paragraph to another. • The piece has clear ending, but it is somewhat dull or underdeveloped, or does not adequately tie up the piece.	• The piece lacks clear organization. • For the most part, the lack of good organization gets in the way of the conveyance of the main ideas and key details. • The piece does not have a clear beginning or ending. • Ideas are not developed in any clear sequence, or the sequence is distracting. • The piece does not move along smoothly from one sentence or paragraph to another. • Important ideas or details seem to be missing or out of place. • The piece leaves the reader feeling confused.
VOICE	• The writer has left a personal stamp on the piece. A reader knows there is a person behind the writing. • It is clear that the writer knows what audience and purpose he/she is reaching. • The writer engages the audience. • The writer shows passion, commitment, originality, and honesty in conveying the message. • The voice used (level of personal closeness) is appropriate for the purpose of the piece.	• The writer has left a personal stamp on the piece, but this is not as strong or consistent as it might be. The reader is not always sure of the writer's presence. • It is not always clear that the writer knows his/her audience and purpose. • The writer engages the audience some, but not all of the time. • The writer shows some passion, commitment, originality, and honesty in conveying the message, but this is inconsistent.	• The writer has not left any personal stamp on the piece. The writing feels detached. • There is little sense that the writer is speaking to the audience, or clearly knows the purpose of the writing. • There is little or no engagement of the audience. • The writer shows little or no passion, commitment, originality, and honesty in conveying the message.
CONVENTIONS	• There is clear control of capitalization, punctuation, spelling, and paragraphing. • There is consistent use of correct grammar and language usage. • The strong use of conventions strengthens the communication of the work's meaning. • The piece needs little editing/revision.	• There is some control of capitalization, punctuation, spelling, and paragraphing. • There is inconsistent use of correct grammar and language usage. • The uneven use of conventions sometimes interferes with the meaning. • The piece needs much editing/revision.	• There is poor control of capitalization, punctuation, spelling, and paragraphing. • There is a lack of correct grammar and language usage. • Poor use of conventions obscures meaning. • There are multiple errors; the piece needs extensive editing/revision.

A score of 4 may be given for papers that fall between 3 and 5 on a trait. A score of 2 may be given for papers that fall between 1 and 3.

Collecting

Once you choose your topic for writing, get busy collecting. This step in the writing process is very important to creative thinking. It is also a step that is critical to gathering enough content to cover your topic.

- Get as much raw material as possible that pertains to your topic.

- Keep collecting until you get past the ordinary stuff to the fresh and unusual.

- Don't quit this stage too soon! Too many ideas are better than too few.

Collect:

facts
fragments
ideas
observations
phrases
words
sentences
questions
facts
memories

Amusement Park Sensations

screams coming from all directions
nose-tickling sweetness of cotton candy
lines snaking back and forth
stomach-dropping thrill
roar of waterfalls at the water rides
bulging boxes of yellow popcorn
greasy sausages dripping with mustard
squeals of delighted riders
the tomatoey smell of pizza and spaghetti
ticket booths like soldiers in the paths
clickety-clack of wheels on rails
tinny music of the carousel
the tingle of the ice cream truck
noisy marching bands
crazy characters in kooky costumes
drop fast enough to stop your heart

Places I'd Rather Not Visit

the dentist's chair
an emergency room
a sinking boat
a sewage treatment plant
a war zone
my sister's piano recital
a piranha pool
the bottom of a bird cage
inside a bee hive
a lion's mouth
an opera rehearsal
a burning building
the bottom of a crevasse
the principal's office
a cuckoo clock repair shop

Facts about koala bears

looks like teddy bear
live in trees
protected species
marsupial
active at night
young called joey
no tail
population in decline
habitat disappearing

mother carries young koala in pouch
25-30 in. long, 15-30 lbs
brown, gray fur on most of body, white belly
many have disease called chlamydia
sharp claws, long toes
joey stays in pouch 7 months
found in Australia
live in eucalyptus trees, sleep in trees during day
eat leaves and shoots of eucalyptus trees

Ways to collect:

brainstorm
research
interview
search
read
ask questions

Organizing

There is no best way to organize your ideas for writing. The only "rule" about organizing is that you should do it!

Find a method, tool, or process to organize each time you write. It's helpful to connect ideas in some visual way.

There are many possibilities for methods to organize. The tool you choose will depend on the writing genre, the time you have, and your personal preference.

Try these:

clusters	webs	diagrams	outlines
charts	note cards	tables	lists
story maps	timelines	grids	

Places I'd rather not visit!

dangerous
- a sinking ship
- a runaway train
- a piranha pool
- a lion's mouth
- a war zone
- a burning building

Boring or Disgusting
- the bottom of a bird cage
- an opera rehearsal
- a sewage treatment plant
- my sister's piano recital

scary
- a dentist's chair
- an emergency room
- the principal's office
- the bottom of a crevasse
- inside a beehive

Amusement Park Sensations

Sounds
- screams coming from all directions
- clickety-clack of wheels on rails
- roar of waterfalls at the water rides
- squeals of delighted riders
- tinny music of the carousel
- the tingle of the ice cream truck
- noisy marching bands

Sights
- lines snaking back and forth
- bulging boxes of yellow popcorn
- ticket booths like soldiers in the paths
- greasy sausages dripping with mustard
- crazy characters in kooky costumes

Smells
- nose-tickling sweetness of cotton candy
- the tomatoey smell of pizza and spaghetti

Feelings
- stomach-dropping thrill
- drop fast enough to stop your heart

Koala Facts

Appearance
looks like teddy bear
no tail
brown, gray fur, white belly
sharp claws, long toes
25–30 in. long, 15–30 lbs

Habitat
Australia
live in trees
eat leaves and shoots of
  eucalyptus trees
sleep in eucalyptus trees
habitat disappearing

Species, Behavior
marsupial
active at night
mother carries young koala
  in pouch
young called " joey"
joey stays in pouch 7 months

Status
population in decline
habitat threatened
protected species
many have disease called
  chlamydia

Effective Words

Words are the building blocks of your writing. They need to be the right ones, and they need to work for your purposes in the writing. Choose your words carefully.

Here is some advice to help you polish your word choice. Note that each bit of advice on this page is followed with an ordinary example, followed by an example of better word choice.

Use words that are precise.

General: a **rough** trail
Precise: a **treacherous** trail
General: a sleepwalker **walking** around the house at night
Precise: a sleepwalker **stumbling** around the house at night

Use words that are interesting.

Ordinary: When the jewel thief held out his hand, it held a pretty diamond necklace.
Interesting: The thief's **clenched** fingers **uncurled**; in his palm lay an **exquisite** diamond necklace.
Ordinary: She drove a beat-up old car.
Interesting: Her **ancient** car was **battered** and **rickety**.

Use active words.

Passive: The shark **seemed** to be smiling.
Active: The shark **sneered** as he passed by.
Passive: The January wind **was** cold and icy.
Active: A cold and icy January wind **bit** my nose.

Use words that are fresh and original.

Ordinary: That waiter has a **sour attitude**.
Fresh: That waiter has a **vinegary personality**.
Ordinary: Dark clouds swirled, pouring out heavy raindrops
Fresh: **Petulant** clouds **threw tantrums, sputtering** out wet torrents.

Better Grades & Higher Test Scores / READING & LANGUAGE gr. 4–6

The examples on this page show effective use of words for each piece of advice.

Use words in unusual ways.

A cream-cheese moon oozed toward the midnight end of the city.

Bus # 27 groaned when twelve Sumi wrestlers climbed on board.

Fuzzy shadows purpled all the treetops on the ridge.

Use words that evoke images.

Waves of warm, yellow popcorn air caressed my nose.

Every time my sister chews gum, I hear cows walking through mud.

The traffic light winked its yellow eye at me.

How lucky the lilac bush is to spread its toes in the warm, velvet mud.

Use figurative language.

Snow peaks on the fencepost like sugary meringue-drop swirls.

That pesky wave chased me all the way down the beach, grasping at my heels.

My mailbox mocks me with its empty, careless yawn.

Living with Maxie is as dangerous as living near an active volcano.

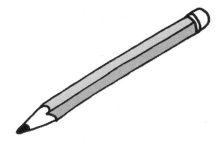

Get Sharp Tip #11
A few well-chosen words are better than a whole string of adjectives and adverbs.

Last night's moon
A single silver sliver
A lone light in a slate sky

Avoid these over-used words.

amazing	delicious	funny	kill	quiet
angry	destroy	get	little	right
ask	difference	go	look	run
awful	do	good	love	say
bad	dull	great	make	scared
beautiful	end	gross	move	show
begin	enjoy	happy	neat	slow
big	explain	hate	new	stop
brave	fair	have	nice	story
break	fall	help	old	take
come	false	hide	part	tell
cool	fast	hurry	place	think
cry	fat	important	plan	true
cut	fear	interesting	pretty	ugly
dangerous	fly		put	unhappy
dark				wrong

Clear, Interesting Sentences

Smooth, clear, interesting sentences are the heart of your writing. You can choose all sorts of wonderful, fresh words and phrases, but if you aren't able to combine them into clear sentences, your writing won't be very effective. Here are some hints to help you strengthen your writing style with sentences that are meaningful, clear, natural-sounding, and interesting to read.

News Flash!
A torrential downpour has swelled the reservoir at Lost Creek Dam! Tons of water billowed over the perimeter, and drowned the unsuspecting valley below. This is the most devastating flash flood in fifty years!

Use each sentence to express a complete idea.

Make sure each sentence has a reason for being included. Each sentence should state a main idea or add something to support the main idea. Watch out for sentence fragments, run-on sentences, or sentences that just ramble.

Make sentences interesting.

Interesting sentences add more meaning to the writing. They also hold the reader's attention.

You can make sentences interesting . . .

. . . by including colorful adverbs and adjectives.

Less interesting: *An avalanche chased the skiers.*

More interesting: *A sudden avalanche, roaring fiercely, chased terrified skiers.*

. . . by including phrases.

Less interesting: *Matilda Mars decided to sue the town of Prospect.*

More interesting: *With great reluctance, Matilda Mars decided to sue the town of Prospect for failing to protect her from deadly scorpions.*

Less interesting: *We met Tabatha Twister while she was working.*

More interesting: *We met Tabitha Twister, the famous contortionist, while she was working on a new position called "The Pretzel."*

. . . by varying the sentence structure.

Less interesting: *Pierre loved cream puffs, and he was angry because the bakery used artificial cream.*

More interesting: *Pierre, a great lover of cream puffs, was angry to find that the bakery used artificial cream in their desserts.*

Write sentences that flow smoothly.

Sentences that are short and choppy don't read smoothly. Neither do sentences that are too long and tangled. Try to write sentences that sound natural. Use sentences of different lengths. Read your writing out loud, and listen to see if it sounds smooth. Combine choppy sentences into longer, smoother ones. Break over-complicated sentences into simpler ones.

Not smooth: *After the lights went out, we saw that long shadows were lurking everywhere and nothing was moving, and it was silent except for scraping sounds.*

Smooth: *The lights went out, long shadows lurked everywhere, and nothing moved. Scraping sounds broke the silence.*

Not smooth: *The back door was locked. The front door was also locked, and the windows were undamaged and locked. Someone got in and took the whole cookie jar and left footprints and since nothing was broken, they must have had a key.*

Smooth: *Though all the doors and windows were locked and there was no sign of a break-in, the cookie jar was missing. The culprit, who must have had a key, left footprints.*

Write sentences that make the meaning clear.

Pay close attention to the meaning of each sentence. Can the reader get the meaning easily? The arrangement of words in a sentence can confuse the reader or make the meaning muddy. Watch out for misplaced phrases, subjects and verbs that don't agree, and pronouns without clear antecedents.

Unclear: *Brad enjoyed his turkey sandwich listening to the radio.*
Clear: *While listening to the radio, Brad enjoyed his turkey sandwich.*

Unclear: *We were frightened by a shark sailing our boat.*
Clear: *A shark frightened us when we were out sailing our boat.*

Unclear: *It was a relief when Andy and she met them and they climbed on their sailboat.*
Clear: *Andy and she were greatly relieved to climb on the sailboat of their friends.*

Write sentences that are concise.

A concise sentence gets to the point without a lot of extra detours or details. Examine your sentences to see that they are not cluttered with unnecessary words and details.

Meaningful Paragraphs

A paragraph is a group of sentences that are related because they cover a specific subject or idea. Paragraphs are used for the many different modes of writing (see pages 130–131). This means a paragraph can explain, define, inform, persuade, or tell part of a story.

But all paragraphs have some things in common. All paragraphs need a beginning, middle, and end. Every paragraph has a main idea. The purpose of the paragraph is to communicate that main idea clearly. A well-written paragraph is carefully planned to state and support the main idea.

The Beginning ⟶

- The beginning of the paragraph lets the reader know the topic of the paragraph.
- Each paragraph needs a topic sentence; usually this is at the beginning.
- The topic sentence names the subject or main idea of the paragraph.
- The topic sentence also gives some unique detail or impression about the subject.

The Middle ⟶

- Most of the sentences in the paragraph make up the middle part.
- These sentences add the details needed to support the main idea.
- These sentences clarify the topic.
- Every sentence must add something to explain or broaden the main idea.
- These sentences should be put in a meaningful sequence.

The End ⟶

- The final sentence wraps up the paragraph.
- This sentence follows the sentences with the details or examples.
- The final sentence restates the paragraph's main idea.

Some paragraphs may seem simple and easy, because they're short. Beware! Paragraphs are more complicated than they look.

Remember, a good paragraph . . .
- . . . states the main idea clearly.
- . . . includes enough details to support the idea.
- . . . uses a variety of sentences.
- . . . includes sentences which begin in different ways.
- . . . has sentences in a clear, sensible order.
- . . . uses well-chosen transitions to connect sentences.
- . . . reads smoothly, connecting words or phrases .
- . . . concludes with a reminder of the main idea.

Topic Sentence →

Supporting Sentences

Concluding Sentence

If Sara had known what she knows now, she would never have tried to pet that parrot. The sign on the cage said, "Please do not touch the bird." But, to Sara, this bird looked so friendly, soft, and harmless. The parrot chattered and whistled at Sara, inviting her to come near. Sara was sure the bird said her name. Polly tilted her head and looked coyly at Sara. Over and over the inviting whistle was repeated. Those colorful feathers just called out to be touched. Without any fear, Sara reached through the bars of the cage to stroke the bird. This is when Polly changed from a coy charmer into a fierce attacker. Sara could not pull her hand away fast enough. The parrot got a firm hold on her little finger with his sharp beak. In her foolishness, Sara had ignored warnings and nearly lost her finger as a result.

Transitions Between Sentences
Some Useful Words & Phrases

about	as soon as	finally	inside	soon
above	as well as	first	lastly	that is to say
across	before	for example	later	therefore
additionally	behind	for instance	likewise	throughout
after	beneath	furthermore	meanwhile	to begin with
after a while	below	in addition	moreover	to conclude
afterward	beside	in comparison	next	to continue
against	between	in conclusion	next week	to elaborate
along with	beyond	in contrast	on the other hand	to emphasize
also	beyond that	in fact	on top of	to restate
although	down	in front of	otherwise	to repeat
among	during	in other words	outside	to summarize
around	even though	in summary	second	today
as a result	even so	in the same way	similarly	yesterday

Successful Compositions

Compositions (such as essays) have a main idea, a beginning, middle, and an end—just like paragraphs. However, a composition is different. A composition covers a longer topic. It is more complex and needs several paragraphs. Writing a good composition takes some skills beyond writing good paragraphs. It requires careful planning and skillful combining of paragraphs.

Some Tips for Good Compositions

The opening paragraph serves as the introduction to the written piece.

A well-written opening paragraph . . .

- grabs the reader's attention
- states the main idea or topic of the whole composition (the thesis statement)
- sets the stage for the rest of the piece

The body includes several paragraphs that develop and support the main topic.

In a well-written body . . .

- each paragraph states a sub-idea and provides details to illustrate or support it
- a new paragraph begins when there is a change to a new subtopic
- paragraphs flow naturally from one to another
- paragraphs are arranged in a logical order
- paragraphs and sub-ideas are organized in order to develop the main idea clearly
- the point of the piece gains strength as paragraphs progress
- information in the paragraphs is accurate
- the language of the paragraphs is colorful and pleasing to the reader

The closing paragraph ties the composition together.

A well-written concluding paragraph . . .

- restates or reviews the thesis
- summarizes the meaning of the composition
- leaves the main point firmly in the mind of the reader
- keeps the reader's attention right to the end

Get Sharp Tip #12
Don't fizzle on the conclusions. Resist the temptation to give in to weariness and settle for a hurried, bland closing. Remember, it is the LAST thing the reader hears from you about your topic. Make it memorable!

Better Grades & Higher Test Scores / READING & LANGUAGE gr. 4–6
Copyright ©2005 by Incentive Publications, Inc., Nashville, TN.

How to Write an Essay

Attention-Grabbing Beginnings

A good beginning catches the reader's attention right away. It gives a hint at what is going to happen or what is going to be argued. Yet, it doesn't give away the whole story, explanation, or argument. A good beginning makes the reader curious enough to continue.

There are unlimited ways to begin. Of course, the way you start will depend on many things, such as the form, purpose, and audience. Your effective beginning might include . . .

- a surprising statement
- a tantalizing or unexpected claim
- an unusual fact

- a fascinating quote
- a question or series of questions
- a brief quip about a famous character
- a strong opinion

ordinary beginning:

Dear Sam,
   I thought you might be interested to know about an experience I had this week.

attention-grabbing beginning:

Dear Sam,
   My right hand still has five fingers. Due to my own stupidity, I could have been writing this letter with only four. Here's what happened.

ordinary beginning:

At last night's school board meeting, high school students staged a protest.

attention-grabbing beginnings:

No one can remember a school board meeting like this one.

There were fireworks over food at last night's school board meeting.

Who dared to deliver rotten meatloaf and slimy pudding to the school board meeting?

"Down with lousy lunches!" was the cry heard at last night's school board meeting.

ordinary beginning:

There is a new policy at our school about how students can dress. Most students don't like it.

attention-grabbing beginnings:

There are groans, complaints, and unrepeatable words being said today as Jackson students learn about the school's new dress code.

T-shirts are nixed. Jeans are out. Shirttails are (tucked) in. Jackson administrators have spoken on the dress code, and students are not happy about it.

Memorable Endings

A strong ending is as important as a good beginning. Like the opening, your conclusion will depend on the topic, form, and purpose of the writing. Yet for each piece of writing, there are many possible ways to wrap it up. That's what your ending must do. It must drive the point home, solidify your argument, or tie up the tale with gusto. However you end, try to write the sentence, paragraph, or line that will leave the reader satisfied with the writing. Your effective ending might include . . .

- a fresh way to restate the thesis
- a short summary of the main points
- a mystery that leaves the reader wondering
- a surprise turn of events
- an unexpected solution
- a lesson or moral
- one more great argument

- a question to the reader
- a final wrap-up quote

ordinary ending:

You see that there is quite a difference between black holes and wormholes.

memorable ending:

So if you do get pulled into a black hole, don't give up hope. Take heart, the black hole just might be linked to a wormhole, and you could escape after all.

ordinary ending:

Learn about what you can do to protect these three species of crocodiles from extinction.

memorable ending:

If you're a crocodile hunter, find another sport. If not, do your part by passing up those crocodile shoes.

ordinary ending:

That's the end of the tale about a lively field trip.

memorable ending:

Yes, this was a lively field trip. But wait until you hear about what happened on the next one!

ordinary ending:

At last, Wilbur Worthington was found. After a mysterious disappearance and three-year absence, he returned to his family. His daughter snuggled in next to her dad in front of the fire, both of them writing in their diaries their own tales of this amazing day.

memorable ending:

At last, Wilbur Worthington was found. After a mysterious disappearance and a three-year absence, he had returned to his family. Though everything seemed normal, his young daughter still wondered. As she watched him write in his journal at the end of that amazing day, she wrote this in her own journal: "I was so sure my dad was left-handed like me."

Get Sharp: Writing Guide

Strong Voice

Voice is the way a writer uses language to show his or her unique personality and feeling about the topic. Your voice is expressed in your writing through many of the techniques and devices you use: word choice, choice of form and format, structure of sentences, tone, topics you choose, sequence and organization of the writing, and use of dialogue.

Voice can be...
. . . casual or formal.
. . . folksy or snooty.
. . . fresh or traditional.
. . . intimate or distant.
. . . earthy or pristine.
. . . sober or cheery.

To find your voice . . .

- be yourself
- choose topics that interest you
- know your audience
- care about saying something to your audience
- show your passion for the idea or message
- be original—use your own ideas
- show your commitment to expressing the ideas
- keep your writing honest (Write what you really feel.)
- write in the style and voice you use in your own diary
- write as if you were talking honestly to your best friend
- let readers know something about your values and opinions

This writer described some guests at a costume party. Her voice shows that she has a good sense of humor. She seems to be having fun with the writing. Her writing is down-to-earth with a touch of pretend haughtiness fitting for the subject. She speaks directly to the reader.

- *Fiona is dressed as a jolly black cat. She makes sure the other guests notice as she swings her tail and lavishly licks her paws. Her outrageous dance with the giant mouse catches everyone's attention.*

- *Lucy, who dresses as a character named Lady Laticia, brashly shows off her beauty and grace. She just knows everyone is fascinated by her. But if you are not a handsome, wealthy prince, she won't waste her time on you.*

- *Little Prince Mischief (Peter in disguise) is so small that the guests hardly notice him. He lurks under tables and behind curtains, eavesdropping and spying. Occasionally, he slips a gooey cream puff inside a lady's shawl or tucks an appetizer into a tall hairdo.*

- *As Judge d'Éclair, Arthur behaves like a terribly important man. He hovers close to the plentiful food at the lavish table. Oh, how he loves to eat! If you stop to chat with him, do bring along a pastry or two.*

- *Charlie does an amazing impersonation of Count Pompous. He struts about the great hall with a frilly hat and silver-bowed high-heeled boots. He will probably keep his nose in the air the entire evening.*

Editing & Revising

Here's an easy-to-use plan to guide you through the response and revision stages of the writing process. The first P and the Q are response tactics: Praise and Question. The last P is the revision tactic: Polish. Writers of all ages can make improvements in their writing by remembering these three steps:

The P-Q-P Plan for Editing & Revision

P = Praise

Writers point out successes by telling each other . . .

. . . what's strong

. . . what's good

. . . what's effective

. . . what works

. . . what caught their ear or eye

. . . what's pleasing

. . . what sparked a thought

. . . what taught them something

. . . what surprised or delighted them

> **Crash!** was a great choice for your opening sentence! It grabbed my attention right away.

Ask someone else to read what you have written and give you clear, specific "praises" for the parts you've written well.

Some examples of helpful praise:

- *It was a good idea to string all those short words together in this part. It made the girl seem very much in a hurry.*

- *I liked the way you repeated the **t** sound over and over in this poem. That gave a marching rhythm to the poem.*

- *I like the wet words for your rain poem. My favorites were:* **slosh...slurpy...slush...drizzle...slop...** *and* **splatter**.

- *The ending was a great surprise. It really caught me off guard.*

- *The part about the alligator swallowing the umbrella was my favorite! It was so unexpected.*

- *I like the part about the **squirmy, squishy, soft,** and **mushy** worm. The internal rhyme is pleasing.*

- *Tom, your title, "The Food No Kid Should Eat," made me want to listen to your paragraph.*

- *It was such a good idea to end the argument with a question. That really made me question the safety of tattoos, too.*

- *These two sentences right here really show your sense of humor.*

Q = Question

Writers ask questions that will help the author review and think about the writing to . . .

> . . . realize where things may not be clear
>
> . . . hear where something is missing
>
> . . . notice where something could be stronger, funnier, more suspenseful, more informative (and so on)
>
> . . . consider what could be changed, added, or removed

> Could you replace the word "nice" with a more descriptive word, such as "luxurious"?

This is not harsh criticism. No outside opinion is forced on the writer. That's the reason for using the question form. A question is stated and left for the author to answer. Find someone you trust to read your writing and ask you specific questions—questions that will inspire you to clarify and improve your writing.

Some examples of helpful questions:

- *Could you add a few sentences in your autobiography to tell about your preschool years?*
- *I'm confused about the difference between a black hole and a wormhole. Are they the same?*
- *It can't be too easy to lose a tuba. How did your tuba get lost anyway?*
- *I felt as if you gave away the ending too soon. Could you add something to prolong the suspense?*
- *Could you replace the word **went** with a different word in two of the three places you used it?*
- *What is your opinion about this topic? I'd like to get more of a feel for your voice.*
- *How did the girls get inside the volcano in the first place? That's unclear.*
- *Are all the crocodile species you mentioned endangered? I can't tell from your essay.*
- *Didn't the gorilla have to escape from the zoo before he sat on the mayor? If so, shouldn't this sentence come before this one?*

P = Polish

> Polishing my report is even more satisfying than polishing my fingernails.

After gaining some responses from others, the author decides what input to use:

> . . . what suggestions to discard or include
>
> . . . what changes to make
>
> . . . which feedback is important

Then, the author adds this information to his or her own ideas to put to use in a new draft. It is unlikely that all of the responses can be used. That, finally, is up to the author to decide. When you are ready to write a final draft, make the changes you believe are necessary. Check the spelling and mechanics (or ask someone to assist you with this), and complete your polished copy.

Editor's Guide

Get Sharp Tip #13

Don't think of editing as a chore. Instead, think of it as a gift—a second chance for you, the writer. It's a chance for you to make your writing say what you **really want** it to say. Also, it's a chance to spark your originality, giving your writing a unique flavor that will make people glad they read it!

_____ Substitute stronger words (*more colorful, more specific*).

_____ Replace inactive verbs with more active, lively ones.

_____ Eliminate repetitive or unnecessary words.

_____ Add more interesting words (*fresh, rich, original, energizing*).

_____ Add words or phrases that create or add to a certain mood.

_____ Rearrange words within a sentence to clarify the meaning.

_____ Rearrange words or sentences for smoother flow.

_____ Rearrange words or sentences for more interesting sound.

_____ Expand sentences to include more detail.

_____ Make sure main ideas are well-developed and to the point.

_____ Make sure each sub-idea is developed in its own paragraph.

_____ If needed, include more powerful, effective details.

_____ Expand or rearrange paragraphs to improve clarity and focus.

_____ Make sure each paragraph has clear organization.

_____ Rearrange sentences in the paragraphs for clearer meaning.

_____ Rearrange sentences or paragraphs for better sequence.

_____ Vary sentence length, structure, and rhythm within paragraphs.

_____ Vary transitions between sentences or paragraphs; make them smooth.

_____ Eliminate repetitive or unnecessary ideas.

_____ Break up excessively long sentences.

_____ Add dialogue where it would be effective.

_____ Examine beginning; revise to make it more inviting.

_____ Examine ending; make sure it is memorable and gives clear closure.

_____ Decide if the written piece accomplishes the purpose.

_____ Adapt content and form to fit the audience.

_____ Include literary techniques that make the writing more interesting or appealing (*e.g: personification, onomatopoeia, hyperbole, understatement, exaggeration, foreshadowing, or irony*).

_____ Include figures of speech (*metaphors, similes, idioms, puns*).

_____ Replace ordinary titles with strong, "catchy" titles.

_____ Remove bias from piece (*unless called for*).

_____ Revise to strengthen voice (*liveliness, originality, personality, conviction, voice, good communication with audience*); make sure a personal flavor is evident.

_____ Examine pieces for correct conventions (*punctuation, spelling, capitalization, paragraphing, grammar and usage*).

Steps for Writing a Report

Cool!

1. Choose a topic.

- Think of what you want to learn about that topic.
- Write a list of subtopics or categories you need to explore.
- Write a list of questions you'd like to answer on the topic.

Do . . . ➡ **Don't . . .**

✓ **Choose a topic that is manageable.**

✓ **Choose a topic that has enough information available to develop it.**

✓ **Choose a topic that is too big.** *(War)* or *(Animal Diseases)*

✓ **Choose a topic that is too small.** *(Stomach Ailments of Pintos)*

✓ **Choose a topic that is too vague.** *(People Who Travel)*

✓ **Choose a topic that is too obscure.** *(Mosquito Psychology)*

2. Find resources.

- Look for sources that will provide the information you need.
- Head for the library. Look for books, magazine articles, newspapers, and encyclopedias.
- Search for information on CDs, videos, and the Internet.
- Don't forget to consult people, too. Some good information can be gained from interviews.

Skateboarding Equipment

skateboard deck (7.5" recommended)
trucks (bullets recommended)
bearings
skate shoes
knee pads, wrist guards, elbow pads

Source: Skateboard City website,
(www.skateboard-city.com/beginners guide)

3. Take notes.

- Write down bits of information. Write phrases, sentences, facts, or quotes.
- Write each piece of information on a separate card.
- At the top of the card, write a key word or phrase title to show the subtopic or subcategory.
- Write the source on each card (the complete name of the author, article, book or magazine, dates, and page numbers).
- Keep researching until you find enough details, examples, or information for each of the categories you chose.

Skateboard Tricks—Roast Beef

The trick is like the Ollie except that you have your front hand in between your knees when you pop. While in the air, move your hand behind your knees and the board and grab. Then, let go and come back down to earth.

(Source: Arnold, T.J. Skateboarding for Everyone.

Dangers of Skateboarding

— sprains, fractures, abrasions
— broken arms, wrists, ankles
— head injuries, face injuries
— 60,100 children under age 15 in 2002
— most injuries occur under age 14
— death due to collision with vehicles

(Source: "American Assn of Pediatrics
Skateboard Safety Policy" (2002)
www.Riley Children's Hospital.com

164

4. Sort & organize the note cards.

- Group together the cards with the same key word titles.
- Make a pile for each category.
- Organize the cards in a sensible sequence within each category.
- Place the category piles into a sensible order.

5. Make an outline.

- Write each category as a main idea in outline.
- Under each category, write the supporting details or examples (or subcategories).
- If necessary, list sub-subcategories under the subcategories.
- Do your outline carefully. A complete organized outline will make the writing easier.

6. Write an introductory paragraph.

- Start the report with something catchy that will get the reader interested in your topic.
  Include a thesis statement.
- Make sure your introductory paragraph lets the reader know the general idea of the report.

7. Write the body of the report.

- Write carefully from your outline, referring to your notes as needed.
- Build a paragraph on each subtopic topic.
- Include a topic sentence for each paragraph.
- Add details to support each main idea.
- Make smooth transitions between the sentences and paragraphs.

8. Write a concluding paragraph.

- Use this to repeat the main point of the paper, summarize the main points, or conclude with a generalization.
- Finish with a sentence that has punch—one that readers will remember.

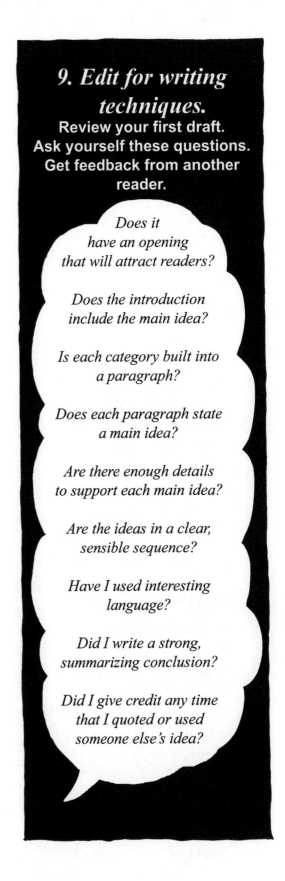

9. Edit for writing techniques.

Review your first draft.
Ask yourself these questions.
Get feedback from another reader.

Does it have an opening that will attract readers?

Does the introduction include the main idea?

Is each category built into a paragraph?

Does each paragraph state a main idea?

Are there enough details to support each main idea?

Are the ideas in a clear, sensible sequence?

Have I used interesting language?

Did I write a strong, summarizing conclusion?

Did I give credit any time that I quoted or used someone else's idea?

Better Grades & Higher Test Scores / READING & LANGUAGE gr. 4–6

Get Sharp: Writing Guide

10. Proofread for conventions.

- Check for sense, fluency, and completeness of the sentences.
- Check for correct grammatical construction.
- Check for correct spelling, capitalization, and punctuation.

11. Revise to write the final draft.

- Make use of the information you gained from steps 9 and 10.
- Make the changes and corrections you feel are necessary.
- Decide on a format (handwritten, typed, etc.) and write the final copy.

12. Add extra materials to text.

- Decide what you might add to make your report more instructive or interesting.
- Add drawings, diagrams, lists, charts, maps, graphs, timelines, and surveys.

13. Choose and write a good title.

- Make sure your report has an accurate and inviting title.

14. Add a list of sources used (bibliography).

- Make a list of the sources you used for information in your report.
- Write these in alphabetical order *(by last name of author, or by title if there is no author).*
- Attach this to your report.

15. Share.

- Find a way to show off, share, publish, or display your finished report.

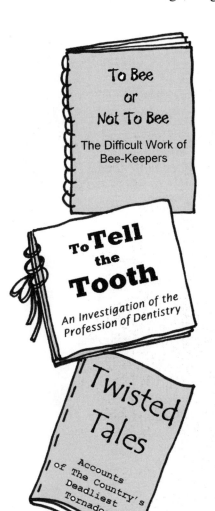

Follow this form for bibliography entries:

Book: Author last name, first name. <u>Title.</u> Place: Publisher, Date.

Encyclopedia Article: "Title." <u>Encyclopedia.</u> Volume, pages. Date.

Magazine Article: Author last name, first name. "Article Title." <u>Magazine</u> (Date of Publication): page numbers.

Newspaper Article: Author last name, first name. "Title," <u>Newspaper,</u> day, month, year.

CD: "Title." CD-ROM. <u>Title of CD.</u> Publisher, Date.

Video: <u>Title.</u> Videotape. Production Company, Date.

Internet Article: — Author last name, first name. "Title." (Date) Name of website. URL.

Writing a News Article

A **news article** is a short nonfiction form that presents a factual account of a current event.

How to Write a Good News Story

1. Get the facts. Answer the questions *who, what, when, where,* and *how*. Gather information by interviewing people who were involved in the event or situation. Try to interview other people who are knowledgeable about the subject. Always write down the precise words that are said to you.

2. Write an opening sentence. This is called a *lead*. This gives the story's main idea and grabs the interest of the reader.

3. Write the body of the story. Include all the details needed to tell the known facts about the story.

4. Create a headline. A headline needs to be short and attention-getting. It is not always a complete sentence. Make sure your headline gives some clue about the story.

WOODLAND TIMES

Woodcutter Praised for Daring Rescue

(Red Bluffs California, UPI)

Quick thinking and bold action by a woodcutter saved the life of a local girl yesterday. Woody Axle was awarded a medal of honor today for rescuing Ms. Red R. Hood from the jaws of a hungry wolf. Mr. Axle reported that he was chopping east of town when he heard cries at about 3 p.m. He entered the 286 Apple Lane house, found the girl trapped by a wolf, and overpowered the wolf with his axe.

According to Mrs. Agatha R. Hood, grandmother of the girl and owner of the home, she was alone when the wolf forcibly entered the house around midday Monday. The wolf allegedly snatched her bonnet and gown, tied her up, and locked her in the closet. It appears the wolf then donned her clothing, climbed into her bed, and awaited the granddaughter's arrival.

Young Ms. Hood was treated for a broken arm, abrasions, and bruises. The grandmother was unharmed.

The SPCA has issued a complaint about the cruel treatment of the wolf, a member of an endangered

(continued, page 5, column 2)

A word of warning: Beware of wolves in grandmas' clothing.

Writing a Short Story

- A **short story** is a form of fiction that can be read in a relatively short amount of time.
- The action and setting of a short story is far more limited than in longer pieces, such as novels.
- The tale told in the story can be real, or it can be imaginary (fantasy).
- Some short stories are science fiction.
- A short story has a conflict, a problem, or complication that is the center of the story. The statement of this conflict, its development, and resolution are part of the story plot.

I'm writing a short story about myself from the third person point of view.

Ask

Professor Know-it-all

She knows a lot!

How does a writer create a character?

Answers:

. . . by describing the character's appearance or personality

. . . by describing the character's behavior, actions, thoughts, and feelings

. . . by writing what the character says

. . . by showing what other characters say, think, or feel about him or her

Short Story Elements

point of view

The **point of view** of the story is the angle or perspective from which the story is told. The point of view changes depending upon who is telling the story.

first person point of view—The narrator telling the story is one of the characters in the story (uses the pronouns *I* and *we*).

third person point of view—The narrator is an observer, standing outside the action of the story (uses the pronouns *they, she, he,* and *it*).

characters

A short story develops through the actions of one or more characters. A short story has just a few characters. Characters are brought to life in the story through **characterization** (the creating of a character).

setting

The **setting** is the time and place (or times and places) where the story's action happens.

theme

The **theme** is the central idea or message of the story (*e.g., jealousy can poison a person's life; sometimes losing is better than winning; courage is not a lack of fear*).

mood

Mood is the atmosphere or feeling the writer creates in the story. The writer uses language skillfully to cause a particular emotional response in the reader (*e.g., annoyance, fear, impatience, anticipation, suspense, empathy*).

plot

The **plot** is a series of events or situations related to the action of the story, usually involving some sort of a problem or conflict.

Plot Structure:

exposition—the introduction to the characters and setting

rising action—introduces and develops the conflict of the story to a point of high intensity

climax—the highest point (most intense point) of action in the story

falling action—the events that follow the climax, usually started by some turning point

resolution—the ending of the conflict or solving of the problem

dénouement—any details or parts of the story that follow after the resolution

Tips for Writing a Good Short Story

Get Sharp Tip #14
After you write a story, set it aside for a few days. Then come back and take a fresh look at it.

- Make reading a constant part of your life. Read good stories written by a variety of authors. This will give you ideas for your own writing. More importantly, it will give you models for good story writing.

- Review the elements of short stories. Include them all in your story.

- Find an idea for your story. Look nearby—in your own life. Think about people you know who are interesting characters; review your journal for things that have interested you; watch for ordinary or extraordinary events that you could describe; notice things you feel strongly; notice things that have changed.

- When you have a general idea for a story, think about the theme—the message or idea you want readers to get from your story. Settle on this before you begin writing.

Stay with just a few characters. A story can get complicated with too many characters. Choose a few to develop well. Include some dialogue in your story to show who your characters are.

Start a new paragraph each time you begin a quotation from a different speaker.

I think this will be my best ghost story ever.

Better Grades & Higher Test Scores / READING & LANGUAGE gr. 4–6
Copyright ©2005 by Incentive Publications, Inc., Nashville, TN.

Get Sharp: Writing Guide

Writing a Letter

Basic Parts of a Letter

The heading includes your address and the date. In a business or formal letter, the heading has a second part, called the inside address. This is the name and address of the person to whom you are writing. Skip at least one line after the heading. (In a business letter, skip four or more lines.)

The greeting or salutation speaks to the person you are writing. It begins with the word, "Dear" (capitalized), and is followed by the name of the person receiving the letter. In a personal letter, a comma follows the name. In a business letter, a colon follows the person's name. Skip one line after the greeting.

The body is the main part of the letter. Often, the first line of the body is indented. If this is indented, all paragraphs must also be indented. Keep the paragraphs in a letter fairly short. Skip one line after the body and between paragraphs.

The closing has a capital beginning its first word. A comma always follows the closing. In a friendly letter, the closing can be personal *(Love, Your friend, Sincerely, With love, Affectionately, Your buddy)*. In a business letter, the closing should be formal *(Yours truly or Sincerely)*.

The signature — Always sign your letter. In a business letter, your name is also typed or printed below your signature.

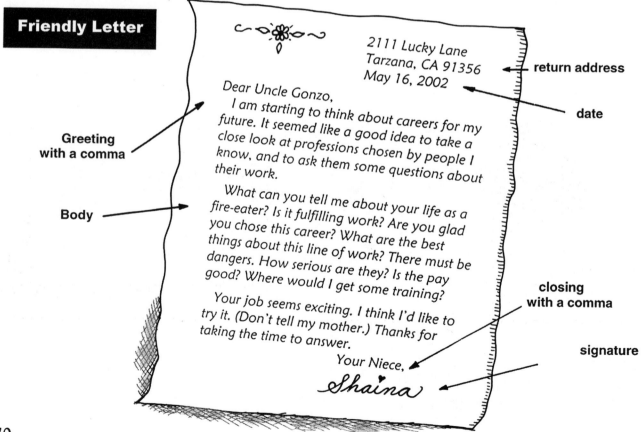

Friendly Letter

2111 Lucky Lane
Tarzana, CA 91356
May 16, 2002

← **return address**

date

Dear Uncle Gonzo,
I am starting to think about careers for my future. It seemed like a good idea to take a close look at professions chosen by people I know, and to ask them some questions about their work.

**Greeting
with a comma**

Body

What can you tell me about your life as a fire-eater? Is it fulfilling work? Are you glad you chose this career? What are the best things about this line of work? There must be dangers. How serious are they? Is the pay good? Where would I get some training?

Your job seems exciting. I think I'd like to try it. (Don't tell my mother.) Thanks for taking the time to answer.

Your Niece,
Shaina

**closing
with a comma**

signature

Business Letter

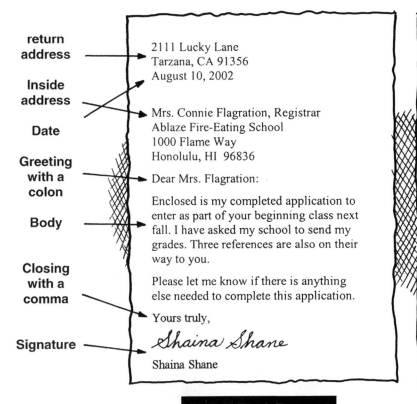

return address → 2111 Lucky Lane
Tarzana, CA 91356
Inside address → August 10, 2002

Date

Mrs. Connie Flagration, Registrar
Ablaze Fire-Eating School
1000 Flame Way
Honolulu, HI 96836

Greeting with a colon → Dear Mrs. Flagration:

Body → Enclosed is my completed application to enter as part of your beginning class next fall. I have asked my school to send my grades. Three references are also on their way to you.

Please let me know if there is anything else needed to complete this application.

Closing with a comma → Yours truly,

Shaina Shane

Signature → Shaina Shane

Full Block Form

2111 Lucky Lane
Tarzana, CA 91356
August 10, 2002

Mrs. Connie Flagration, Registrar
Ablaze Fire-Eating School
1000 Flame Way
Honolulu, HI 96836

Dear Mrs. Flagration:

Enclosed is my completed application to enter as part of your beginning class next fall. I have asked my school to send my grades. Three references are also on their way to you.

Please let me know if there is anything else needed to complete this application.

Yours truly,

Shaina Shane

Shaina Shane

Semi-Block Form

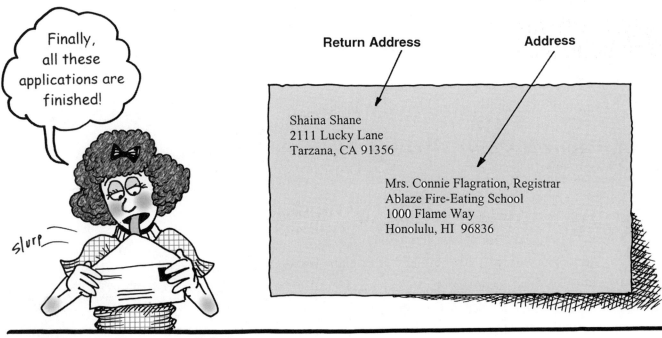

Return Address

Address

Shaina Shane
2111 Lucky Lane
Tarzana, CA 91356

Mrs. Connie Flagration, Registrar
Ablaze Fire-Eating School
1000 Flame Way
Honolulu, HI 96836

Finally, all these applications are finished!

slurp

Expository Writing

The purpose: to explain or inform

Examples: essay, book report, research paper, news article, instructions

Tips for Your Expository Writing

- Choose a creative, fresh approach to explaining the topic.
- Investigate your topic before you write. Use a variety of resources.
- Use reliable, well-supported evidence for your explanation.
- Include fresh, unusual examples.
- Present your facts, examples, or opinions in an organized manner.
- Go beyond just stating the facts.
- Interpret or evaluate the facts, showing that you understand them well.
- Choose a particular approach for your organization, such as . . .
    - *. . . how-to-do steps for the reader to follow*
    - *. . . compare and contrast similarities and differences*
    - *. . . identify and explain the causes and effects*
    - *. . . give a detailed and broad explanation of an idea*
    - *. . . analyze an idea—break it down into its parts and show how the parts work together as a whole*

Narrative Writing

The purpose: to recount an event or series of events

Examples: short story, poem, biography, anecdote

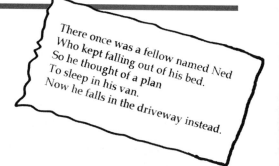

Tips for Your Narrative Writing

- Use time as your way of organization. Unless you specifically choose to jump back and forth in time, narration is usually told in chronological order.
- Choose a fresh, creative approach to telling your story.
- Keep the focus on a particular event; don't wander off too far on minor events.
- Pay attention to characterization. Make your characters come alive for the reader.
- Be aware of your audience as you write. Make sure the approach and language are appropriate and appealing for the audience.
- Use vivid anecdotes and details to keep the story alive for the reader.
- Include some interpretation or analysis of the events, so the reader understands their importance to the story.
- Make sure the story has a clear beginning, middle, and end.

172

Get Sharp: Writing Guide

Persuasive Writing

The purpose: to convince readers to respond in some way (to agree with something, change attitude or behavior about something, desire something)

Examples: advertisement, editorial, petition, argument

Tips for Your Persuasive Writing

- Choose a topic that is of interest currently to many people, at least to many people in the group that will be your readers or listeners.
- Choose a topic about which you have strong opinions and feelings.
- Choose a creative, fresh approach to arguing for your viewpoint.
- Know and state clearly what your viewpoint is.
- Gather reliable, sensible arguments to back up your position.
- Do research, if necessary, to have credible sources behind your arguments.
- State the alternative view or views. Show that you know the other side.
- Carefully "combat" each opposing argument, showing the flaws or weaknesses in each.
- Use words and phrases that are authoritative and convincing.
- Give good examples and illustrations to show why your viewpoint works.
- Make the examples specific and interesting. Use real-life stories.
- Present at least one strong example or story to back up each point in your argument.
- Present your arguments in an organized manner.
- Carefully build your argument so that it gains strength as the writing moves along.
- Use your two strongest arguments first and last.
- Write a strong conclusion that wraps up all the arguments.

Descriptive Writing

The purpose: to "paint a picture" of a person, place, thing, or idea

Examples: travel brochure, character study, catalog entry

Tips for Your Descriptive Writing

The new neighbor's garbage can collection had an odor that could choke an elephant. Steamy streams of grease snaked up from more than fifty cans. Most of them overflowed with growing tentacles of mold.

GAG!

- Write about a person, place, thing, event, or idea that you know well.

- Spend time observing the subject of your description.

- Take notes, collecting details and observations.

- Pay attention to the physical characteristics of the person, place, event, or thing.

- Use all your senses to observe the subject.

- Talk to others about the subject. Gather their feelings and reflections.

- Notice the way other people respond to the person, place, event, or thing.

- If you're describing a person, interview him or her. Write down some specific quotes the person says.

- Recall particular incidents involving the person, place, event, or thing.

- After you have collected observations and details, decide what the main impression is that this subject has made on you. Use this as your main idea or thesis.

- In your introduction, use an anecdote, quote, or vivid description that will immediately cause the reader to "picture" the person, place, event, or thing.

- Write sentences that add to an ever-broadening picture you're trying to show of the subject. Only include things that relate to the point you are making.

- Work to paint a colorful picture of the subject. Use specific, vivid adverbs and adjectives, and specific, active verbs in your description.

- Include figurative language, especially metaphors that compare the subject imaginatively to something the reader will understand.

- End your description with a final feeling or bit of information that emphasizes the importance of this person, place, or thing to you or to others.

Imaginative Writing

The purpose: to entertain with make-believe events

Examples: fairy tale, science fiction story, myth, ghost story

Tips for Your Imaginative Writing

- Choose a unique, fresh approach and form.

- Use language that surprises the reader and draws in her or him .

- Include figurative language to enrich the tale (alliteration, metaphor, personification, etc.).

- Develop interesting characters. Since the writing is imaginary, you can make them unusual, even outlandish!

- Include some dialogue, imagery, foreshadowing, and other literary elements.

- Choose words and phrases that spark the imagination. Avoid ordinary ways of describing events or characters.

- Make sure the beginning lets the reader know this will be no ordinary tale.

Personal Writing

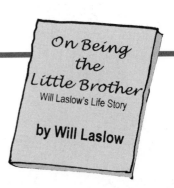

The purpose: to express the writer's personal opinions, insights, questions, reflections, or perspectives

Examples: diary, journal, autobiography, reflection on a poem

Tips for Your Personal Writing

- Focus on putting yourself honestly into the writing.

- Let your personal perspective shine through. Avoid being swayed by what someone else might think, or what you feel you're "supposed" to say.

- Reflect on the topic seriously. Connect it to your personal experiences and observations.

- Include concrete examples and anecdotes to support your thoughts and ideas.

- Write as if you are writing for yourself or a close friend. Use a natural style.

- Allow your passion and commitment for the topic to show.

- Make sure the opening and closing let the reader know this is a personal opinion or reflection.

Get Sharp: Writing Guide

Public Speaking

There are many times when you will need to speak in front of an audience—even if that is a very small audience. You might give a speech for any one of many purposes: to tell a story, to share information, to convince someone about something, to report on a book, to recite a poem, to interpret a poem, to take part in a debate, or to narrate an event or a multimedia presentation. In each situation, there is one basic purpose for giving a speech: you want to communicate some idea or feeling. You also want your audience to hear, understand, and respond favorably.

Kinds of Speeches

Impromptu speech—a speech given without advance preparation

Usually there is very little or no warning that you'll need to give a speech. All of a sudden, in a school assignment, or in a real life situation, you need to say something on some topic or in response to some event. If you're lucky, you might get a few seconds to brainstorm or collect your thoughts, but don't count on it!

You might give an impromptu speech when . . .
- someone makes a statement and asks you to give your opinion (in front of a group).
- you get an award or honor you were not expecting.
- you walk into a surprise party (and it's for you)!

A tree frog can walk up a window.

The frog has pads on its fingers and toes.

The pads ooze a sticky substance.

Memorized speech—a speech that you have written and memorized, word for word

A memorized speech is carefully planned and written, then memorized precisely.

You might prepare and memorize a speech when . . .
- you are going to receive an award, and you know you'll have to respond.
- you want to run for an office, and you'll need to make a campaign speech.

Extemporaneous speech—a planned speech, given with the help of notes

An extemporaneous speech spares you the need to memorize every word, because you have help from your notes. However, it feels more spontaneous (like an impromptu speech) because your language doesn't have to stick to a memorized script.

You might give an extemporaneous speech when . . .
- you've been assigned to give a speech in school (and allowed to use notes).
- you want to share an opinion at a meeting.

Speaking Troubles

Students often have troubles with their speaking. Maybe you have some of the same problems. It's quite common to be nervous about giving a speech. Follow these tips for better speaking.

SPEAK UP!

DISINTERESTED DORA

"There is nothing at all interesting about snakes."

An effective speech has a topic that interests the speaker.

BORING BOBBY

"Here are the names of the 47 scientists who have studied the snakes..."

An effective speech has a topic that interests the audience.

UNORGANIZED UMA

"And, now...to begin...and ..to start ...um..."

An effective speech is well-planned and well organized.

MARTHA MUMBLER

"Snakes can mummmbe.. mummmble... and another fact mummmbbble.. remember... muummmbble.."

An effective speech can be heard and understood by the audience.

SUPERCILIOUS SAM

"The obsequious nature of the extraneous data precludes the cognitive dispostion of the species..."

An effective speech uses natural language.

NERVOUS NANCY

"Ananaconandadas snakes....I mean anancondanaa...oh, I mean...ahh... anacondas..."

An effective speech is given in a friendly, relaxed manner.

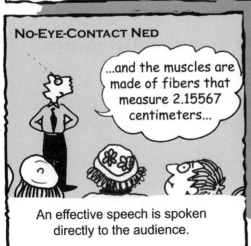

NO-EYE-CONTACT NED

"...and the muscles are made of fibers that measure 2.15567 centimeters..."

An effective speech is spoken directly to the audience.

INAPPROPRIATE IZZIE

"In 1847 a scientist wrote a paper examining the stucture of the Latin names of the genus for this animal..."

An effective speech fits the audience and the occasion.

Get Sharp: Speaking Guide

Preparing for a Speech

Get prepared! It's the best way to feel more confident and have better success with public speaking.

Steps for Preparing a Speech

1. Choose the topic.

Select a topic that is important or interesting to you. It can be a new topic for you if you are going to do research. Otherwise, choose something with which you are very familiar.

2. Decide the purpose and the audience.

Be sure about the reason for giving the speech and who the listeners will be. Ask yourself these questions:

- *What is the purpose for giving the speech?*
- *Will I share information, tell how to do something, compare some things, or try to convince someone about something?*
- *What do I want to accomplish?*
- *Who is the audience?*
- *What will be interesting to the audience?*
- *What questions will they have that I should try to answer?*
- *What objections will they have that I should consider?*

Get SharpTip #15
Are you nervous about giving your speech? The best defenses against speech anxiety are good preparations and practice.

3. Find information and take notes.

First, write down what you already know about the topic. Write questions you would like to answer about the topic. Search a variety of references to answer your questions and learn about the topic. Interview people to get more information. Write down key ideas, questions, phrases, and facts about the topic. Write down direct quotes or specific statistics you might want to use in your speech. If you plan to quote someone or use an exact statistic, write down the source. Write a key word or subtopic label on each card.

4. Organize your material.

Gather all the notes together into subtopic or category groups. Organize the groups into a sensible sequence.

5. Plan the timing.

Know how much time you have for the speech. This will help you with the organization. You may need to drop some of the subtopics or points. If your material seems too skimpy to fill the time, you may have to do some more research.

6. Write an introduction.

Create an attention-grabbing introduction—one that makes the audience eager to hear the whole speech. In the first few sentences, make the topic or purpose of the speech clear to the audience. You might start with . . .

> *. . . a startling fact*
> *. . . a funny anecdote*
> *. . . an explanation of your interest in the topic*
> *. . . a question or group of questions*
> *. . . an interesting quote*
> *. . . a demonstration or illustration of your topic*

7. Write the body of the speech.

Write the main points. Describe or explain each point clearly. Give interesting examples. Move the points along smoothly. Don't overwhelm the listeners with facts, dates, and statistics. Use examples that make a point and capture the listeners' interest.

8. Write a conclusion.

End your speech by reminding the listeners of the main point. Be sure about what you will say at the end. Make your final sentences statements with a punch. Leave the listeners satisfied, amused, ready to act, or fascinated with the topic.

9. Memorize the speech OR prepare your note cards.

Write the information that you will need in order to move the speech along smoothly. Put this on 3" x 5" or 4" x 6" note cards. Write clear, specific introductory information—maybe even word-for-word. Write the ending clearly, too. Write neatly on your cards so you will be able to read the information quickly and easily.

10. Memorize your introduction and conclusion.

Know exactly what you will say to start and end the speech. Don't leave either part up to chance.

11. Practice.

Rehearse your speech. Do this in private, on a tape recorder, in front of a mirror, or in front of a video camera. If you wish, rehearse in front of a friend who will give you feedback.

12. Practice.

Review the tips on page 180. Use the advice while you practice.

Giving a Speech

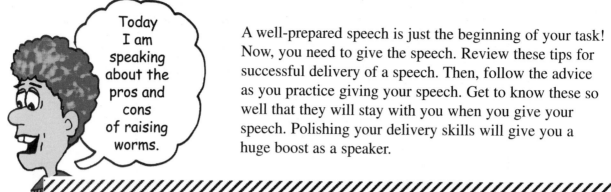

Today I am speaking about the pros and cons of raising worms.

A well-prepared speech is just the beginning of your task! Now, you need to give the speech. Review these tips for successful delivery of a speech. Then, follow the advice as you practice giving your speech. Get to know these so well that they will stay with you when you give your speech. Polishing your delivery skills will give you a huge boost as a speaker.

10 Things to Remember
When Giving a Speech

1. **Confidence** Your planning **will** pay off! You **do** know more about the topic than the audience. Believe that the audience wants to hear what you have to say.

2. **Posture** Stand straight, but not stiff. Relax. Don't slump, slouch, or bounce around. Don't sway. Do move a little. This will help to keep you relaxed.

3. **Hands** Make a plan for your hands. Don't let them dangle awkwardly by your side, nervously pull at your hair, or absent-mindedly scratch your nose. Use your hands to hold your note cards, and for gesturing or demonstrating. Let your hands relax, and use them naturally.

4. **Language** Talk as if you were speaking to someone. Use your own language. Don't use big words.

5. **Smoothness** Plan ahead for how you will move from one idea to the next.

6. **Tone** Use a friendly, natural tone. You don't want to sound timid and hesitant. Nor do you want to sound arrogant or impersonal. Avoid a monotone sound.

7. **Volume** Speak loudly enough so listeners can hear you, but don't shout.

8. **Speed** Don't rush. A common speaking problem is talking too fast. Practice brief pauses. This gives the listeners a chance to absorb your latest point.

9. **Contact** Look at your audience. Keep eye contact and talk directly to the people as individuals. Look at different faces as you speak.

10. **Enthusiasm** Show enthusiasm for your topic and keep that enthusiasm up—from the start to the very end.

Speaking Scoring Guide

Peers, teachers, or parents in responding to a speech given by a student may use this. Students may also use this guide for self-evaluation after a speech. It can be used for preparation and practice, as well as for assessment.

TRAIT	Score of 5	Score of 3	Score of 1
CONTENT & IDEAS *(main ideas, supporting details, appropriateness to audience and purpose)*	• Main ideas are clear and focused. • Main ideas, purpose stand out clearly. • Main ideas are well-supported with details and examples relevant to topic. • Ideas fit the audience and purpose well. • Ideas are interesting and command audience attention. • Content is creatively presented. • Content includes a variety of sources, viewpoints, or examples. • Conclusions reached are based on strong evidence. • The speaker shows strong insight into the topic.	• Main ideas are mostly clear and focused. • Main ideas, purpose are mostly clear.. • Details and examples are used but may be limited or repetitive. • Most details are relevant to the topic. • Ideas fit the audience and purpose somewhat. • Ideas are mostly interesting and command audience attention some of the time. • Some ideas are creatively presented. • Content includes different sources, viewpoints, or examples, but variety is limited. • Some, but not all conclusions reached are based on strong evidence. • The speaker shows insight into the topic. • All in all, the speech is a successful attempt to present coherent ideas and details effectively to the audience.	• The speech lacks clarity and focus. • Main ideas are hard to identify. • Ideas are not supported well with details and examples. • The purpose is not clear. • Details given are not relevant. • Ideas do not fit the audience or purpose. • Ideas have little sparkle and do not command audience attention. • Content is presented with no creativity.. • Conclusions reached are not based on any evidence. • The speaker shows little insight into the topic.
ORGANIZATION *(system of organization including introduction, main body, transitions, and conclusion)*	• Organization allows the main ideas and details to be conveyed well. • A strong, creative introduction grabs the listeners' attention. • The speech moves along from one idea fluently, with smooth transitions. • Details and examples are well-placed in the speech so as to maintain interest and strengthen the main point. • The speech has a strong, creative conclusion that fits the purpose and strengthens the message.	• Organization is recognizable, but is weak or inconsistent in places. • For the most part, the organization allows the main ideas and details to be conveyed. • The introduction has a beginning that is recognizable but not compelling. • The speech moves along from one idea relatively well, but some parts are choppy or transitions awkward. • Details and examples are mostly well-placed in the speech so as to maintain interest and strengthen the main point. • Conclusion fits the purpose and strengthens the message, but may be uncreative or unmemorable.	• Little or no organization is evident. • Poor organization interferes with communication of message. • Introduction is missing or irrelevant. • Speech does not flow smoothly. There are no transitions between ideas. • Details and examples have little relevance or purpose. • The conclusion is missing or irrelevant.

A score of 4 may be given for speeches that fall between 3 and 5 on a trait. A score of 2 may be given for speeches that fall between 1 and 3 on a trait.

Better Grades & Higher Test Scores / READING & LANGUAGE gr. 4–6
Copyright ©2005 by Incentive Publications, Inc., Nashville, TN.

Get Sharp: Speaking Guide

SPEAKING SCORING GUIDE, continued

TRAIT	Score of 5	Score of 3	Score of 1
LANGUAGE USE *(language use which communicates main points; correctness of grammar/usage; use of language appropriate to the purpose and audience)*	• Language is fresh and colorful. • Language communicates with and interests the audience. • Proper English language is used, unless slang or jargon is chosen to fit the purpose well. • Speech uses language creatively. • Terms used are pronounced and explained clearly. • Grammar and usage are correct.	• Language is somewhat original, but does not always work well in the speech. • The language communicates the point but does not have a strong impact on the audience. • For the most part, proper English language is used; slang or jargon may interfere with the purpose at times. • There are attempts at creativity, but they are not always successful. • Terms used are sometimes, but not always, pronounced and explained clearly. • Grammar and usage are is mostly correct.	• Language very ordinary • Language unclear. Some words are the wrong words. • Language does not work to communicate the main ideas. • Language, including slang and jargon, is used inappropriately or improperly. • Terms are not used or are not explained or are used improperly. • Grammar and usage are frequently incorrect. Poor grammar interferes with the meaning of the message.
DELIVERY *(pronunciation, enunciation, eye contact, fluency, rate, volume, tone, body movements, and gestures)*	• Speaker has very clear (and correct) pronunciation and enunciation. • Speaker maintains good eye contact with audience. • Rate, tone, and volume fit the purpose and lend to good communication of the message. • Speaker's delivery engages audience and keeps their attention. • Delivery is very smooth. • Interesting and appropriate use of gestures, facial expression. • Body movements do not detract from the effectiveness of speech.	• Pronunciation and enunciation are sometimes less than clear. • Eye contact is minimal. • Rate, tone, and volume are inconsistent. • Speaker's delivery engages audience and keeps their attention only part of the time. • Delivery is choppy in some places. • Interesting and appropriate use of gestures, facial expression some of the time; at other times gestures and expressions are nonexistent or inappropriate. • Some body movements interfere with effectiveness of the speech.	• Speaker has very poor pronunciation and enunciation. • There is no eye contact with audience. • Rate is too fast or too slow, volume is too soft or too loud, tone is monotone. • Speaker is not able to command audience attention with delivery. • Delivery is halting and interferes with communication of the message. • Gestures and facial expressions are not used at all or are distracting or inappropriate. • Body movements are distracting.

GET SHARP →

in

READING and WORD MEANING

Purposes for Reading

Just think of all the different things you read each day—signs, ads, news headlines, reminders on the refrigerator, phone numbers, calendars, maps, menus, textbooks, test questions, directions, puzzle clues, CD labels, movie reviews, e-mail, stories, novels, your sister's diary, notes from friends, and Internet website information. You have a different purpose for different kinds of reading. The **purpose** is the reason you are reading. To get the most out of your reading, it's good to understand your purpose for reading before you even begin.

The purposes for your reading will generally fall into one of the following categories:

Reading for Personal Enjoyment & Experience

Get Smart Tip #16
Don't rush your personal reading. Slow down and notice all the words, sounds, and ideas.

Much of your reading is for the purpose of **pure enjoyment or expansion** of your world and mind. Here are some examples: you want to find out something about a person or group, a place, or an idea; you want to explore a different culture; you want to enjoy a good story; you want to laugh at some jokes.

Follow these suggestions for effective personal reading:

- Notice the setting. Picture it in your mind.

- Get to know the characters.

- Identify the main idea or story conflict right away.

- Watch for delicious words and phrases. Reread them for enjoyment.

- Read poems aloud to appreciate the special sounds and rhythms.

- Relate the reading to what you know and how you feel.

- Relate the reading to your personal experiences.

- Get involved in the material. Ask yourself questions like these:

    How would I feel in this setting?

    How would I solve this problem?

    When have I been in a situation like this character is in?

    Whom do I know like this character?

    What do I already know about this topic?

    What will happen next? What would I like to see happen?

I always enjoy a good story about daredevils!

Daring Do

Reading to Find Information

When you **read to find information**, you are often trying to find an answer to a specific question. You are probably looking in reference books, journals, newspapers, ads, or Internet sources. When you read for information, follow these suggestions:

- First, identify clearly what you need to find. That way you won't waste time looking at things you don't need.

- Skim each source. Ask these questions:

  What is the purpose of this material?

  What is the exact source of the fact or information?

  Is this a reliable source?

  Does the material or site name the author?

  How current is the information?

- Scan the material to find the topic you are seeking.

- Take notes on the information you find.

- Review graphics that might expand on the information.

Reading to Learn

Sometimes you read because **you want to learn and remember something**. Generally, when you read for this purpose, you are reading nonfiction—articles, newspapers, magazines, nonfiction books, and textbooks. Follow these suggestions for reading to learn:

- Plan plenty of time to do the reading well.
- Don't rush through the assignment.
- Start by skimming the material to get an overview of the structure and contents.
- Think ahead of time about what you already know on this subject.
- Determine your purpose for the reading. What do you need to learn?
- Read all the titles, subtitles, and headings first.
- Read the questions at the end, if there are any.
- Read the vocabulary words, if any are introduced.
- Read through one section at a time.
- Stop after each section and think about what it said. Take notes.
- Summarize each section in your mind or notes.
- Reread anything that was confusing.
- Follow the SQ3R Strategy for an effective method to get more out of your reading. (See page 187.)

Get Sharp Tip #17
Before you start, have an idea what you're looking for.

Get Sharp Tip #18
Allow plenty of time for reading to learn. You can't do it in a rush.

Reading Methods

The way you read changes according to the kind of material you read and the purpose for the reading. When you start reading, there is something you need to get from the material, or something you hope will happen when you read. So, you will be constantly adjusting the method of reading to fit those needs and hopes.

3 Different Reading Methods

Scanning — a quick look through written text to find specific facts or particular information

When you **scan,** run your eyes quickly over the material, watching for a key word or phrase. This helps you locate the part that will give you the information you need. When you find this, change to another reading method—slowing down to read this portion closely.

Example: *You scan through a flier, which describes a sale on electronic equipment, until you find the section showing the kind of device you want to buy. Then, you switch to careful reading to get the details of the equipment, including the sale price.*

Skimming — a quick overview of the whole piece, to get a general idea of the content

When you **skim,** closely read headlines, titles, subtitles, headings, captions, and words in bold type. Closely read opening and closing paragraphs, and anything labeled "conclusion" or "summary" or "results." Don't forget to skim graphics too.

Example: *You skim over a menu to see what kinds of things they serve and the general categories. Then you switch to careful reading, choosing some parts of the menu to examine carefully, and possibly ignoring other parts altogether.*

Close Reading — a slow, careful reading of all the material, taking time to enjoy or think about each sentence, paragraph, or section

When you **read closely,** stop after each sentence, paragraph, or section, to think over what you have read. Notice the main idea before you go on. Look up the meanings of any unfamiliar words. Take notes and underline key points.

Examples: *You read closely when you are reading an assignment from your textbook, or when you read a book, story, or poem for enjoyment.*

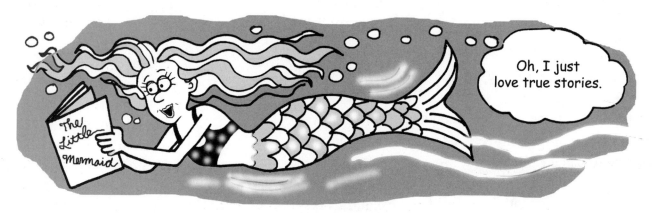

Oh, I just love true stories.

The Little Mermaid

Better Grades & Higher Test Scores / READING & LANGUAGE gr. 4–6

The SQ3R Strategy

The **SQ3R Reading Strategy** is a method for helping you get the most out of your reading when you are reading to study or learn information. Use the SQ3R Strategy right now to learn about this method. Get to know all five steps—and practice them in order.

1. S = SURVEY

Survey (skim) the material to get a general understanding of what's in it. Notice these things:

- the organization of the material
- the title or heading and subheadings
- the introduction, conclusion, and summary
- review questions at end of chapter
- pictures, diagrams, and illustrations
- graphs or tables
- words in boldface, color, or italics
- captions under pictures or graphics

These strategies really helped me!

2. Q = QUESTION

While you are surveying, and before you read, ask yourself:

- What do I already know about this subject?
- What is the point of this material?
- What is the author trying to say?
- What did the teacher say to look for when reading this?
- What point is made by each graphic aid?

Turn each title, heading, or subheading into a question. Write down these questions to use as you read.

3. R = READ

Read the material closely, one section at a time. As you read:

- Look for answers to the questions you wrote.
- Pay close attention to the main ideas.
- Study the graphic aids and their captions.
- Go back and read any confusing sections.
- Take notes. Write down main points or key ideas.

4. R = RECITE

Stop after each section, and:

- Talk to yourself. Restate what you just read.
- Try to summarize it succinctly.
- Take notes on the part you read.
- Write down main points and key ideas.
- Write down important definitions.
- Underline important points.

5. R = REVIEW

When you finish your reading:

- Try to say the answers to the questions you wrote.
- Reread the main headings and restate the main ideas you now know.
- Review your notes, definitions, and summaries.
- Reread the questions at the end of the material. Recite the answers.

Finding Main Ideas

One of the most important reading comprehension skills is the ability to **find the main idea** in any written work. Often the main idea is stated in the first sentence or paragraph. (In a poem, the main idea is often found in the first few lines.)

Sometimes the main idea is **literal**. This means it is stated very clearly. It is obvious!

Sometimes the main idea is **implied.** This means it is stated less directly.

Be alert for both ways of presenting the main point.
Notice the literal and implied main ideas from the following passages.

Mischievous Millie was always watching for a good chance to stir up excitement with the help of her pet tarantula, Tom. The tarantula showed up strutting along a Thanksgiving dinner table, slinking along an empty pew during a church service, and balancing on the classroom windowsill during a math test. Once, a whole restaurant full of people emptied in seconds when Tom showed up between the pages of a menu. Tom terrified children and adults and caused a stir wherever he went. This always delighted Millie.

Main Idea:
Millie enjoyed using her pet tarantula to shock and scare people.

Dinner for two, please.

I'll have the French-fried flies, cobweb soup, and earwig salad.

Main Idea:
Though most records are set with people doing an activity, some records are set with non-activity.

Most records are set with active feats
Of speed or strength or skill.
But did you know that prizes go
To folks who just stay still?

To win their fame, some dive from planes
Or juggle two-edged swords.
Some walk on ropes, or wrestle snakes,
Or surf through air on boards.

But records, too, are broken
For doing nothing at all.
For standing still, sitting in trees,
Or relaxing on a wall.

You can imagine that walking on water is a rather tough thing to do. Yet, it seems that walking on your hands may be even harder. The world records for the two events hint at this. A water-walker covered 3502 miles on skis to set the record. The person who walked on his hands, however, could cover only 970 miles.

Main Idea: It is probably harder to walk on hands than to walk on water.

Celery, they say, is good for you to eat. It is one of those healthy vegetables that's full of fiber. I know this is true, but celery has a problem.

Celery can be a tasty, treat, too. Try it with coated with cream cheese and chopped walnuts. Or fill the little troughs with peanut butter and raisins. I've tasted these treats. I know they're good. But celery has a problem.

The problem with celery is the strings. They stick in your teeth and get caught in your throat. If you're going to enjoy the health and taste benefits of celery, you will have to get used to the strings.

Main Idea: Though celery is tasty and good for you, anyone who eats it has to deal with the strings.

Stubborn Spider Evades Extinction

Reporters swarmed a suburban home today to get a picture of an unusual spider. An itsy spider with only seven legs has been climbing up a waterspout every day for two months. The owners of the home say they have tried more than a dozen different plans to capture, kill, or relocate the spider, all without success. When rain washes through the waterspout, it seems to be gone. When the sun comes out, the spider returns to crawl up the waterspout.

Main Idea: Some homeowners tried for two months to get rid of a spider, but never succeeded.

I'm a pretty good climber for a seven-legged spider.

Better Grades & Higher Test Scores / READING & LANGUAGE gr. 4–6
Copyright ©2005 by Incentive Publications, Inc., Nashville, TN.

Get Sharp: Reading Comprehension

Identifying Details

Details are the examples that give more information about a topic. To understand the meaning of a written passage, the reader needs to be able to find the examples or details that support the main idea. Keep your eye sharp for those details, and you will get more out of your reading.

Find details in passages...

Surfing began as long ago as the 17th century in the Pacific Islands. Surfing began in California in the 1950s, and was made popular by surf movies and a successful singing group, "The Beach Boys." Thousands of people now surf in places around the world. You can surf on a shortboard, a longboard, or with no board. (This is called "bodysurfing.") A surfer can ride a snowboard or sailboard. A sky surfer rides a surfboard in the air while freefalling.

With careful reading, you can learn . . .
. . . where surfing began
. . . how long ago surfing began
. . . when surfing came to California
. . . things that made surfing popular
. . . different ways to surf

Surfers spend a lot of time waiting. They lie or kneel on the board and paddle beyond the place where the waves break. Then they wait. When a wave over three feet tall heads for the shore, the surfer paddles to get ahead of its crest (the place where the wave is breaking). Just when the wave is about to pick up the surfboard and carry it along, the surfer stands up. The surfer uses body weight to steer the surfboard. He must keep the board along the vertical face or wall of the wave. If she gets it right, the surfer can enjoy a nice ride for several minutes, moving at a good speed—up to 10 miles an hour. Or, if she doesn't get it right, she can **wipe out** (be sent smashing beneath the water by the tremendous weight and force of a monstrous wave).

With careful reading, you can learn . . .
. . . how surfers ride a wave
. . . how surfers begin their ride
. . . when the surfer stands up
. . . where the surfboard rides the wave
. . . the speed of the ride
. . . what happens when things go right
. . . what happens when everything does not go right

Find details in graphics . . .

Pay close attention to graphics such as illustrations, ads, charts, graphs, tables, diagrams, posters, tickets, and maps. There are plenty of details to be read in many graphic presentations.

STRANGE & AMAZING JOURNEYS

Journey	Distance	Time It Took	Person	Year
backwards run	2,100 mi	107 days	Arvind Pandya	1984
walking on stilts	3,008 mi	107 days	Joe Bowen	1980
unicycle trip	3,261 mi	44 days	Akira Matsushima	1992
leap frog trip	996 mi, 352 yd	244 hr, 43 min	14 Stanford University students	1991
walking on hands	870 mi	55 days	Johann Jurlinger	1990
wheelchair journey	24,901 mi	2 years	Rick Hansen	1985-1987
lifeboat trip	800 mi	17 days	Ernest Shackleton party	1916
polar sled journey	3,740 mi	220 days	6-member party	1989-1990
horse-drawn journey	17,200 mi	7+ years	the Grant family	1991-1998
walk on water	3,502 mi	59 days	Remy Bricka	1988
lawnmower journey	3,366 mi	42 days	Ryan Tripp	1997

With careful reading you can learn . .

. . . the names of the unusual journeys

. . . the length, time, and date of each trip

. . . the name(s) of the traveler(s)

. . . the name and age of the lost cat

. . . the cat's owner and phone number

. . . details of the cat's description

. . . the date, time, location of the concert

. . . the name of the performing group

. . . the price of the ticket

. . . the location of the seat

Ticket 079254

Rolling Boulders
Rock Concert
Half Moon Theater
2727 Crescent Street
Sunday, May 8 · 8:00pm
$25.

Loge D21

LOST CAT

Name: Roamer
orange tiger cat
5 years old
Left ear chewed
slightly overweight

Loves to roam
Last seen on the corner
of Elm and Maple Streets
on Thursday, 25th

Please notify Elena.
555-7734
Desperate!
Cat is asthmatic- he needs medication!

Find details in titles and captions . . .

Don't miss the good information that is given in titles and captions. Read them closely. Often, you can pick up a main idea for a whole article, essay, or other written work.

SKYDIVING SCHOOL

Kip Farnsworth sky dives to a win Sunday during the national Collegiate Parachuting Championships. He won in the freestyle skydiving category, where the sky diver performs airborne gymnastic maneuvers before deploying the parachute.

FreeFall! magazine for sky divers

With careful reading you can learn . . .

. . . the name of the sky diver

. . . an idea of what freestyle skydiving involves

. . . the name of the competition

With careful reading you can learn . . .

. . . the names of records set or broken

. . . the dates of the records

. . . exact details of some records

. . . who set or broke some of the records

The Gazette, December 12, 2002
300 SKY DIVERS SET WORLD RECORD IN FREEFALL FORMATION

The Tribune   *December 10, 1979*
Man Eats Record 19 Bananas in 2 Minutes

City Sun Times--------------July 24, 2000
Local Woman Wins Fire-Eating Contest Yesterday

The Chronicle   *Saturday, July 20, 2002*
Boomerang Contest Begins Next Thursday

Separating Fact from Opinion

A **fact** is something that is based on truth. Generally, a fact can be proven.

An **opinion** is one individual's personal viewpoint or feeling about a subject.

A sharp reader will be skilled at separating fact from opinion in written material. There is nothing wrong with an author writing his or her opinions. A problem develops when opinions are stated as if they are factual information.

Interview With Jet Skier

Interviewer: How did the idea of jet skiing develop?

Jet Skier: A motorcycle racer named Clayton Jackson was concerned about injuries that resulted from motorcyclists crashing into hard pavement. He came up with the idea of a motorcycle-like vehicle that works in water (where the falls would be softer). *He was a genius*.

Interviewer: What are the dangers?

Jet Skier: *Oh, jet skiing is perfectly safe*. The water is soft, so *you can't get hurt*.

Interviewer: How much does a jet ski cost?

Jet Skier: *Jet skis are very affordable. Anyone can own one.*

Interviewer: Why is jet skiing so popular?

Jet Skier: Boaters and non-boaters of all ages can have the experience of jetting around out on the water. *Everybody who tries it loves it.*

In this interview, many of the skier's statements give facts about the sport. Notice the statements *in italics.* These are stated as fact, but are actually the personal opinions of the jet skier.

Identifying Cause & Effect

Understanding cause and effect involves two skills: seeing what specific happening **causes** or sparks an event (or response), and recognizing what specific **effects** (results) came about because of a certain event or action. A sharp reader will also be alert to passages that describe causes and effects. Look for the causes and effects in the cures described here.

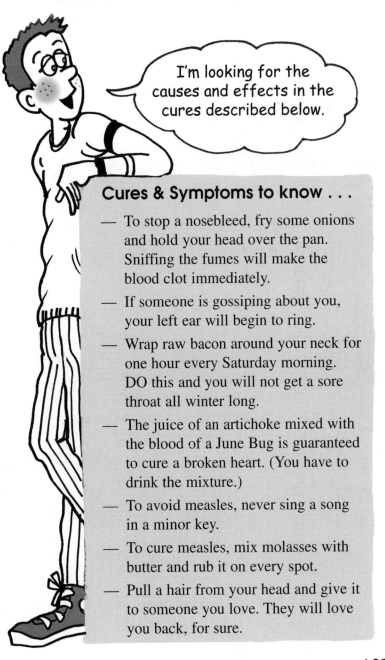

I'm looking for the causes and effects in the cures described below.

Cures & Symptoms to know . . .

— To stop a nosebleed, fry some onions and hold your head over the pan. Sniffing the fumes will make the blood clot immediately.

— If someone is gossiping about you, your left ear will begin to ring.

— Wrap raw bacon around your neck for one hour every Saturday morning. DO this and you will not get a sore throat all winter long.

— The juice of an artichoke mixed with the blood of a June Bug is guaranteed to cure a broken heart. (You have to drink the mixture.)

— To avoid measles, never sing a song in a minor key.

— To cure measles, mix molasses with butter and rub it on every spot.

— Pull a hair from your head and give it to someone you love. They will love you back, for sure.

Generalizing

To **generalize** is to use specific details you have read to help you get a general understanding about the topic. When you make a generalization about something you've read, make sure that the written material provides enough examples or details to support your generalization.

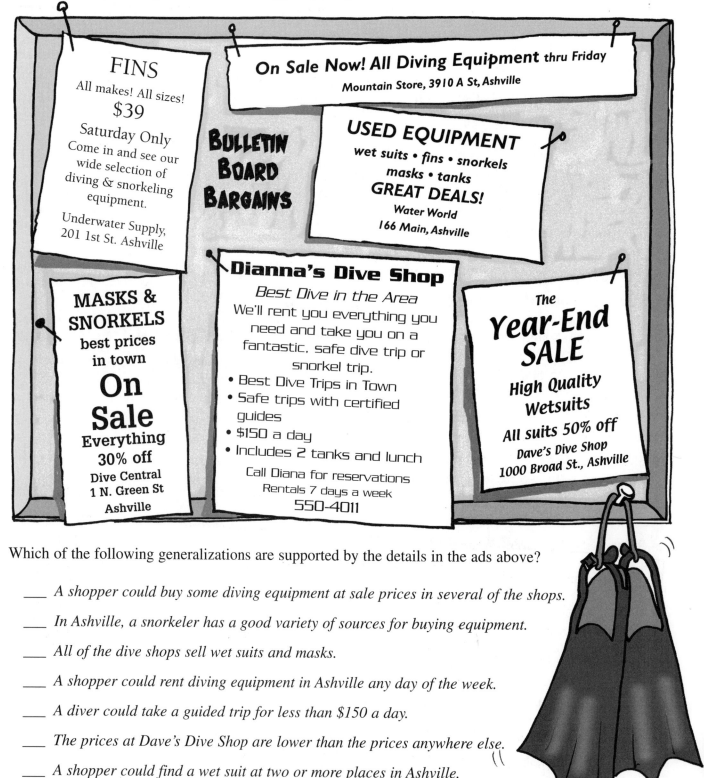

FINS
All makes! All sizes!
$39
Saturday Only
Come in and see our wide selection of diving & snorkeling equipment.
Underwater Supply,
201 1st St. Ashville

On Sale Now! All Diving Equipment thru Friday
Mountain Store, 3910 A St, Ashville

BULLETIN BOARD BARGAINS

USED EQUIPMENT
wet suits • fins • snorkels
masks • tanks
GREAT DEALS!
Water World
166 Main, Ashville

MASKS & SNORKELS
best prices in town
On Sale
Everything
30% off
Dive Central
1 N. Green St
Ashville

Dianna's Dive Shop
Best Dive in the Area
We'll rent you everything you need and take you on a fantastic, safe dive trip or snorkel trip.
• Best Dive Trips in Town
• Safe trips with certified guides
• $150 a day
• Includes 2 tanks and lunch
Call Diana for reservations
Rentals 7 days a week
550-4011

The Year-End SALE
High Quality Wetsuits
All suits 50% off
Dave's Dive Shop
1000 Broad St., Ashville

Which of the following generalizations are supported by the details in the ads above?

____ *A shopper could buy some diving equipment at sale prices in several of the shops.*

____ *In Ashville, a snorkeler has a good variety of sources for buying equipment.*

____ *All of the dive shops sell wet suits and masks.*

____ *A shopper could rent diving equipment in Ashville any day of the week.*

____ *A diver could take a guided trip for less than $150 a day.*

____ *The prices at Dave's Dive Shop are lower than the prices anywhere else.*

____ *A shopper could find a wet suit at two or more places in Ashville.*

Inferring

To **infer** is to make a logical guess based on information. When you make an inference about something you have read, make sure the inference is based on examples, details, and information actually provided in the text.

THINGS I'VE READ THIS WEEK

A. a recipe for salsa and salmon ice cream sundae

B. my sister's diary

C. a poster advertising my favorite word, "argyle"

D. an argument promoting pet slugs

E. five poems about compost

F. a report on the eyeballs of anteaters

G. a tall tale about a cricket who saved the world

H. several Internet studies about the uses of earwax

I. directions for getting to the city dump

J. an invitation to an earthworm beauty contest

K. the ingredients in all the frozen dinners at the market

L. definitions for all the words in my dictionary that begin with *g*

M. a poster promoting a day to wear your clothes inside out to school

Which can you reasonably infer based on the list of Sam's reading?

_____ Sam has unusual interests.

_____ Sam had a boring week.

_____ Sam's parents are unhappy with his choice of reading material.

_____ Sam has a good sense of humor.

_____ Sam is a member of a group that tries to protect animals.

_____ Sam does a lot of reading.

_____ Sam has the ability to make use of many sources of written information.

Better Grades & Higher Test Scores / READING & LANGUAGE gr. 4–6
Copyright ©2005 by Incentive Publications, Inc., Nashville, TN.

Get Sharp: Reading Comprehension

Predicting

To **predict** is to make a statement about what will happen. When you make a prediction about something you've read, make sure that the written material provides some basis on which to make your prediction.

Each of the selections below is just right for making predictions. As a reader, you will want to know what would happen next. See the predictions that another reader has made.

Prediction:
Bob will not be able to stay awake. He will fall asleep and the fire will go out.

It was warm when the camping trip began. The weather turned cold without warning. The campers had not brought warm clothing or warm sleeping bags. They decided that they must keep a fire going all night in order to stay warm. They made a plan to take turns staying awake to add wood to the fire.

Bob was the third fire-keeper. He was awakened at 3 a.m. and stumbled sleepily to the fireside. Staying awake was not going to be easy. He slouched down by the fire, yawning and grumbling. To stay awake, Bob jiggled, wiggled, clapped is hands, recited poems, and sang silly songs. No matter how hard he tried, his eyelids kept tugging toward the ground, and his head kept falling toward his hands.

Court Case # 473

Mrs. Grundy claims that the neighbors' dog is repeatedly digging up her tulips and tulip bulbs. She is asking for $600 to pay for replacement bulbs and damage to her lawn. She has receipts for the costs and photos of a small Dalmatian digging in her garden.

Her neighbors, the Jeffersons, claim that they do not own a dog. A city official testified that the law required dogs to be kept on leashes except when on their own property. This same official brought city records showing that a Dalmation puppy is registered to the Jefferson family.

Prediction:
Judge Law will order the Jeffersons to pay the costs and will fine them for breaking the leash law.

Drawing Conclusions

A **conclusion** is a general statement made after analyzing examples, details, or facts. It involves an explanation that you develop through reasoning. When you draw a conclusion about something you have read, make sure that the text has enough evidence to support your conclusion. Different readers may draw different conclusions from the same material.

Thirteen Thrills on Thirteen Hills

No doubt you have waited in line for at least two hours for the opening of the gates to *The Twister*. Like the hundreds in line behind you, you don't regret the long wait for a chance to ride this new upside-down, triple-loop, heart-stopping roller coaster. While you wait, you can begin to imagine the screams and screeches that will soon be coming from your own throat.

You will be nervous, excited, and impatient to get on. If you didn't have trust in the safety of this coaster, you wouldn't be here at the front of the line. Though you will be the first paying customer ever to ride *The Twister*, you are sure it will be safe. You don't want to know how it works; you just want to ride!

Now you're on the ride. A moving chain pulls the car to the top. When the car gets to the peak of the hill and starts to curve over, gravity pulls it down the steep incline. At the very top of each hill, your body keeps going up out of your seat because of inertia. You feel like you are flying, but soon the gravity has you back in your seat again. At every curve and every upside-down loop, centripetal force pushes you against your seat. This is why you don't fall out. Finally, friction slows down the coaster and stops it.

All too soon, the ride is over. You enjoyed every minute of it. Your stomach is still upside down, but you're feeling fairly stable. You want to get on *The Twister* again—right away!

Here are some conclusions different readers drew after reading this:

*The **Twister** is a brand new ride, opening for its first day.*

Many customers are eager to try the new roller coaster.

The author is an experienced roller coaster rider.

The author is confident that he or she knows what the rider will feel.

The author has done some research about how roller coasters work.

Better Grades & Higher Test Scores / READING & LANGUAGE gr. 4–6   *Get Sharp: Reading Comprehension*

Evaluating

When you **evaluate** a piece of writing, you make a judgment about something in it. Evaluations should be based on evidence. Evaluations do include opinions, but these opinions should be supported or explained by examples from the written text. When you evaluate writing, ask such questions as:

How well does the writer make the point or accomplish the purpose?
Are the conclusions reached based on good examples and facts?
Is this believable?
Does it make sense?
Is it realistic?
Is the writer biased?

> *Are you shocked at the idea of cuddling with a boa constrictor? Many people are. They couldn't imagine choosing this animal for a pet. If you listen to my experience, you will change your mind. You might even go looking for a pet boa this very afternoon.*
>
> *My pet boa, Brewster, was given to me for a birthday gift. I've kept him in my room for three years. He eats live mice and lives happily at our house.*
>
> *You would like a boa constrictor, too. You could give him or her a name you like. This snake will be your friend. There is no better pet in the world. Your pet would be longer than most other pets, and more unusual. Go shopping for a boa constrictor today.*

Evaluation:
The writer's purpose seems to be to convince readers that a boa is a good pet, but the writing is not convincing. His essay is full of general statements. He does not give much information about having a boa as a pet. There is little here for the reader to learn. When the essay ends, the reader has few reasons to go out and buy a boa constrictor.

Evaluation:
The writer set out to show how much she hates spinach. She does a good job of making her point by using many strong examples. I believe that she is serious about this.

> Don't ask me to eat spinach, 'cause
> The taste I could not stand.
> I'd rather swallow goldfish live,
> Or gulp a cup of sand.
>
> I'd eat my cell phone, chew CDs,
> Munch my earphones any day—
> But eat some spinach with my lunch?
> Never, nope, no way!
>
> You can torture me with scorpions,
> Hang snakes from all my walls,
> Fill my bathtub with piranhas,
> Push me over Niagra Falls.
>
> You can swear to light my underwear,
> Feed me motor oil in steady drips.
> No matter what you threaten—
> Spinach will never touch my lips!

Identifying the Author's Purpose

Every piece of literature is written for a purpose. The **purpose** is the reason for the writing, or what the writer hoped to accomplish. As a reader, you should try to figure out the purpose of the writing when you start reading. That way you will get more out of your reading. Also, you will be able to judge whether or not the writer accomplished the purpose.

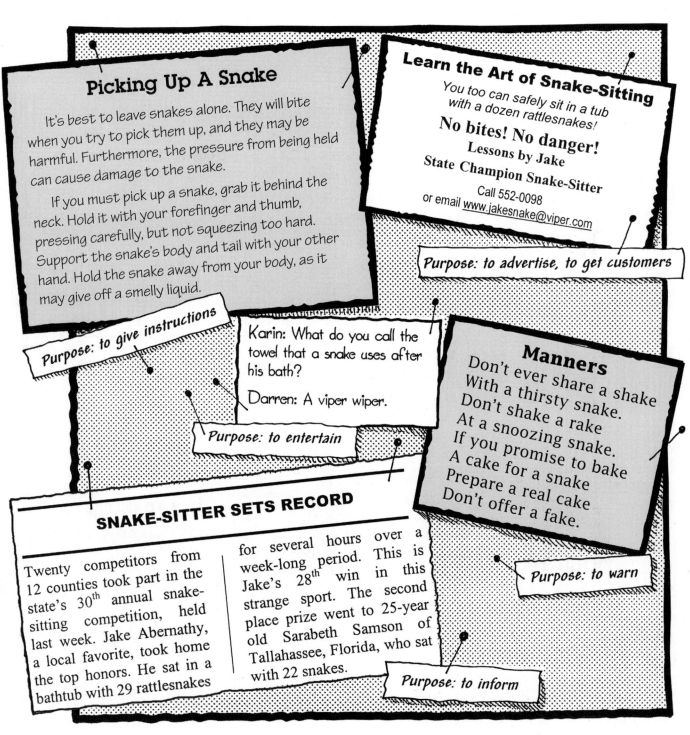

Picking Up A Snake

It's best to leave snakes alone. They will bite when you try to pick them up, and they may be harmful. Furthermore, the pressure from being held can cause damage to the snake.

If you must pick up a snake, grab it behind the neck. Hold it with your forefinger and thumb, pressing carefully, but not squeezing too hard. Support the snake's body and tail with your other hand. Hold the snake away from your body, as it may give off a smelly liquid.

Purpose: to give instructions

Learn the Art of Snake-Sitting

You too can safely sit in a tub with a dozen rattlesnakes!

No bites! No danger!

Lessons by Jake
State Champion Snake-Sitter
Call 552-0098
or email www.jakesnake@viper.com

Purpose: to advertise, to get customers

Karin: What do you call the towel that a snake uses after his bath?

Darren: A viper wiper.

Purpose: to entertain

Manners

Don't ever share a shake
With a thirsty snake.
Don't shake a rake
At a snoozing snake.
If you promise to bake
A cake for a snake
Prepare a real cake
Don't offer a fake.

Purpose: to warn

SNAKE-SITTER SETS RECORD

Twenty competitors from 12 counties took part in the state's 30th annual snake-sitting competition, held last week. Jake Abernathy, a local favorite, took home the top honors. He sat in a bathtub with 29 rattlesnakes for several hours over a week-long period. This is Jake's 28th win in this strange sport. The second place prize went to 25-year old Sarabeth Samson of Tallahassee, Florida, who sat with 22 snakes.

Purpose: to inform

Identifying the Audience

Usually, when a writer works on a piece of writing, she or he has an audience in mind. The **audience** is a person or a group who the author hopes will read the writing. The author hopes the audience will appreciate the writing, learn from it, act on it, or respond in some way. Of course, the audience is closely tied to the purpose of the piece.

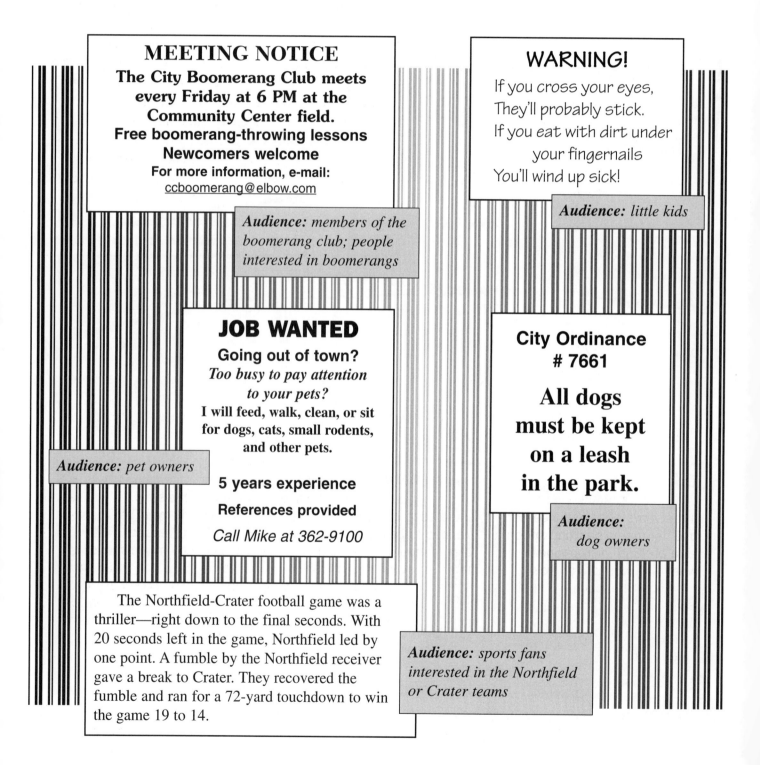

MEETING NOTICE
**The City Boomerang Club meets
every Friday at 6 PM at the
Community Center field.
Free boomerang-throwing lessons
Newcomers welcome**
For more information, e-mail:
ccboomerang@elbow.com

Audience: members of the boomerang club; people interested in boomerangs

WARNING!
If you cross your eyes,
They'll probably stick.
If you eat with dirt under
your fingernails
You'll wind up sick!

Audience: little kids

JOB WANTED
Going out of town?
*Too busy to pay attention
to your pets?*
I will feed, walk, clean, or sit
for dogs, cats, small rodents,
and other pets.

5 years experience
References provided
Call Mike at 362-9100

Audience: pet owners

**City Ordinance
7661**

**All dogs
must be kept
on a leash
in the park.**

*Audience:
dog owners*

The Northfield-Crater football game was a thriller—right down to the final seconds. With 20 seconds left in the game, Northfield led by one point. A fumble by the Northfield receiver gave a break to Crater. They recovered the fumble and ran for a 72-yard touchdown to win the game 19 to 14.

Audience: sports fans interested in the Northfield or Crater teams

Identifying the Author's Tone

The **tone** in a piece of literature is the approach a writer takes toward the topic, or the attitude the writer has toward the topic. Pay attention to the tone. It will give you clues about the author's beliefs and biases, as well as his or her purpose for the writing.

Some critics think that slug racing is **silly**. Well, we think they are silly, too!

Every year, in August, hundreds of visitors flock to Prairie Creek Redwoods State Park to take part in or watch a perfectly useless activity—the annual Banana Slug Derby. Believe it or not, people stand around and watch sticky yellow creatures slide along a "race track." The slugs look like scrunched, confused bananas with horns. The spectators act like fools, cheering for animals that don't even know what they are doing. Someone even spends money on prizes and trophies for this ridiculous competition. There's a wonderful ocean nearby this California park, and hundreds of rewarding things to see and do in the state. So why would anyone use up a good summer weekend to hang around slugs and slug-lovers?

Tone: **critical, mocking**

Identifying Point of View

Someone tells each story. When you look for the **point of view**, you find who is telling the story, and whether or not they, themselves, are inside the story or an outsider looking in.

Tammy has been a-singin' her heart out since she was just three years old. I watched her use her mama's mixing spoon as a pretend microphone when she was just an itsy-bitsy girl. She just stood there and belted out the tune, "Your Cheatin' Heart," at the top of her little lungs. I always knew she'd end up being a star.	I headed for Nashville at age 16 with my guitar over my shoulder and a song in my head. I planned to be a star. Ten years later, without a dollar to my name, no work, and no hit songs, I headed out of town. No one wanted my singin', my song-writin', or my guitar playin'. It's a town that will break your heart and your bank account.	Singer James Twang has a new hit. His song, "Don't Send Me That E-mail That Breaks My Heart," leaped to the top of the country music charts last week. It took only three weeks for this to reach number one. Fans hope that Twang will be nominated for best new artist in the upcoming Country Music Awards.
Point of View: *second person, narrator in the story*	***Point of View:*** *first person, narrator writing about self*	***Point of View:*** *narrator outside the story*

Identifying the Author's Bias

Bias is the writer's personal opinion about the topic. Watch for clues to the author's bias in each written piece. If the author lets a bias show, that can influence the way the subject is presented to the reader. This might be interesting to the reader, but it can also twist information or leave out important facts. Bias is particularly a problem in a piece that pretends to be neutral.

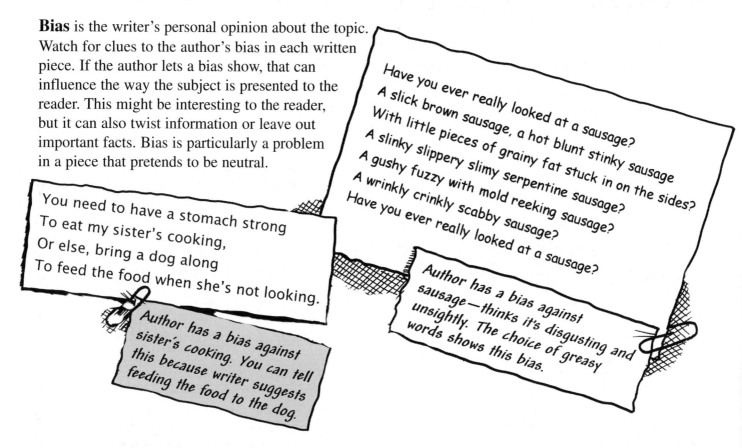

Have you ever really looked at a sausage?
A slick brown sausage, a hot blunt stinky sausage
With little pieces of grainy fat stuck in on the sides?
A slinky slippery slimy serpentine sausage?
A gushy fuzzy with mold reeking sausage?
A wrinkly crinkly scabby sausage?
Have you ever really looked at a sausage?

You need to have a stomach strong
To eat my sister's cooking,
Or else, bring a dog along
To feed the food when she's not looking.

Author has a bias against sister's cooking. You can tell this because writer suggests feeding the food to the dog.

Author has a bias against sausage—thinks it's disgusting and unsightly. The choice of greasy words shows this bias.

Identifying Stereotype

A **stereotype** is a false idea (usually uninformed or unexamined) that someone has about a person or a group of people. Be alert for stereotyping in written pieces—particularly in works that are intended to present facts or information. Usually bias can be found right alongside stereotype in passages.

Dear Editor: The city must have better ways to spend the taxpayers' money than on a skateboard park. We need a better library, more traffic lights, and fewer potholes. Instead, the city council wants to encourage the teenagers, who already waste time, to hang around doing nothing useful. A skateboard park would fill the area with sloppily dressed, lazy teens. Their noise and bad language would downgrade the city center. Surely, there would be graffiti on every store window. Any area given over to teens will have a negative impact on the city. I urge all City Council members to come to their senses and vote against a skateboard park.

Sincerely,
Joe Jones

obvious stereotyping of teenagers and skateboarders as lazy, sloppy, and poorly behaved

202

Analyzing Characters

Characterization is a writer's way of explaining the people in a story or other piece of writing. Readers observe the characters, think about them, and respond in some way.

Since Ginger Georges moved into the old brick house down the street, our neighborhood has never been the same. We had a feeling something exciting was happening when a purple, paint-splattered SUV pulled up behind a moving van last October. Out scampered a wild-haired child with clothes on backwards and balloons tied to her pigtails. She hurried across the yard, walking on her hands, and stuck out a foot to shake my hand.

Ever since then, the neighborhood has been hopping. Every weekend, Ginger stirs up a shocking new activity. One Saturday, she built a giant scarecrow on her roof. The next, she entertained us all by balancing drinking glasses (full of water) on her chin. Another time, she made a sandwich that reached across her entire yard. She has eaten record numbers of pickled eggs, raced pet mice inside roller-skates up and down the driveway, climbed ladders upside down while holding a flaming torch in her teeth, and made a paper clip chain that circled the whole neighborhood.

She loves to organize crazy events for the neighbors. We've joined her for everything from bathtub races to cricket-spitting contests. She's announced an egg-balancing derby and an onion-peeling race for next month. Like all the neighbors, I can't wait to see what Ginger will do next.

To analyze a character, you can ask questions about the person and the way the author presents the character. For practice, ask yourself these questions about the character in the example above.

- *Is the character believable?*
- *What is likable (unlikable, annoying, disturbing, etc.) about the character?*
- *When I read about this character, do I feel a strong response?*
- *What is my response to this character? Why do I respond this way?*
- *Would I like to know this character? Is this character like me in any way?*
- *Have I had any similar problems or been in the same situation?*
- *Does this character remind me of anyone I know?*
- *If I were in this story, would I behave in the same way the character did?*
- *What are the author's feelings about this character?*
- *Has the author done a good job of making the character "come alive"?*

Identifying Literary Devices

Literary devices are techniques authors use to make writing effective. Look for them and appreciate the color, interest, and power they add to writing.

Literary Terms and Devices

alliteration — the repetition of consonant sounds at the beginnings of words
flimsy flippers flailing and flopping

allusion — a reference in one piece of literature to something else that is well known (It may be part of another piece of literature, an object, a person, or an event.)

anecdote — a short tale of an incident, generally highly interesting or comical

antagonist— the character in a story who struggles against the main character

bias— the writer's personal opinion about the topic (usually a stubbornly held opinion)

character — a person (or animal) who takes part in a story

characterization— the act of creating or describing a character in a written work

cliché — an overused expression

climax— the highest point of suspense in a story

conflict — a problem or struggle between two people, things, or ideas in a story

crisis — turning point in the plot of the story

dialogue — conversation of two or more characters in a literary work

drama — story told by actors taking the parts of characters

dramatic irony — the situation in some dramas where the audience knows something that the characters do not

fiction— prose writing that tells a story

figure of speech — words, phrases, or sentences that are meant to be taken imaginatively rather than literally (pun, idiom, proverb, metaphor, oxymoron, hyperbole, personification, simile)

HAVE YOU HAD YOUR CLICHÉ TODAY?

flashback — part of a story, play, or story-poem that tells about events which happened earlier than the current setting of the story

foreshadowing — the author's way of giving readers hints about something that might happen later in a story, play, or poem-story

genre — the form or type of literature (*such as poem, joke, essay, novel, epitaph*)

hyperbole — an extreme exaggeration used for a particular purpose in a written piece

It was so cold that even the polar bear wore a parka.

idioms — a phrase or expression whose meaning is different from what the words say literally
He put his foot in his mouth.

image — a mental picture created in the mind of the reader by the words the writer uses
a slice of silver-slivered moon
in a plum-purple sky

imagery — the use of images in a passage

irony — a situation in literature in which something is different than it appears; or when there is a difference between what is spoken and what is meant

metaphor — a figure of speech in which something is compared to an unlike thing; one thing is written about as if it were another
Life is a can of spaghetti surprises.

meter — the pattern of beats in a poem

As I was going up a stair
I saw a cat that wasn't there.

There is a stress on every other syllable in this poem, beginning with the second one (I).

mood — the feeling or atmosphere created by the writer

moral — the lesson taught by a piece of literature

narrator — the person telling the story

novel — a long work of prose fiction

novella — a work of fiction that is shorter than a novel but longer than a short story

onomatopoeia — the use of words that sound like the thing or noise they name

bang, pop, hiss, splat, sizzle, bark

oxymoron — an expression made up of two words which seem to contradict each other

paradox — a statement that is actually true, though it seems to go against common sense

parody — a work that makes fun of another work by imitating some aspect of the other writer's style

personification — a figure of speech in which human characteristics are given to nonliving things

> *Midnight grabbed me and dragged me into its shadows.*

plot — series of events that make up a story

A plot involves a central conflict, or problem. The problem is introduced, builds to a climax, and is eventually resolved in some way.

poetry — a kind of language which is written in lines, and has more emphasis on sounds and rhythms than ordinary (prose) writing

point of view — the angle or perspective from which a story is told

prose — writing that is not drama or poetry Prose is generally written in complete sentences and paragraphs, and can be either fiction or nonfiction.

protagonist — the main character in a story, usually one which faces a problem or conflict

proverb — a saying that gives some wisdom in a sneaky way; often the meaning is something other than what the words say literally

> *A rolling stone gathers no moss.*

pun — a figure of speech which uses double meaning to make a play on words

> *Teachers have a lot of class.*

resolution — the ending or solving of the conflict in a story, play, or poem-story

rhyme — repetition of similar sounds at the ends of words

rhyme scheme — the pattern of the rhyming lines in a poem

rhythm — the pattern of beats in a line of poetry or prose

satire — writing that makes fun of the shortcomings of people, systems, or institutions for the purpose of enlightening readers or bringing about a change

setting — the time and place of a story

simile — a metaphor where two things are compared using **like** or **as**

> *She was as prickly as an artichoke.*

stereotype — a false idea (usually uninformed or unexamined) that someone has about a person or a group of people

style — the way an author chooses and arranges words in getting a message across or telling a story

symbolism — the use of symbols (concrete objects) to stand for ideas in a written work

theme — the main idea or message of a text

tone — the writer's attitude or approach toward the subject or toward the writing

understatement — the opposite of exaggeration; bringing attention to a subject by treating it as if it is less important or less powerful than it really is

voice — the way a writer's personality shows through in their writing

Identifying Figurative Language

Figurative language is a way of using language that expands the literal meaning of the words and gives them a new meaning or twist. When authors use *figures of speech*, it makes the language more colorful and vivid. It sparks the reader's imagination and brings the subject to life. Watch for the way good writers use figures of speech, such as hyperbole, idioms, puns, metaphors, oxymorons, proverbs, similes, or personification. *(Read about these on pages 138–141, and 204–206.)*

Look for figurative language in the examples below.

I'm getting hungry for some lemon meringue pie.

YELLOW
Yellow never wants help
But steps right out on its own
Throwing bright flashes everywhere.
Yellow dashes through flower gardens,
Splashes on fried eggs,
Drips on traffic lights,
And wraps itself around bananas.
Yellow is bigger than the sun,
Brighter than the day.
It reaches out from spotlights
Like lemon-streaked fingers
Grabbing attention.
Yellow never gives up.
Yellow is BOLD.

BROWN is gingerbread baking.
Homework is **BROWN**.
It's climbing out of bed on a cold morning,
Getting in fights with your friend,
Eating something you don't like.
It's as smooth as a chocolate shake
And as loud as a complaining cow.
BROWN is thinking of people starving.
Being punished is **BROWN**.
BROWN is failing a test
Or having your foot fall asleep.

Personal Response to Reading

A **personal response** can be described as the reader's feelings, opinions, and questions about something she or he has read. It is not likely that you will ever read anything without some personal response. But sometimes you might be asked to write or tell a personal response. Get in the habit of paying attention to your own reactions and feelings about something you have read.

When you read, ask yourself questions such as these:

How do I feel about this passage?

How do I identify with this?

What experiences, memories, emotions are stirred up by this?

What words, phrases, lines, or ideas appeal to me? Why?

What writing techniques seem most effective?

> I love the joke about the girl with the ring in her nose.

1000 JOKES

Frostbite in Montana

How cold is cold? Do you think you have ever been REALLY cold? Well, listen to this and then you can decide.

Last winter when I visited my Uncle Fred in Montana, I found out about cold. The first morning I was there, it was so cold that the chickens laid frozen eggs and the cows gave ice cream instead of milk. The next day, my words froze as I spoke and dropped to the ground and shattered. On the third day, I spilled my hot chocolate and it landed in a puddle in the snowbank. Instantly, we had a chocolate cream pie ready to slice up for dessert after lunch. On my last day, the dog's shadow froze on the ground the minute he stepped out of the house. Uncle Fred wrote to me that the shadow did not thaw until April.

That's the last time I will visit Montana in the winter. Uncle Fred says I should come in August. He wants me to see the chicken lay scrambled eggs from the terrible heat.

B was born with a bang!
It's brainy, brawny, beautiful.

B builds bridges,
Has a billion in the bank,
And barbeques beef on the balcony.

B buzzes, bites, bops, and booms.
It bedazzles and bewilders.

B is always on its best behavior,
Except when it **blunders**,
        blabbers,
            or **belches**.

Body Piercing—Cool or Risky?

Is it cool to poke holes in your body to insert fabulous jewelry? Or, is body piercing is downright dangerous? It can be both.

Body piercing is a hot fad in many cultures today. With the help of a needle or piercing gun, people by the thousands are getting jewelry inserted into their ears, noses, navels, lips, upper ears, tongues, and other spots on the body. People of many ages seem to enjoy decorating their body with jewelry that is held in place by fastening it through a hole in some body part.

There's more to piercing than decoration. Generally, piercing is painful and done without taking anything to dull the pain. There are no guarantees that the person doing the piercing is using clean equipment or safe methods. Frequently, piercing is followed by infections and allergic reactions to the jewelry. Some infections that get into the bloodstream can affect the whole body. Others can cause long-lasting damage to body parts. All infections are dangerous. Upper ear cartilage is especially prone to infections that can cause permanent deformity. Tongue piercing can lead to pain, uncontrollable salivation, swallowing problems, impaired speech, loss of taste, gum damage, and chips or fractures in teeth.

A careful customer of body piercing will learn about the risks, take them seriously, and find out how to avoid them. Is the glittery jewelry worth the risk to your health? You have to decide for yourself. Don't make the choice without knowing the facts.

Creative Book Reports

Do you need to do a book report? Unless you have a particular form to follow, think about doing something different. There are many ways to show that you have read a book, explain what you have learned from it, or share your response to it.

Try one (or several) or these ideas for your book reports.

Advertisement — Make a poster, banner, T-shirt, or magazine ad that advertises your book.

Book in Costume — Dress up as one of the characters and tell the story from a first person point of view. *(Or make a mask of a character, and do the same.)*

Book Review — Write a book review to be printed in the school newspaper.

Changed Parts — Create a different beginning, middle, or ending for the story.

Changed Sequence — Retell the story in a different sequence. Make sure it makes sense!

Character Portrait — Write a description of one of the main characters.

Paint a portrait or caricature to accompany the description.

Complaints — Write a letter to the main character of the book.

Ask a question, protest some situation, make a complaint or suggestion, etc.

Comic Book — Rewrite the book as a comic book.

Compare Illustrations — Compare the illustrations of two books.

Tell how the illustrations influence the reader.

Crossword Puzzle — Make a crossword puzzle using ideas, new words, or names from a book. Give the puzzle to someone who has read the book. Make enough copies to keep on hand for others who read the book.

Diary — Write a diary from the main character's viewpoint to explain the events of the story.

Drama — Turn the book (fiction or nonfiction) into a drama. Perform it.

E-mail — E-mail the author, asking questions about his or her writing process, asking questions about purposes or themes in the book, or suggesting some changes that might improve the book.

Interview — Make a list of questions you would ask one of the characters in the book if you could interview him or her.

Joke book — After reading a joke and riddle book, make a scrapbook of original jokes and riddles.

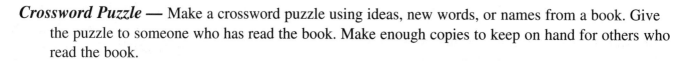

Letter — Write a letter recommending (or not recommending) the book to a friend or relative in another city. Or, write a letter to the school librarian telling why she or he should recommend the book to other classes.

Missing Facts — For a nonfiction book, write a list of 10-20 questions or facts that are NOT covered in the book.

Movie Comparison — Read a book that has been made into a movie. Write an essay comparing the movie to the book

New Point of View — Re-write the story from the point of view of a different character (or an animal or inanimate object in the story).

New Genre — Rewrite the story as a poem, advertisement, essay, TV script, myth, tall tale, fable, or other form of literature.

News Article — Change the story into a feature news article with a headline that tells the story as it might be found on the front page of a newspaper in the town where the story takes place.

Online Review — Log onto an Internet book-selling site that has a place for reader's reviews of books. Add your own review to the collection.

Picture Book — Rewrite the story as a picture book. Use simple vocabulary so that the book may be enjoyed by younger students.

Poetry Scrapbook — If your book is a poetry book, make a scrapbook containing 15 or 20 of your favorite poems.

Puppet Show — Make three or four simple puppets of characters in the book. Prepare a short puppet show to tell the story to the class.

Retell without Words — Retell your story to an audience without using any spoken or written words.

Sequel — Create an outline for a sequel to the book.

Timeline — After reading a book about history or a historical fiction, make a timeline or calendar to show the important events of the story.

Top 10 Facts — After reading a factual book, make a list of 10 important facts you found in the book.

Top 50 Smashing Words — After reading any book, make a list of 50 phrases or sentences that show effective word use.

Travel Poster — Make a travel poster inviting tourists to visit the settings of the book.

20 Questions — Prepare a list of questions to ask another reader to help find out if that person has a good understanding of the book.

Web Synopsis — Add a synopsis of the book to your website. Create illustrations to go along with the review.

The book, *Pinocchio*, is better than the movie.

Reading Performance Assessment Guide

Have the student read a sample orally. Then, check the following areas of performance. The performance descriptions given indicate a level of high competency in each area.

Oral Reading Performance

Pace
- Pace mostly or always matches a pace of normal conversation.

Flow
- Reading is consistently smooth with few disruptions.
- Student corrects errors quickly and smoothly.

Phrasing
- The phrasing and breathing are natural.
- The student mostly or consistently uses appropriate-length phrases for conversing, including some long phrases.
- The student includes natural expression within the phrases.

Does her reading flow smoothly?

Retelling

Clarity
- The retelling is very clear and organized, showing good understanding of the whole piece and the correct sequence.

Completeness
- The retelling contains a clear and accurate telling of the main point or idea.
- The retelling includes all the main events, points, or developments.
- The retelling includes important details.
- The retelling covers the story in the correct sequence.

Oral Response to Comprehension Questions

Main Idea
- When questioned, the student can clearly explain the main idea(s).

Details
- The student can identify specific details that support the main idea or that describe characters, setting, or plot development.

Personal Connection
- The student can relate events, situations, or feelings from the piece to her or his own life experiences.

Inference & Evaluation
- The student can make generalizations from text ideas to situations outside of the text.
- The student can make predictions with good text evidence to support them.
- The student can draw conclusions with good text evidence to support them.

Can he tell the main idea?

Written Response to Passage

Comprehension

I can identify the supporting details.

- Student's response shows an understanding of the main point(s) or ideas.

- Student's response shows a clear understanding of the supporting details.

- Student is able to use specific details from the text to support conclusions, interpretations, and opinions.

- Student is able to reach conclusions and form inferences from the text to convey meaning.

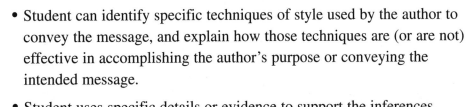

Critical Analysis of Text

- Student can identify the author's purpose.

- Student can identify the author's biases and give specific evidence from the text to demonstrate the biases.

I did notice the author's bias.

- Student can identify specific techniques of style used by the author to convey the message, and explain how those techniques are (or are not) effective in accomplishing the author's purpose or conveying the intended message.

- Student uses specific details or evidence to support the inferences, conclusions, and judgments made about the author's style and the effectiveness of the text.

Making Connections

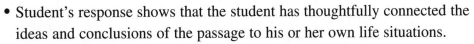

- Student's response makes insightful connections between the ideas or message of the passage to events and circumstances in the world outside of the text.

In this paper, I try to connect my reading to my real life.

- Student's response shows that the student has thoughtfully connected the ideas and conclusions of the passage to his or her own life situations.

- Student can relate personal experiences or feelings that show similarities or differences to events, feelings, or messages from the text.

- Student's response relates the lives, circumstances, or feelings of specific characters in the text to real-life situations.

- Student's response shows that the student has thoughtfully connected the ideas and conclusions of the passage to conclusions and ideas from other written texts.

- Student's response relates the lives or circumstances or feelings of specific characters in the text to those in other written texts.

- Student's response shows that student understands how personal, cultural, or historical factors in the author's life may have affected the style, opinions, message, or purpose of the written work.

Better Grades & Higher Test Scores / READING & LANGUAGE gr. 4–6
Copyright ©2005 by Incentive Publications, Inc., Nashville, TN.

Get Sharp: Literature Skills

Finding Meaning from Context

You're reading along and come across a word that stumps you—you are not sure what it means. You may need to head for the dictionary or glossary to learn the word's meaning. However, you might be able to figure it out from the **context** (setting) of the word in the sentence, line, or paragraph. Pay attention to those clues, and you'll learn the meanings of some new words.

Context Clues in Sentences

Don't breathe those **noxious** fumes from the shellac becasue they will make you very sick.

If *noxious* fumes will make you sick, you can guess that they are *poisonous*.

Were you hurt when we were **candid** with you about how terrible your casserole tasted?

The word *hurt* and the phrase *about how terrible her casserole tasted* help you guess that **candid** means truthful.

Because our guide was **adept** at handling the raft, we made it safely down the raging river with no mishaps.

The guide was able to get the raft through a dangerous situation *(raging river)* safely. This gives a clue that the word **adept** means *skillful* or *competent*.

Julie's constant insults and pushing irritated other students, **instigating** a fight.

Constant insults, pushing and *irritated* are words and phrases that paint a picture of trouble. This helps you conclude that **instigating** means *starting*.

Todd's mouth was **agape** and his face was white when he saw the grizzly bear in the path ahead of him.

Since Todd's face went *white*, you can imagine that he was shocked, and that the position of his mouth (**agape**) was *wide open in shock*.

Hmmm!

Context Clues in Paragraphs or Stanzas

Sometimes it takes more than one sentence to give you enough clues for solving the mystery of a word meaning. Look for the clues in these longer passages to the meanings of the bold words.

I love to go to parties.
They set a happy mood.
The games and dancing draw me,
Though I mostly go for food.
This party has great music.
Where's the snacks? There's not a bite!
Yes, the **paucity** of food disturbs me.
I'll be hungry the rest of the night.

I will never tell! They can threaten to torture me with scorpions, but I will never **divulge** your secret.

You're rude.
You insult with intent.
I'd say you are
Impertinent!

Chester hates water. He hates sunshine. He hates sand. Therefore, his friends were **confounded** when he showed up for the beach party.

All the rest of us are covered with itchy mosquito bite lumps from the camping trip. Charlie has no bumps or itching, though I saw the insects biting him. He must be **immune** to mosquito bites.

I heard there was a **dearth** of tickets available. That's why I went down to the auditorium at dawn to get in line for the opening of ticket sales at noon today.

Angie has shown that she is an **eclectic** musician. Her show combines rock music with country music, classical music, jazz, blues, and hip-hop.

Better Grades & Higher Test Scores / READING & LANGUAGE gr. 4–6
Copyright ©2005 by Incentive Publications, Inc., Nashville, TN. *Get Sharp: Vocabulary & Word Meaning*

100 Great Vocabulary Words to Know

abase — to humiliate
abrupt — sudden
aggravate — to irritate

aghast — shocked

amicable — peaceable friendly
astonish — amaze
audacious — bold
avarice — greed
bellicose — hostile, warlike
bizarre — very strange
brawn — strong, muscular
buoyant — able to float
cache — something hidden
calamity — disaster
cease — stop
chide — scold
conceal — hide
contemptuous — scornful
cower — crouch in fear
dearth — short supply
deride — ridicule
dismal — dull, depressing
divulge — reveal
doleful — sad
emulate — imitate
fatuous — foolish
fetid — rotten-smelling
foe — enemy
foible — small flaw or error
frenetic — frantic
furtive — sneaky

garish — outlandish, tacky
garrulous — talking too much
glum — sad, gloomy
gourmand — lover of food
grotto — cave
hoodwink — deceive
horde — mob
illicit — illegal
illusory — imaginary
impeccable — without flaw
impertinent — rude
impetuous — impulsive
indelible — permanent
jeer — laugh at
jocose — playful
jovial — jolly
languid — listless, indifferent
luminous — shiny
macabre — gruesome
malevolent — evil
mediocre — average, ordinary
miniscule — tiny
moniker — nickname
morose — dark and gloomy
murky — dark, unclear
noxious — harmful to health
nuisance — a bother
obstinate — stubborn
obstreperous — stubborn
obtuse — blunt
onus — blame
pallid — pale
perilous — dangerous
petulant — impatient
placid — tranquil
plethora — excess
prevaricate — lie (fib)
punctual — on time
quandary — doubt

query — question
rampant — widespread
rancor — deep spite or malice
random — without a pattern
recede — to move away from
repose — act of resting
requisite — required
sagacity — wisdom
savory — tasty
scrupulous — conscientious
stationary — not moving
sullen — gloomy, grumpy
superb — exceptional
surfeit — excess
tariff — tax

tedium — boredom

tenuous — flimsy
timorous — shy
turgid — swollen
urbane — refined
undulate — move in waves
unseemly — indecent
vacillate — fluctuate
valiant — brave
vacuous — empty
veritable — true
vindicate — clear from blame
volatile — explosive
wane — lessen, shrink
wraith — a ghost
yore — a time long past
zenith — highest point

Better Grades & Higher Test Scores / READING & LANGUAGE gr. 4–6

Connotation & Denotation

The **denotation** of a word is its dictionary definition.

The **connotation** is all of the ideas and images suggested by a word. The connotation may be different for different readers. When you read, connotation helps you imagine a rich context for a simple word.

The **denotation** of **giant** is . . . a person or thing of great size and strength.

PIRATE

denotation — one who robs on the high seas

connotation — a mean-spirited, grungy character (usually wearing a patch over one eye and having a wooden leg) associated with danger, adventure, mystery, swords, people walking planks, great works of literature, buried treasure, treasure maps, deserted islands, gold and silver, talking parrots, a skull and crossbones flag, etc.

MUSIC

denotation — the science of ordering tones

connotation — wonderful, colorful, and pleasing rhythmic sounds for dancing

ROLLER COASTER

denotation — a steep, sharply banked, elevated railway with small open passenger cars operated as an attraction at amusement parks and fairgrounds

connotation — a wild, terrifying amusement park ride that speeds up and down hills, jerking screaming passengers and upsetting stomachs

GOSSIP

denotation – petty and groundless rumors, usually of a personal nature

connotation — juicy secrets and harmful stories whispered behind someone's back

The **connotation** is much broader. The word **giant** stirs up all kinds of images and ideas of . . . a huge, frightening, hairy creature that looks strange, growls, and threatens people.

But some of us are actually very sweet.

Meanings of Prefixes

prefix	meaning	examples
a-	not	atypical, atheist
ab-	away, from	abnormal, abound
alti-	high	altitude, alto, altar
ante-	before	antecedent, anterior
anti-	against	antibody, antifreeze
auto-	self	autobiography
bi-	two	bicycle, biannual
cent-	hundred	century, centimeter
circum-	around	circumference
co-	together, with	coexist, cooperate
con-	together, with	concert, connect
contra-	against	contradict, contrast
counter-	against	counteract
de-	away, down	depart, dehumanize
dec-	ten	decade, decagon
deci-	tenth	decimal, decibel
di-	two	dissect, diagonal,
dis-	apart from	dislocate, distance
dis-	not, opposite	disallow, disapprove
equi-	equal	equilateral
ex-	from	expel, exit, exclude
extra-	beyond	extracurricular

prefix	meaning	examples
fore-	in front	forward, forefinger
hyper-	above, over	hypersensitive
hypo-	under, below	hypodermic
il-	not	illegal, illegible
im-	not	immature, imperfect
in-	not	inactive, incomplete
inter-	between, among	interact
ir-	not	irrational, irregular
kilo-	thousand	kilometer, kilowatt
micro-	small	microphone
mid-	middle	midair, midnight
mill-	thousandth	millimeter, milliliter
mis-	wrong	misfortune, misspell
mono-	one	monotone, monolith
multi-	many	multitude, multiply
non-	not	nonsense, nonsmoker
over-	over	overactive, overspend
para-	beyond, beside	parallel, paramedic
poly-	many	polygraph, polygon
post-	after	postdate, postscript
pre-	before	precaution, prefix
pro-	before, forward	produce, pronoun
quad-	four	quadrilateral
re-	again	reclaim, redo, repaint
retro-	backwards	retrograde, retrofit
se-	aside, apart	seclude, segregate
semi-	half	semicircle, semigloss
sub-	under	submarine, subplot
super-	over	supercede, superego
tele-	far away	telegram, telescope
trans-	across	transplant, transpolar
tri-	three	triangle, tripod
ultra-	beyond	ultramodern
un-	not	unclear, uneven, unfair
uni-	one	unicorn, unicycle
with-	against	withhold, withdraw

The **quadrupeds** are **cooperating** to make my **transpolar** journey **extraordinary**.

Meanings of Suffixes

prefix	meaning	examples
-able	tending to, able to	*enjoyable, lovable, payable, perishable, conquerable*
-age	state of being, place of, result of	*anchorage, orphanage, shrinkage, wastage*
-al	relating to	*electrical, theatrical*
-an	belonging to	*American, urban*
-ance	state of being	*importance*
-ant	one who	*immigrant, occupant*
-ar	one who	*beggar, scholar*
-ary	one who	*missionary, visionary*
-ate	to make	*irrigate, saturate,*
-cy	state or quality of	*lunacy, piracy*
-en	have nature of	*ashen, broken, earthen, golden*
-en	to make or become	*blacken, fatten, lengthen, whiten*
-ence	state of	*difference, excellence*
-ent	one who	*resident, president*
-ery	place where	*bakery, nursery*
-er	more	*faster, lighter, nicer*
-er	one who	*baker, preacher*
-est	most	*cleanest, deepest*
-ful	characterized by	*awful, beautiful, helpful, masterful, plentiful*
-fy	make or form into	*clarify, glorify, horrify*
-hood	state of rank	*adulthood, falsehood*
-ible	like or capable of being	*terrible, audible, permissible, visible, impossible, reversible*
-ic	pertaining to, like	*angelic, artistic, athletic, classic*
-ical	pertaining to, like	*magical*
-ish	having nature of	*bluish, childish*
-ism	act or quality of	*heroism, pessimism*
-ist	one who	*artist, biologist*

prefix	meaning	examples
-less	without	*friendless, ageless*
-like	resembling	*childlike, lifelike*
-ly	in the manner of	*actively, happily*
-ment	resulting state action or process	*amazement, commitment,*
-most	most	*aftermost, foremost*
-ness	state of being	*blindness, gladness,*
-or	person who	*actor, auditor, debtor*
-ous	state or condition having quality of	*courageous prosperous*
-ry	state of being	*rivalry, revelry, finery*
-ship	office, profession, art, or skill	*championship, fellowship, hardship*
-some	resembling	*handsome, lonesome*
-ion	act, process, state	*action, collection*
-tion	act, process, state	*clarification*
-ure	act, process	*adventure, failure*

Due to our **expertise**, he can be **optimistic** about the **possibility** of this **adventure** becoming **successful**.

Get Sharp: Vocabulary & Word Meaning

Meanings of Common Roots

root	meaning	example
act	act or do	*actor*
ami	friend	*amiable*
ann	year	*annual*
aqua	water	*aquatic*
astr	star	*astronaut*
brev	short	*brevity*
cap	head	*captain*
card	heart	*cardiac*
celer	fast	*accelerate*
chron	time	*chronology*
clam	cry out	*exclaim*
crypt	hidden	*cryptic*
cycle	circle, wheel	*tricycle*
cir	circle, wheel	*circumvent*
cit	speak, talk	*citation*
civ	city	*civilian*
cred	believe	*credible*
culp	blame	*culprit*
dic	speak	*dictate*
don	give	*donate*
dorm	sleep	*dormant*
dom	rule	*dominate*
dox	opinion	*orthodox*
duc	lead	*conductor*
dur	hard	*durable*
dynam	power	*dynamite*
fer	bring, carry	*transfer*
fin	end	*final*
flam	fire	*flammable*
form	shape	*format*
fract	break	*fracture*

Look! It's a **quickly accelerating projectile!**

root	meaning	example
frag	break	*fragment*
fug	flee	*fugitive*
geo	earth	*geology*
glyph	carving	*hieroglyphics*
graph	write	*autograph*
grat	pleasing	*gratitude*
greg	crowd	*congregation*
gyr	whirl	*gyrate*
ign	fire	*ignite*
ject	throw	*eject*
labor	work	*laboratory*
lib	book	*library*
lith	stone	*lithograph*
loc	place	*locate*
lucr	money	*lucrative*
lum	light	*luminous*
lun	moon	*lunar*
manu	hand	*manufacture*
mar	sea	*marine*
morph	sleep	*morphine*
mort	death	*mortal*
mob	move	*mobile*

Get Sharp: Vocabulary & Word Meaning

Yes! Its **luminosity** is clearly **visible**!

root	meaning	example
mon	warn	*admonish*
mot	move	*motion*
mov	move	*movement*
mur	wall	*mural*
mut	change	*mutate*
noct	night	*nocturnal*
nat	born	*native*
nom	name	*nominate*
oper	work	*operator*
pac	peace	*pacify*
ped	foot	*pedal*
pel	push	*propel*
pend	hang	*suspend*
petr	stone	*petrify*
phon	sound	*phonics*
pod	foot	*podiatry*
pop	people	*popular*
port	carry	*portage*
posit	place	*position*
pus	foot	*octopus*
pyro	fire	*pyrotechnics*
radi	ray	*radiate*

root	meaning	example
rot	turn	*rotate*
scend	climb	*descend*
sci	know	*science*
scrip	write	*transcript*
sculpt	carve	*sculptor*
sect	cut	*dissect*
sed	sit	*sedentary*
sol	sun	*solar*
son	sound	*sonar*
soph	wise	*philosopher*
strict	bind	*restrict*
stat	stand	*stationary*
tang	touch	*tangible*
tard	slow	*tardy*
tele	far	*telephone*
tempor	time	*temporal*
term	end	*terminate*
terr	earth	*territory*
therm	heat	*thermal*
tort	twist	*torture*
turb	spin	*turbulent*
vac	empty	*vacate*
vali	strong	*valiant*
vanqu	conquer	*vanquish*
verb	word	*verbose*
view	see	*review*
vict	conquer	*victory*
vid	see	*video*
vis	see	*visible*
vit	life	*vitality*
viv	life	*revive*
volv	roll	*revolve*
wit	know	*wittingly*

221

Confusing Words

Some words are easily confused with other words because they sound similar or because they have similar meanings. Pay close attention to the differences in the meanings of these pairs of words.

ability (power) — **capacity** (condition)

accede (to agree) — **exceed** (to surpass)

accept (to receive) — **except** (to exclude)

adapt (to adjust) — **adopt** (to accept)

all ready (completely prepared) — **already** (previously)

allude (to refer to) — **elude** (escape)

The footprints to which reporters **alluded** have **eluded** the searchers.

assure (to set a person's mind at ease) — **insure** (to guarantee life or property against harm)
ensure (to secure from harm)

avenge (to achieve justice) — **revenge** (retaliation)

avoid (to shun) — **avert** (to turn away)

between (refers to two persons, places, or things) — **among** (refers to more than two)

clench (to grip something tightly, as hand or teeth) — **clinch** (to fasten firmly together)

complement (something that completes) — **compliment** (an expression of praise)

confidant (one to whom secrets are told) — **confident** (assured of success)

Better Grades & Higher Test Scores / READING & LANGUAGE gr. 4–6

deny (to contradict) — **refute** (to give evidence to disprove something)

fatal (causing death) — **fateful** (affecting one's destiny)

graceful (refers to movement) — **gracious** (courteous)

impassable (impossible to travel through or cross) — **impassive** (devoid of emotion)

imply (to hint or suggest) — **infer** (to draw conclusions based on facts)

latter (the second of two things mentioned) — **later** (subsequently)

mania (craze) — **phobia** (fear)

nauseated (to feel queasy) — **nauseous** (causing queasiness)

Get Sharp Tip #21
Pay special attention to the differences (in meaning) between those words that sound a lot alike.

obliged (feeling a debt of gratitude) — **obligated** (directed to follow a certain course)

older (refers to persons and things) — **elder** (refers to only one person)

persecute (to oppress or harass) — **prosecute** (to initiate legal or criminal action against)

piteous (pathetic) — **pitiable** (lamentable) — **pitiful** (very inferior or insignificant)

practically (almost) — **virtually** (to all intents)

precipitant (rash, impulsive) — **precipitate** (to hurl downward) — **precipitous** (extremely steep)

principal (chief) — **principle** (basic law or truth)

raise (to move upward; to build; to breed) — **rear** (to bring up a child) — **rise** (to ascend)

rare (of unusual value and quality, of limited supply) — **scarce** (refers to temporary infrequency)

regretful (sorrowful) — **regrettable** (something that elicits mental distress)

reluctant (unwilling) — **reticent** (refers to a style that is characteristically silent or restrained)

repel (drive off; cause distaste or aversion) — **repulse** (to drive off; reject by means of discourtesy)

respectfully (showing honor and esteem) — **respectively** (one at a time in order)

specific (explicitly set forth) — **particular** (not general or universal)

stationary (immovable) — **stationery** (matched writing paper and envelopes)

trivial (insignificant) — **tiny** (small)

223

Homophones

Homophones are words that sound alike, but have different meanings. Here are a few of the hundreds of homophones in the English language.

acclamation — acclimation
acts — axe
ail — ale
air — heir
aisle — I'll — isle
all — awl
aloud — allowed
ant — aunt
arc — ark
ascent — assent
assistance — assistants
ate — eight
attendance — attendants
aught — ought
aye — eye
bail — bale
bait — bate
bald — bawled
bare — bear
bard — barred
baron — barren
bass — base
beau — bow
beech — beach
beet — beat
bee — be
berry — bury
berth — birth
better — bettor
bier — beer
billed — build
blue — blew
bore — boar
bowled — bold
border — boarder
burrow — borough
bow — bough
breach — breech
break — brake
bred — bread
bridle — bridal
but — butt
bye — by — buy

caller — collar
canon — cannon
canopy — canapé
canvas — canvass
capital — capitol
cache — cash
carrot — carat
ceiling — sealing
cell — sell
cellar — seller
census — senses
cent — sent — scent
chance — chants
chord — cord
cite — sight — site
close — clothes
coarse — course
colonel — kernel
compliment — complement
concur — conquer
coral — choral
caught — cot
council — counsel
creak — creek
cruise — crews
currant — current
cymbal — symbol
days — daze
dense — dents
descent — dissent
do — due — dew
die — dye
doe — dough
draft — draught
dual — duel
earn — urn
elicit — illicit
ewe — you — yew
feat — feet
find — fined

fir — fur
flew — flue
flea — flee
flour — flower
for — four — fore
forth — fourth
fowl — foul
gait — gate
gamble — gambol
gilt — guilt
gnu — new — knew
grate — great
grisly — grizzly
grater — greater
groan — grown
hail — hale
hair — hare
hall — haul
hay — hey
heal — heel
hear — here
heard — herd
higher — hire
him — hymn
holy — holey — wholly
hole — whole
hour — our
idol — idle
incidents — incidence
in — inn
knap — nap

*I wish someone would **hire** me at a much, much **higher** salary!*

DOG WALKER

Get Sharp: Vocabulary & Word Meaning

Better Grades & Higher Test Scores / READING & LANGUAGE gr. 4–6

knead — need
knight — night
knot — not
know — no
knows — nose
lead — led
leak — leek
lean — lien
leased — least
liar — lyre
lie — lye
lone — loan
maid — made
mail — male
main — mane — Maine
manner — manor
marshal — martial
meddle — medal — metal
miner — minor
mite — might
morning — mourning
navel — naval
nay — neigh
none — nun
or — oar — ore
ode — owed
one — won
oh — owe
owed — ode
paced — paste
packed — pact
pail — pale
pain — pane
palate — palette
patience — patients
paws — pause
piece — peace — peas
peak — peek — pique
peal — peel
pear — pair — pare
peer — pier
plain — plane
pole — poll
pore — pour
pray — prey
prays — praise
pried — pride

principal — principle
prints — prince
profit — prophet
rain — rein — reign
raise — rays — raze
rap — wrap
read — red
read — reed
real — reel
right — write — rite
ring — wring
rowed — rode — road
roe — row
rose — rows
rote — wrote
rot — wrought
rung — wrung
rye — wry
sail — sale
scene — seen
scent — sent — cent
scull — skull
sea — see
sealing — ceiling
seam — seem
seas — sees — seize
seed — cede
seen — scene
sense — scents — cents
serf — surf
sew — sow — so
shear — sheer
shoe — shoo
shone — shown
shoot — chute
side — sighed
slay — sleigh
soar — sore
soared — sword
some — sum
son — sun
stair — stare
stake — steak
stationary — stationery
steel — steal
straight — strait
tacks — tax

After we finish reading *The Tale of the Cat's Tail*, let's read the story about the pale pail.

The Tale of the Cat's Tail

tail — tale
taut — taught
team — teem
tear — tier
tear — tare
teas — tease
tense — tents
their — there
threw — through
throne — thrown
thy — thigh
thyme — time
tide — tied
toad — towed
toe — tow
told — tolled
too — to — two
vale — veil
vane — vain — vein
wade — weighed
wail — whale
wait — weight
wave — waive
way — weigh — whey
weak — week
wear — where — ware
were — whir
whether — weather
which — witch
whole — hole
while — wile
whine — wine
wood — would
wrapping — rapping
yolk — yoke

225

Get Sharp: Vocabulary & Word Meaning

Analogies

An **analogy** shows relationships between words in two pairs of words. In each pair, the words must have the same relationship. To solve an analogy with a missing word, you must first discover the relationship in the completed pair. There are many different kinds of relationships used in analogies. Some of them are shown here.

Synonyms

Peril is to *danger* as *hectic* is to *chaotic*.

Noisy is to *clamorous* as *splendid* is to *superb*.

Perfect is to *faultless* as *mimic* is to *imitate*.

Savory is to *tasty* as *boring* is to *dull*.

Rotten is to *smelly* as *shun* is to *avoid*.

Frugal is to *stingy* as *scoundrel* is to *crook*.

Cordial is to *friendly* as *morass* is to *swamp*.

Genuine is to *real* as *coarse* is to *rough*.

Antonyms

Criticize is to *praise* as *slander* is to *truth*.

Amateur is to *professional* as *continue* is to *cease*.

Lazy is to *energetic* as *instigate* is to *stop*.

Clumsy is to *graceful* as *triumph* is to *defeat*.

Buoyant is to *sinkable* as *punish* is to *reward*.

Disapprove is to *condone* as *greed* is to *generosity*.

Agile is to *clumsy* as *haughty* is to *friendly*.

Categories

Physician is to *professional* as *miner* is to *laborer*.

Cedar is to *evergreen* as *oak* is to *deciduous*.

Sleet is to *precipitation* as *hurricane* is to *storm*.

Dolphin is to *vertebrate* as *anemone* is to *invertebrate*.

Stomach is to *digestion* as *artery* is to *circulation*.

Rigatoni is to *pasta* as *shrimp* is to *crustacean*.

Better Grades & Higher Test Scores / READING & LANGUAGE gr. 4–6
Copyright ©2005 by Incentive Publications, Inc., Nashville, TN.

Degree

Flurries is to blizzard as sprinkles is to downpour.

Warm is to scalding as cool is to freezing.

Death is to injury as disastrous is to troublesome.

Cub is to lion as kid is to goat.

Evening is to night as dawn is to morning.

Function

Mitt is to baseball as bucket is to drip.

Umbrella is to rain as awning is to sunshine.

Vocal chords are to voice as strings are to piano.

Siren is to sound as chocolate is to taste.

Baker is to oven as dentist is to drill.

Location

Foot is to toes as hand is to fingers.

Channel is to television as station is to radio.

Squid is to ocean as antelope is to tundra.

Laces are to shoes as buttons are to shirt.

Hairdo is to head as roof is to house.

Word Structure

Mice is to mouse as berries is to berry.

Worried is to worry as frenzied is to frenzy.

Boyhood is to boy as neighborhood is to neighbor.

Semiconductor is to conductor as extraterrestrial is to terrestrial.

Fruitcake is to cake as sandstorm is to storm.

Other Relationships

Hiss is to snake as growl is to tiger.

Yellow is to banana as green is to celery.

Smoke is to fire as rain is to clouds.

Surgeon is to operate as detective is to investigate.

Diamond is to hard as copper is to flexible.

Raindrop is to rainstorm as bee is to swarm.

Idioms

Idioms are "sayings" peculiar to a particular language or group. The meaning of the expressions cannot necessarily be understood from the words themselves. The meanings have come to be understood over time—often to mean something very different from what the words actually say. Here are a few of the thousands of idioms in the English language.

a bad egg
a bee in your bonnet
a bone to pick
a drop in the bucket
a finger in every pie
a flash in the pan
a lion's share
a long row to hoe
a pain in the neck
a splitting headache
almighty dollar
an ace in the hole
an axe to grind
back to square one
bark up the wrong tree
bats in the belfry
be a good egg
be on top of the world
between the devil and the
  deep blue sea
behind the 8 ball
bite the bullet
bite the dust
bite your head off
blows my mind
blow off steam
blow the test
break the ice
bring home the bacon
burn the candle at both ends
bury the hatchet
by the skin of my teeth
call her on the carpet

carry a torch for her
chew the fat
chicken out
chip off the old block
chip on your shoulder
come in out of the rain

Hold your horses!

I wish she'd get off my back!

Don't get on your high horse!

cook your goose
cry your eyes out
deep in thought
died with his boots on
doesn't amount to a hill
  of beans
don't beat a dead horse
don't bite off more than
  you can chew
don't cry over spilled milk
don't cry wolf
don't give me any lip
don't make a mountain
  out of a molehill
dressed to the nines

eager beaver
easier said than done
eat crow
eat humble pie
eye to eye
face the music
fly the coop
get cold feet
get it off your chest
get forty winks
get off my back
get off my case
get on board the gravy train
get on your high horse
give a tongue lashing
got an earful
have your cake and eat it too
hit it off
hit the nail on the head
hold a candle to
hold your horses
hold your tongue
in a pretty pickle
in hot water
in the bag
in the doghouse
in the nick of time
in the pink
in the red
it's right down my alley
jump the gun
just under the wire
keep a stiff upper lip

keep your shirt on
kick the bucket
kick up your heels
knock it off
knock the fur out
lay an egg
left holding the bag
lend me a hand
let the cat out of the bag
lie through your teeth
look a gift horse in the mouth
lose your cool
lose your head
lose your shirt
lost his marbles
mad as a hatter
make a beeline
make hay while the sun shines
make no bones about it
make your mouth water
mint condition
more fun than a barrel of
   monkeys
more than one way to skin a cat
nose to the grindstone
not worth a hill of beans
nothing to shake a stick at
off the record
on the bandwagon
on the money
on the nose
on top of the world
once in a blue moon
out of the frying pan into the fire
out on a limb
out to lunch
paint the town red
pass the buck

pay through the nose
plain as the nose on your face
pull strings
pull the wool over your eyes
put a sock in it
put on the dog
put your foot in your mouth
puttin' on the Ritz
raining cats and dogs
rake over the coals
read you the riot act
red letter day
right up my alley
run it into the ground
sadder but wiser
see eye to eye
shoot the breeze
shoot the bull
skeleton in your closet
skin the cat
sleep like a top
sour grapes
spill the beans
split hairs
spring a leak
stab someone in the back
stay until the bitter end
stick your neck out
straight from the
   horse's mouth
swallow it hook, line,
   and sinker
sweating blood
take heart
takes the cake
talk through your hat
talk turkey
the apple of my eye

the black sheep
the handwriting's on the wall
the lady is a fox
things are touch and go
tickled pink
till the cows come home
too many irons in the fire
under her thumb
under the gun
up the creek without a paddle
upset the apple cart
wants cash on the barrel
wear your heart on your sleeve
went bananas
wolf in sheep's clothing
worth his salt
yell your head off

I wanted to shoot the breeze with my friend, but I really let the cat out of the bag when I spilled the beans about the surprise party.

I jumped the gun about the news, and now I'm in a pretty pickle!

Puns & Proverbs

pun — a word or a phrase used in a way that gives a funny twist to the words. Puns often make use of double meanings of words.

Is it any surprise that a girl named Robin Steale would grow up to be a thief?

It's a drain on our budget to hire a plumber.

"Don't drop the eggs!" cracked the grocer.

A clockmaker works overtime.

My surgeon is so funny; she keeps me in stitches!

Is a barber who works in a Library called a Barbarian?

Our optometrist is Seymour Clearly.

Claude Severely is an ex-lion tamer.

To win a relay race, swimmers pool their efforts.

proverb — a brief saying that presents a truth or some bit of useful wisdom

A bird in the hand is worth two in the bush.
A fool and his money are soon parted.
An apple a day keeps the doctor away.
A stitch in time saves nine.
Absence makes the heart grow fonder.
Better safe than sorry.
Blood is thicker than water.
Curiosity killed the cat.
Don't change horses in the middle of the stream.
Don't count your chickens until they're hatched.
Don't cut off your nose to spite your face.
Don't hang your dirty linen in public.
Every family has a skeleton in its closet.
Fools rush in where angels fear to tread.
Good fences make good neighbors.
He who hesitates is lost.
It is no time to send for the doctor when the patient is dead.
It never rains but it pours.
It takes two to tango.
Laughter is the best medicine.
Look before you leap.

Money is the root of all evil.
Never look a gift horse in the mouth.
No news is good news.
Practice what you preach.
Rats desert a sinking ship.
Spare the rod and spoil the child.
Strike while the iron is hot.
The early bird gets the worm.
There's more than one way to skin a cat.
Too many cooks spoil the broth.
Two heads are better than one.
You can lead a horse to water, but you can't make him drink.
You can't tell a book by its cover.
Where there's smoke, there's fire.

230

Oxymorons & Palindromes

oxymoron — a combination of two words that seem to contradict each other

My new hat is pretty ugly!

act naturally	found missing	open secret
almost exactly	freezer burn	original copies
alone together	fresh-frozen	plastic silverware
bittersweet	friendly fire	pretty ugly
black light	good grief	sanitary landfill
calm wind	jumbo shrimp	seriously funny
childproof	half naked	silent scream
civil war	holy war	small crowd
clearly misunderstood	ill health	terribly pleased
deafening silence	industrial park	unbiased opinion
definite maybe	minor crisis	vaguely aware
designer jeans	minor miracle	virtual reality
double solitaire	modern history	working vacation
exact estimate	more perfect	
even odds	old news	

palindrome — word or phrase that reads the same forwards and backwards

a nut for a jar of tuna	I did, did I?	radar	We panic in a pew.
a Santa at NASA	I prefer pi.	racecar	Wontons? Not now.
a Toyota	I saw I was I.	re-paper	Yreka bakery
Ana, nab a banana.	kayak	Rise to vote, sir.	
bird rib	level	senile felines	
Boston, O do not sob.	Ma has a ham.	solos	
Dee saw a seed.	Ma is a nun, as I am.	so many dynamos	
Del saw a sled.	Mad am I, Adam!	star comedy by	
Delia failed.	Madam, I'm Adam.	democrats	
Do geese see god?	Name no one man.	Stella won no wallets.	
Don't nod.	Never odd or even	Step on no pets.	
Dot sees Tod.	Niagara, O roar again.	straw warts	
Dr. Awkward	No devil lived on.	Too bad, I hid a boot.	
Dumb mud.	No garden, one dragon.	too hot to hoot	
Ed is on no side.	No lemons, no melon.	top spot	
Evade me, Dave.	Pa's a sap.	tuna nut	
Eve	party-trap	Was it a bat I saw?	
God saw I was dog.	peep	Was it a cat I saw?	
He stops spots, eh?	Poor Dan is in a droop.	Was it a rat I saw?	

Olson is in Oslo!

Wow!

Common Acronyms & Abbreviations

AC	alternating current	F	Fahrenheit
A.D.	anno Domini (*Latin for "in the year of the Lord" or "since the birth of Christ"*)	FAQs	frequently asked questions
		F.B.I.	Federal Bureau of Investigation
a.m.	ante meridiem (*midnight to noon*)	ft.	foot, feet
anon.	anonymous	i.e.	id est (*that is*)
apt.	apartment	I.Q.	Intelligence Quotient
ASAP	as soon as possible	I.R.S.	Internal Revenue Service
assoc.	association	K	kilo (*1000*)
asst.	assistant	k.	karat
atty.	attorney	kg	kilogram
A.S.P.C.A.	American Society for the Prevention of Cruelty to Animals	l	liter
		lb.	pound
B.A.	Bachelor of Arts (*college degree*)	M.D.	Medical Doctor
B.C.	before Christ	min.	minute
bps	bites per second	ml	milliliter
B.S.	Bachelor of Science (*college degree*)	mm	millimeter
C	centigrade or Celsius	mph	miles per hour
c.	copyright	mpg	miles per gallon
cal.	calories	no.	number
CD	compact disc	oz.	ounce
C.I.A.	Central Intelligence Agency	p.m.	post meridiem (*noon to midnight*)
cm	centimeter	POW	prisoner of war
C.O.D.	cash on delivery	P.S.	post script
C.P.A.	certified public accountant	pt.	pint
C.P.R.	cardiopulmonary resuscitation	qt.	quart
CPU	central processing unit	R.N.	registered nurse
CST	Central Standard Time	RR	railroad
D.A.	district attorney	R.S.V.P.	please respond
DC	direct current	S.A.S.E.	stamped, self-addressed envelope
D.D.S.	doctor of dental surgery	St.	street, saint
dept.	department	t.	ton
DNA	deoxyribonucleic acid (*basic genetic material*)	UFO	unidentified flying object
		URL	Uniform Resource Locator
DVD	digital video disc	v. or vs.	versus
ed.	editor, edition	w	watt
e.g.	exempli gratia (*for example*)	www	world wide web, Internet
e-mail	electronic mail		
enc.	enclosure, encyclopedia		
ESP	extrasensory perception		
EST	Eastern Standard Time		
esp.	especially		
et al.	et alia (*and others*)		
etc.	et cetera (*and so forth*)		

I'm going to buy a new CD and a DVD ASAP!

Get Sharp: Vocabulary & Word Meaning

Better Grades & Higher Test Scores / READING & LANGUAGE gr. 4–6

INDEX

A

abbreviations, 232

acronyms, 232

adjective clauses, 90

adjectives, 80–81, 84, 90

adverb clauses, 91

adverbs, 82–83, 85, 91

advice to parents

about writing, 144–145

how to use the book, 11–12

student motivation, 14–17

advice to students

getting motivated, 14–16

how to use the book, 11–12

advice to teachers

how to use the book, 11–12

agreement

pronoun, 98–99

subject-verb, 96–97

alliteration, 138, 204

allusion, 204

analogies, 66, 226–227

analyze, 33

anecdote, 204

antagonist, 204

antecedents, 98

anyway and *anyways*, 102

appositives, 69

articles, 81

assessment

reading, 212–213

speaking, 181–182

writing, 146–147

assignment notebook, 22

assignments, 22

assonance, 138

audience, identifying, 200

B

bad and *badly*, 105

ballad, 133

beginnings, 156, 158, 165

beside and *besides*, 102

between and *among*, 102

bias, 32, 202, 204

blank verse, 133

C

can and *may*, 104

capitalization, 106–107

cause and effect, 32, 193

character, 204

characterization, 138, 168, 203, 204

checking mechanics in writing, 143

cinquain, 133

clarity, sentences, 153

classify, 30

clauses, 90–91, 92

cliché, 204

climax, 169, 204

close reading, 49, 186

closings, 156, 159

collecting for writing, 142, 148

comma use, 108

comparative

adjectives, 84

adverbs, 85

compare and contrast, 32

compositions, 156–159

conclusions, 156, 159, 165

conflict, 169, 204

confusing words

meaning, 222–223

spelling, 120–121

usage of, 102–105

conjunctions, 87

yourself, 23
good and *well*, 104
grammar, 68–95
    parts of speech, 68–87
    phrases and clauses, 88–91
    usage, 96–105

H

haiku, 134
headlines, 167
health, 24
helping students with writing, 144
homophones, 224–225
how to use this book, 11–12
how come and *why*, 104
hyperbole, 139, 205
hypothesize, 32

I

identify bias, 32
idioms, 205, 228–229
images, 151, 205
imagery, 139, 205
imaginative writing, 130, 131, 175
impromptu speeches, 176
independent clauses, 91
infer, 31, 195
infinitives, 75
infinitive phrases, 89
information skills, 36–49
    Internet, 39, 46–47
    library, 44–45
    listening, 48
    reading, 49, 185
    references, 36–41
interjections, 87
Internet, 39, 46–47
irony, 139, 205

L

lay and *lie*, 104
let and *leave*, 103
letters, 170–171

business (formal), 171
    friendly, 170
library
    card catalog, 44–45
    computer catalog, 45
    finding information in, 44–45
    organization, 42–43
limerick, 134
literature skills
    identifying audience, 200
    identifying bias, 202
    identifying details, 190–192
    identifying cause and effect, 193
    identifying figurative language, 207
    identifying literary devices, 204–206
    identifying point of view, 201
    identifying purpose, 199
    identifying stereotype, 202
    identifying tone, 201
    separating fact from opinion, 193
logical thinking, 34
lyric poetry, 134

M

main ideas, 188–189
memorized speeches, 176
metaphor, 139, 205
meter, 205
modes, writing 130–131
mood, 139, 168, 205
moral, 205

N

narrative writing, 130–131, 172
narrator, 205
negatives, usage of, 100
news articles, 167
nonessential clauses, 91
nonessential phrases, 89
note taking, 56–57, 164–165
novel, 205
novella, 205
nouns, 68–71

O

objects, 78, 98–99
ode, 134
onomatopoeia, 140, 205
openings, 156, 158
organization
    assignments, 22
    for studying, 18–23
    for writing, 142, 149
    schedules for study, 20–21
    space to study, 18
    supplies for study, 19
    time for study, 20–21
    yourself, 23
outlining, 52–55, 165
oxymoron, 205, 231

P

palindrome, 231
paradox, 205
parody, 205
paragraphs, 154–155, 165
paraphrasing, 50–51
parent advice
    student motivation, 17
    use of the book, 11–12
participles, 75
participial phrases, 89, 101
parts of speech, 68–87
    adjectives, 80–81, 84
    adverbs, 82–83, 85
    conjunctions, 87
    nouns, 68–71
    objects, 78
    interjections, 87
    prepositions, 86
    pronouns, 72–73
    verbs, 74–79
personal writing, 130, 131, 175
personal response to reading, 208–209
personification, 140, 206
persuasive writing, 130, 131, 173

phrases, 88–89, 92
plot, 169, 206
plot structure, 169
plural nouns, 68, 70–71
poetry, 132–134, 206
polishing writing, 143, 162
possessive
    nouns, 71
    pronouns, 73
praises for writing, 143, 161
predicates, 92
predict, 31, 196
prefixes, meanings of, 218
prepositions, 86
P-Q-P Plan for Writing, 161–162
prepositional phrase, 88
process, writing, 137, 142–143
pronouns, 72–73, 98–99, 100
    agreement, 98
    usage, 98–99, 100
propaganda, identify, 34
prose, 132, 206
protagonist, 206
proverb, 206, 230
public speaking, 176–182
punctuation, 108–111
    apostrophe, 111
    colon, 110
    comma, 108
    dash, 110
    ellipsis, 109
    exclamation point, 109
    hyphen, 110
    italics, 111
    parentheses, 109
    period, 109
    question mark, 109
    quotation marks, 111–113
    semicolon, 110
pun, 140, 206, 230
purposes
    reading, 184–185, 199
    writing, 199